Legislating Foreign Policy

Also of Interest

Presidential Leadership and National Security: Style, Institutions, and Politics, edited by Sam C. Sarkesian

The Politics of Resource Allocation in the U.S. Department of Defense, Alex Mintz

Congress and the Presidency in U.S. Foreign Policymaking: A Study of Interaction and Influence, 1945-1982, John T. Rourke

Inside the Legislative Process: The Passage of the Foreign Service Act of 1980, William I. Bacchus

The Legislative Veto: Congressional Control of Regulation, Barbara Hinkson Craig

*The Illusion of Presidential Government, edited by Hugh Heclo and Lester Salamon

*The President, the Budget, and Congress: Impoundment and the 1974 Budget Act, James P. Pfiffner

Inside the Bureaucracy: The View from the Assistant Secretary's Desk, Thomas P. Murphy, Donald E. Nuechterlein, and Ronald J. Stupak

Rhetoric and Reality: Presidential Commissions and the Making of Public Policy, Terrence R. Tutchings

The Hoover Commissions Revisited, Ronald C. Moe

*Available in hardcover and paperback.

A Westview Special Study

Legislating Foreign Policy
edited by Hoyt Purvis and Steven J. Baker

Beginning with the premise that Congress has reasserted its role in U.S. foreign policy, the authors of this book describe, analyze, and evaluate how Congress is exercising its formal and informal powers and responsibilities. Five policy studies examine congressional action in major policy areas, placing Congress's behavior in the institutional and political contexts necessary to an understanding and evaluation of the congressional role; in combination, the studies provide an insightful look at some major developments in recent U.S. foreign policy.

Hoyt Purvis is director of the Fulbright Institute of International Relations at the University of Arkansas. He served for many years as an aide to Senator J. W. Fulbright and then as foreign/defense policy adviser to Senate Majority Leader Robert Byrd. *Steven J. Baker* is associate professor of international policy studies at the Monterey Institute of International Studies; Dr. Baker was a SALT II consultant and foreign policy adviser to Senator Byrd.

Legislating Foreign Policy

edited by Hoyt Purvis
and Steven J. Baker

Westview Press / Boulder and London

A Westview Special Study

Copyright © 1984 by Westview Press, Inc.

Published in 1984 in the United States of America by Westview Press, Inc.,
5500 Central Avenue, Boulder, Colorado 80301; Frederick A. Praeger, President
and Publisher

Library of Congress Catalog Card Number: 84-50372
ISBN: 0-86531-794-1

Composition for this book was provided by the editors
Printed and bound in the United States of America

10 9 8 7 6 5 4 3 2 1

Contents

Preface

This volume is the result of a collaborative effort that began while the editors worked together as congressional staff members concerned with foreign policy and defense issues. After leaving Washington, and while both served on the faculty of the University of Texas, that collaboration continued and work began in earnest on this book.

Based on both our governmental and teaching experience, we see a need for greater attention to the congressional role in foreign policy and international security affairs. Although there have been some noteworthy contributions to the study of Congress' role in the formation and conduct of American foreign policy, too often academic and journalistic treatments of the subject have tended to view Congress' role negatively and out of context. While Congress' shortcomings are thoroughly discussed and analyzed here, we proceed from the conviction that Congress _is_ a factor in American foreign policy, if sometimes only a subordinate factor, and that it is essential to examine Congress' foreign policy involvement in a broader perspective.

American foreign policy cannot be understood without a recognition of the congressional role. Likewise, the congressional role cannot be understood without a recognition of the importance of the legislative process, of politics, and of congressional personalities and procedures.

While we have drawn heavily on our own experience and research in preparing this book, we have also had the benefit of the efforts of three individuals who have worked with us in research and analysis of the congressional role in foreign policy. The contributions of John Opperman, J. Philip Rogers, and Tura Campanella are an important part of this volume.

This book builds around five policy studies, which examine and analyze the role of Congress in a wide range of policy areas. Rather than describing a single case, these chapters (3 through 7) place Congress' behavior in the issue, institutional, and political contexts that are necessary to an understanding and evaluation of Congress' performance.

The book begins with an introductory overview, providing a framework within which the congressional role should be considered, as well as some specific examples of the formal and informal interaction between the legislative and executive branches, and the direct and indirect congressional influence.

Chapter 2 introduces explicit criteria for evaluating the congressional performance, and in the concluding chapter the congressional role in each of the policy study areas is evaluated on the basis of those criteria.

Congress reasserted its foreign policy prerogatives in the early 1970s, and much of the existing literature focuses on that important period. Legislating Foreign Policy looks at how Congress is exercising the powers and responsibilities that it earlier recaptured. Each of the policy studies includes a major set of issues dealt with by Congress in the late 1970s and early 1980s. However, there is an effort to provide a broader historical perspective, and each policy study relates the development of these issues over a longer period. In particular, Chapter 3 focuses on U.S. relations with Turkey as a means of examining the evolution of post-World War II American foreign policy and of the changing pattern of congressional involvement in foreign policy over the years. In a similar vein, Chapter 5 begins its consideration of the congressional role in arms sales by examining the "Country X" loan program, when Congress first delved into executive branch arms sales activities. And, in Chapter 7, the limited congressional involvement at the time of the first strategic arms limitation agreement (SALT I) serves as a contrasting background for the more active congressional role in subsequent arms control matters.

The collective product not only describes and analyzes the congressional role, but provides what we believe is an insightful look at some of the major developments in recent American foreign policy. It is intended to be a book that is instructive in its examination of both process and policy. We hope that it will help illuminate each of these areas.

The concept of this book, as well as its development, resulted from a joint effort by the editors. In addition to our individual contributions, Baker developed the evaluative criteria, while Purvis exercised overall editorial responsibility.

The editors are, of course, particularly indebted to the three other contributors to this volume. Additionally, there are a number of individuals who in various direct and indirect ways have been helpful to us in completing the book. Among those to whom we owe gratitude for their comments or suggestions on various aspects of the book are J. William Fulbright, Bruce Buchanan, Len Weiss, Sidney Weintraub, Richard McCall, and William E. Jackson, Jr. A special acknowledgement is due to Esther Purvis for her support and encouragement. Barbara E. Rieper has been especially helpful in doing the word processing and in preparing the manuscript. We also express appreciation to our former Senate staff colleagues and to Robert C. Byrd, with whom we were privileged to work.

H.H.P.
S.J.B.

1
Introduction:
Legislative-Executive Interaction

Hoyt Purvis

Foreign policy consists of the external goals of a nation and the means adopted to pursue those goals. In United States history, predominance in the making of foreign policy has shifted back and forth between the two institutions entrusted by the Constitution with foreign policy responsibilities--the executive and the legislative branches of the federal government.

However, in the 1930s the United States entered a lengthy period when the executive was to be largely dominant. This was a period of continuing crisis--depression, war, cold war. In the years after World War II, the President retained the pre-eminent position in foreign policy that executives usually have been accorded during wartime. There were a number of major foreign policy initiatives in those post-war years: establishment of the United Nations; the Truman Doctrine and Greek-Turkish aid program; the Marshall Plan; the North Atlantic Treaty; and the "Point Four" aid program. These were moves in which there was some degree of congressional involvement and collaboration, although that collaboration was generally confined to a very limited number of congressional leaders. It is looked upon as an era of bipartisanship in foreign policy, although the depth and durability of that bipartisanship is often exaggerated.

Presidential power increased and the congressional role in foreign policy diminished while U.S. commitments and involvement around the world grew and weaponry became increasingly sophisticated. By the 1960s, the balance between branches of government was further distorted when the influence of television served to strengthen the presidency. Television easily focused on the presidency, while Congress, a more disparate institution, was more difficult to cover, lacking the glamour and singular focus of the presidency. Television reinforced the tendency to look to a single leader.

But, in the mid-1960s, Congress gradually began to

reassert itself in the foreign policy field. That assertiveness increased in the early 1970s in response to the experiences of Vietnam and Watergate.

By the late 1970s, the two branches had settled into an uneasy balance. The executive has the leading role in foreign affairs, but Congress plays an active part at almost every stage, in some cases serving as a check on what are perceived as excesses or potential excesses or errors by the President.

A Stronger Role

Congress has its formal foreign policy powers, some of which have been left dormant at times. The most prominent of these are Congress' constitutional powers --the power to declare war, maintain the armed forces, appropriate funds, and exercise oversight of the execution of laws. The Senate has the special responsibilities of approving treaties and confirming appointments of key officials within the executive branch.

In addition to those constitutional powers, Congress has taken a series of steps to strengthen its involvement in foreign policy. Most notably, Congress sought to reestablish its role in commiting U.S. forces overseas with the War Powers Resolution, enacted in 1973 over a presidential veto. Through other legislative measures, Congress placed restrictions on presidential actions; for example, aid to certain countries was prohibited or made conditional because of objectionable human rights practices or nuclear policies of those countries. Although many of these restrictions applied to Third World countries, in 1974 Congress approved the Jackson-Vanik amendment to the U.S.-Soviet trade bill, requiring freer emigration of Soviet Jewry as a condition of American trade. The move was deeply resented by the Soviet leaders and was seen by some as a primary factor in derailing prospects for real detente between the U.S. and U.S.S.R.

Detailed restrictions on economic and military aid have become commonplace in foreign assistance legislation. Congress also staked out a stronger role for itself by insisting on greater involvement and oversight in such key areas as intelligence and arms transfers. As an example, in the arms sales field, the executive was allowed to proceed with the 1981 sale of AWACS aircraft to Saudi Arabia only after intense scrutiny and some concessions to congressional concerns.

Some of the provisions designed to ensure Congress a voice in various foreign policy and security areas were called into question by a 1983 Supreme Court decision banning the "legislative veto." Under the legislative veto, a provision used primarily in domestic legislation, Congress granted authority to the executive but reserved the right to reject or reverse particular uses of that authority. Despite the Court's action, there were still a number of means by which Congress could exercise its oversight.

War Powers

The Court's legislative veto ruling also raised questions about the War Powers Resolution, specifically the provision allowing Congress, by a concurrent resolution, to force the withdrawal of U.S. troops engaged in hostilities overseas without specific congressional authorization. Many authorities agreed, however, that the other basic War Powers provisions remained intact. (Those provisions require notification to Congress when U.S. forces are sent into hostile or potentially hostile situations or while equipped for combat or in numbers which substantially enlarge U.S. forces already in place; and prohibit the president from keeping troops in hostile situations for more than 60 to 90 days unless Congress gives its authorization.)

Although presidents have frequently questioned the constitutionality of the law, there have been a number of instances of presidental reports to Congress in compliance with the law. For example, not long after the 1983 Court decision, President Ronald Reagan adhered to the War Powers provision on notification when he informed Congress of the dispatch of AWACS and fighter planes to Chad.

However, Reagan and Congress locked horns over the application of the War Powers Resolution to the presence of U.S. Marines in Lebanon. Controversy over the troops in Lebanon heightened in late summer 1983, after several Marines were killed. Initially, Reagan was reluctant to acknowledge that the troops were subject to the War Powers Resolution. But, under congressional pressure, Administration officials worked out a "compromise" agreement with Senate Majority Leader Howard Baker and House Speaker Thomas (Tip) O'Neill, Jr. While the agreement authorized the President to keep U.S. troops in Lebanon for as much as 18 months, it did make the action subject to the War Powers Resolution. Senate Democrats and some House members argued that 18 months was too long, and attempted unsuccessfully to shorten the authorized period. Some claimed that the authorization actually undercut the War Powers Resolution and charged that the President was being given a "blank check," amounting to another Tonkin Gulf Resolution, which Presidents Johnson and Nixon used to claim congressional authorization for the war in Vietnam. Nonetheless, although Reagan was given a long leash by Congress, the major War Powers provisions had been invoked for the first time. Reagan also said that it would be his intention to seek congressional approval if there was a need for any substantial expansion in the number or role of U.S. troops.

A short time later, when U.S. forces invaded Grenada, there was some initial criticism from Speaker O'Neill and others in Congress. However, after a fact-finding mission of House members sent to Grenada by O'Neill reported to him that the action was "justified," the Speaker reversed his position. This reversal came amid evidence of strong public support for President Reagan's action on Grenada.

Congressional Influence

In recent years Congress has been increasingly involved not only in foreign aid and international security issues, but in defense spending as well. It was Congress that pushed for relative decreases in defense spending in the wake of the Vietnam War. Then, in the late 1970s, Congress led the way in insisting on an upturn in defense spending. Still later, it was Congress that insisted on drawing the line on some of the Reagan Administration proposals for massive increases in the military budget.

The Senate has also been increasingly inclined to exercise its constitutional prerogatives on treaties and nominations. Both the Panama Canal Treaties debate and the argument over SALT II, each discussed in this volume, demonstrate the intensity of Senate involvement in the treaty process. The confirmation of presidential appointees is usually routine, with few nominees rejected outright by a Senate vote. But the Senate has become more assertive in its use of the confirmation process--influencing choices, forcing withdrawal of some nominees, and approving others only after lengthy debate.

Informal Processes

Although most studies and analyses focus on those areas of formal congressional authority, the formal powers have been reinforced and supplemented by informal processes of consultation between the President and members of Congress and interaction between congressional staff and the executive branch's foreign policy bureaucracy. Though Congress can have its most obvious impact through the exercise of its formal powers, it can also be influential in a more informal sense. Because of the need to gain congressional support for most foreign policy actions and programs--or the need to at least avert congressional disapproval--the executive frequently engages in a consultative dialogue with Congress. Many issues are negotiated or bartered between the two branches. In some cases policies and proposals are tailored to meet congressional desires without any formal action having been initiated by Congress.

This informal congressional role is manifested in a variety of ways. As noted, although it is rare for the Senate to actually reject a presidential nominee for a position in the foreign affairs field--Senate approval being required by the Constitution for appointments of "ambassadors, other public ministers, and consuls," and by law for various other positions--the Senate can have considerable influence on the selection process. Appointments are ofter "cleared" with key senators. The threat of Senate rejection or a nasty fight over a nomination is often enough to forestall an appointment. The objection of one key senator can in some cases be an effective veto of a potential appointment. Likewise, members of Congress can be influential in helping to determine who does get such appointments.

President Carter sent the nomination of Theodore Sorensen, who had been a top assistant to President Kennedy, for Senate confirmation as director of the Central Intelligence Agency in 1977. But, in the face of strong Senate opposition, Carter withdrew Sorensen's nomination. Some interpreted this as a sign of presidential weakness early in the Carter Administration, and it may have hampered Carter's ability to deal with Capitol Hill. On the other hand, a President can risk souring relations with Congress if he sticks with a nominee despite strong Senate opposition. Carter did stick with the nomination of Paul Warnke as chief arms control negotiator and head of Arms Control and Disarmament Agency (ACDA). Warnke was a man of proven ability, but his views on arms control and defense were anathema to some senators. After much debate, his nomination was approved, but the confirmation was used to "send a message" to the President. Although Warnke received the simple majority necessary for confirmation as arms control negotiator, the vote fell short of the two-thirds that would be required for Senate approval of an arms control treaty. Warnke remained in office until the SALT II Treaty negotiations were nearly complete, and then resigned. It was recognized that the treaty--which faced a difficult time in the Senate-- would not be helped by Warnke's identification with it.

In 1983, a number of senators used the nomination of Kenneth Adelman as head of ACDA as an opportunity to debate the Reagan Administration's arms control policies. Adelman's nomination was opposed by the Foreign Relations Committee, where he encountered criticism for what was seen as a lack of experience and lack of commitment to arms control. Despite the controversy, Reagan ultimately won approval for his nominee, 57-42,

with many senators deferring to the President's choice,
even though expressing doubts about the choice.

Senator Jesse Helms (R-North Carolina) emerged in
the late 1970s as one of the several foreign policy
entrepreneurs in Congress. Helms was particularly
successful at influencing foreign policy appointments
within the Reagan Administration. He used his position on the Foreign Relations Committee and his ability
to rally conservative support to influence several
nominations to foreign policy positions and to block
others. In some cases Helms managed to delay confirmation until he extracted concessions from the
Administration.

One who had Helms' backing for a Reagan Administration position was Ernest Lefever, nominated in 1981 to
be assistant secretary of state for human rights. But
the nominee encountered strong opposition because of
his controversial views on human rights and a series of
contradictory statements. The combined support of
Helms and President Reagan was not enough to save the
embattled Lefever. When the Foreign Relations Committee voted 13-4 against the nomination, with a majority
of the Committee's Republicans among those opposing
Lefever, Reagan recognized that the nomination should
be withdrawn.

This was not a direct confrontation because no
final showdown occurred. The nomination was withdrawn
before a vote was taken on the Senate floor. But it
was an instance where the President had to back down in
the face of overwhelming Senate opposition.

Another Presidential "defeat" came on Reagan's 1982
proposal for production funding for the MX missile with
the "dense-pack" basing system. Presidents seldom experience a direct rebuke on weapons system requests,
just as their nominees are rarely rejected. But, in
this case, Reagan's MX plan was decisively defeated in
the House of Representatives--despite strong lobbying
by the President who called the MX funding absolutely
essential for national security. A House-Senate conference committee did retain some research and development funding, thus keeping the MX alive. And, following the recommendations of a blue-ribbon commission
appointed by Reagan, in 1983 Congress approved some
funding for still another version of MX basing. (At
the urging of some members of Congress, the President,
in return for their support of the MX, did agree to
accept their recommendations on a new approach to arms
control negotiations.) The MX came up repeatedly as
approval and funds were requested for various stages of
research, development, testing, and procurement and had
to go through the congressional authorization and appropriations processes in both Houses. Thus Congress
had numerous opportunities to debate the MX.

Confrontation and Consultation

There are the dramatic examples of confronation between the two branches--the Versailles Treaty in 1919; the disputes over Vietnam and Cambodia; the congressional thwarting of executive branch policies in Turkey and Angola in the 1970s; the later battles over policy in Central America, particular on "covert" aid to anti-government rebels in Nicaragua.

Despite the occasions when Congress has blocked or restricted presidential policies, in the final analysis Presidents usually prevail, even though they may have to modify policies and proposals somwhat. Approval of appropriations for the anti-ballistic missile system (Richard Nixon, 1969), the Panama Canal Treaties (Jimmy Carter, 1978), and the sale of the AWACS to Saudi Arabia (Ronald Reagan, 1981), are examples of bitterly fought battles in which the President prevailed by the narrowest of margins.

But these examples of confrontation and well-publicized battles over foreign policy are certainly less characteristic of legislative-executive relations than the more routine, informal interaction between the two branches. For example, one of the reasons that presidential appointments are routinely approved is that, as noted earlier, they are informally "cleared" in advance with key senators. Few major foreign policy proposals are sent to Capitol Hill that are not the product of intense interaction at the staff level. Trouble results when this procedure is ignored. For example, the Carter Administration proposal to resume military and economic aid to Pakistan in January 1980, was received coolly in Congress due to a lack of groundwork; Congress had been responsible for cutting off aid to Pakistan in 1979.

Similarly, the Carter Administration's surprise announcement in December 1978 of its intention to establish formal diplomatic relations with the People's Republic of China and to terminate the U.S.-Taiwan mutual defense treaty, drew sharp criticism in Congress. The Administration's failure to consult Congress in advance jeopardized support for the action. Even some who favored the move were critical of the lack of consultation. An amendment to the International Security Assistance Act of 1978 had expressed the sense of Congress that the President should consult with Congress before making any changes in China policy. (There were some ardent supporters of Taiwan who would have opposed the Carter policy in any case, regardless of advance consultation. Some of these opponents launched an unsuccessful court action to challenge the President's right to terminate the treaty without congressional sanction.) In its defense, the Carter Administration maintained that the move to formalize relations with China was the logical and anticipated conclusion to a normalization process begun during the Nixon Administration, and was, therefore, no surprise. Although Carter did inform at least one member of the congressional leadership of his plans, the Administration noted that the matter had to be dealt with quietly, so as not to undercut negotiations with the Chinese, who were very sensitive about how the issue was handled. Ultimately, Congress went along with the action, although the terms it included in the Taiwan Relations Act of 1979, which governs the "unofficial" relationship between the U.S. and Taiwan, went considerably beyond what the Administration wanted.

Another Carter initiative which understandably required a high degree of secrecy nonetheless drew criticism from Congress because of the lack of any advance consultation. This was the April 1980 effort to rescue the American hostages in Iran. The fact that the rescue mission failed caused many to question the planning and judgement involved, as well as the lack of consultation. Had the mission succeeded, undoubtedly the criticism would have been muted. Even though many in Congress conceded that the President was justified in maintaining secrecy on plans for the raid, others argued that the matter should at least have been discussed with the top congressional leaders. Ironically, since early stages of the hostage crisis and the subsequent Soviet invasion of Afghanistan, high-ranking State Department officials had been meeting regularly with congressional leaders to discuss developments and possible actions. And only hours before the raid, President Carter discussed a possible rescue missions with Senate Majority Leader Robert Byrd, but gave no indication that such an action was imminent. Later, Carter commented that he probably should have involved Byrd more directly in the planning for the mission.

Informing Congress: The "Pseudo-Crisis"

Despite these problems in executive-legislative consultation, the Carter Administration did consult extensively with Congress on certain other issues. It might even be argued that the Administration's eagerness to inform key members of the Senate inadvertently contributed to the failure to gain approval of the SALT II Treaty. As is discussed in Chapter 7 ("The Senate and Arms Control"), prospects for SALT II approval were badly damaged by the handling of the "discovery" of a Soviet "combat brigade" in Cuba in August 1979. At the time, the outlook for SALT II passage seemed increasingly favorable. The treaty had come through Senate committee hearings in relatively good shape and chances

for Senate approval seemed good--with the addition of
certain reservations and understandings to the final
resolution of ratification. But the handling of the
Soviet-troops-in-Cuba issue dealt a severe blow to SALT
II. The Administration was sensitive to suggestions,
primarily from Senator Richard Stone (D-Florida), whose
constituency included a large Cuban population, that it
was not being sufficiently vigilant in regard to Soviet
activities in Cuba. Stone had raised the matter several times during the Foreign Relations Committee's
hearings on SALT II. When intelligence reports turned
up evidence of some maneuvers by Soviet troops in Cuba,
the Carter Administration felt compelled to react. The
Administration apparently feared that opponents of the
treaty might break the news first. Intelligence information is often leaked in Washington, and members of
Congress and the congressional staff networks have
their own contacts and information sources. Therefore,
the decision was made to inform senior members of Congress, who were away from Washington for the Labor Day
holiday, of the developments.

Chairman Frank Church of the Senate Foreign Relations Committee was one of those informed of the "discovery" of a Soviet "combat brigade." After discussing
the matter with Secretary of State Cyrus Vance and
others by phone, Church said that if the Administration
did not intend to make a public announcement about the
discovery, he would. Church then held a news conference at his Idaho home, and called for "the immediate
removal of all Russian combat units from Cuba" and
later said that the Senate would not ratify SALT II
while the combat troops remained in Cuba. Church's
statements were followed by sweeping, categorical
statements by Administration officials.

Church supported SALT II, but was sensitive to the
fact that some treaty opponents would make a major
issue of the Soviet troops. Church was also facing a
tough re-election campaign in Idaho in 1980 (which he
subsequently lost) and was being strongly criticized
for his leading role in supporting Senate approval of
the Panama Canal Treaties. He had earlier encountered
criticism for his opposition to the U.S role in Vietnam. It is widely believed that Church quickly seized
the "Soviet troops" issue in an effort to prove his
"toughness" on foreign policy and discomfit his critics. Church denied this, but, whatever his intent, the
result was a serious blow to chances for SALT II
approval.

Subsequent information indicated that there was
nothing particularly unusual about the Soviet activities; that the troops had been in Cuba some years; and
that there was no violation of any U.S.-Soviet agreements. Soviet leaders insisted that the troops were
part of a "training center." Gradually, the controversy

died down, but it had caused a costly delay in the
Senate schedule on SALT II. As is portrayed in Chapter
7, with the passing of time the treaty encountered a
number of other serious problems, but the "pseudo-
crisis" over "Soviet troops" undoubtedly hurt the
treaty's prospects.

Intensity of Congressional Interest

All of these experiences, and those featured in the
policy studies in this volume, make clear the complexity and sensitivity of executive-legislative relations. They also make clear the intensity of congressional interest in most foreign policy issues. The
central point is that Congress wants to be in on the
action.

Knowing when Congress should be informed or brought
into a decision-making process, who in Congress should
be consulted, and how consultations should be carried
out, can be thorny problems for the executive. Although presidents often have broad latitude in dealing
with foreign policy, failure to consult and/or inform
Congress or mishandling of the consulatative process
can be a prelude to serious difficulties.

Some members of Congress, particularly those in key
positions, develop their own relationships with some
part of the executive bureaucracy and build an alliance
of interests. On occasion this leads to circumvention
of presidential programs and policies. In August 1981,
Secretary of Defense Caspar Weinberger was reported to
favor the airborne "big bird" mode of deployment for
the MX missile. But Air Force planners, who had been
excluded from the MX decision, let Senate Armed Services Chairman John Tower (R-Texas) know of their
opposition. Tower publicly attacked "big bird" and
effectively shot it down.

In addition to contacts within the executive,
members of Congress can rely on greatly increased
resources and support in dealing with foreign policy,
most notably the much-enlarged (some would say over-
enlarged) congressional staff. The "staff explosion"
since the beginning of the 1970s has meant a doubling
of members' and committee staffs in many cases.

The expanded resources available to Congress can
result in more thorough oversight of executive activities, and better research and investigation. On the
other hand, the growth in staff undoubtedly contributes
to some "make-work" projects within Congress, and, and
turn, the inquiries generated by such projects often
add to the burden of work within the executive branch.

The congressional hearing remains as a primary and
frequently effective means of carrying out the oversight responsibility and of focusing attention on

particular issues. Hearings may deal with specific
legislation or with broader policy questions, such as
the Senate Foreign Relations Committee's hearings on
China policy in the early 1970s. The increased size
and capability of congressional staff can result in
better preparation for the hearings. But the proliferation of subcommittees in Congress sometimes results
in excessive and essentially meaningless hearings.

The importance of congressional travel has
increased too. Overseas trips by members of Congress
have often been labeled as junkets, and unquestionably
there are many congressional trips that fit in that
category. However, travel and meetings with foreign
leaders by influential members of Congress can be
extremely significant. The opportunity for first-hand
observation can be highly valuable in making informed
judgments on key foreign policy issues. This was particularly true in the case of the Panama Canal Treaties, as is depicted in Chapter 4. Senators saw the
canal for themselves, and many realized that it was
highly vulnerable to sabotage or terrorism, and
concluded that it should be defused as a political
issue. They also had a chance to discuss the terms of
the treaties with Panamaian officials and to clarify
and, in effect, renegotiate aspects of the treaties.
In another instance, travel to Iran by Senators Thomas
Eagleton and John Culver raised questions in their
minds about the stability of the Shah's regime, even
though their warnings were unheeded. (See Chapter 5.)
In 1978, when Robert Byrd visited Iran and was asked by
the Carter Administration to give encouragement to the
Shah, he returned with the assessment that the Shah was
unlikely to survive in power. A number of congressional delegations have had meaningful discussions with
Soviet and Chinese leaders. During the Reagan Administration many congressional groups visited El Salvador
for a first-hand view of developments there. A trip to
Grenada in November 1983 by a congressional delegation
led many initially skeptical members to conclude that
President Reagan was justified in sending in American
troops.

All of these examples of congressional involvement
are evidence of the fact that American foreign policy
is a legislative as well as an executive matter. Many
governments in the world today are "authoritarian"
regimes of one type or another, in which popularly
elected legislative bodies, if they exist, have little
or no power. Even in democratic societies, both
parliamentary and presidential, the tendency is to
leave foreign policy questions to the executive and to
the professional foreign service bureaucracy. Most
members of most parliaments are "informed" by the
government about the nation's foreign policy, but have
little direct impact on that policy. Therefore, the

American system of shared powers in foreign policy is
distinctive, and poses some distinctive problems:
sometimes it becomes difficult to conduct foreign policy if there is not a single, authoritative voice;
there is a potential gap between executive commitments
to foreign governments and the approval by Congress
necessary to carry out those commitments; and there is
a tendency for Congress to write into law matters that
elsewhere are left to the discretion of the executive.
Co-determination in foreign policy has its advantages,
but few would deny that it complicates the making of
foreign policy.

This volume describes, analyzes, and evaluates the
strengths and weaknesses of the congressional role in
the foreign policy process. There is every indication
that Congress will continue to play an active role. In
most cases, the President has certain key advantages in
any struggle with Congress. The President retains
greater control of and access to information, the ability to initiate action, and can appeal to the need for
national unity in times of "crisis." Normally, the
Congress, press, and public are reluctant to oppose the
President on critical foreign policy issues, and the
President will usually get the benefit of the doubt.
But Congress does have to be factored into the foreign
policy equation. The critical question, then, is not
whether the executive should be stronger or the congressional role be reduced, or vice versa, but how each
can be strengthened to carry out their respective roles
and to best meet the challenges facing American foreign
policy.

2
Evaluating Congress'
Foreign Policy Performance

Steven J. Baker

Why has Congress grown more active in foreign policy in the past two decades? A variety of factors have been cited to explain this increased congressional role. First, there are broad-scale explanations that transcend a particular institution or time period. For example, there is the argument that there are cycles of executive or legislative predominance in foreign affairs;[1] historical trends, the force of individual personalities, and particular issues favor either predominance by the executive or legislative branch. An alternative broad-scale explanation links the change in Congress' role to a shift in the substance of foreign policy in an interdependent world where the distinction between foreign and domestic politics is less valid that ever before.[2] Blurring the distinction between foreign and domestic affairs implies that the foreign policy preeminence of the executive is less clear: when foreign policy problems impinge on the daily lives of Americans, then Congress has to be as interested in foreign policy as the president.

A second set of explanations at an intermediate level of generality stress structural changes that have occurred in both the executive and Congress, but particularly the latter. For example, the decline of centralized leadership and dispersal of authority within Congress, the growth in the number of subcommittees, the "staff explosion,"[3] are all pointed to as factors making it easier for individual members of Congress, such as Senator Jesse Helms, to become involved in foreign affairs. These structural characteristics are subject to change, but there is little evidence of a trend back towards greater centralization and discipline in Congress. Therefore, the ability of Congress to perform its foreign policy tasks coherently continues to be open to question.

A third set of explanations emphasizes the impact of very specific circumstances--foreign policy crises

13

such as the Vietnam War or Angola, or the succession of weakened and/or ineffectual presidents--Nixon, Ford, Carter. Such explanations would leave room for major short-term variations in the rate and kind of congressional participation in foreign policy, depending on the specific circumstances and on the individual occupying the White House.[4] For example, in the absence of a divisive foreign policy issue or in the presence of a president who was perceived as clear-sighted and able, Congress' involvement in foreign policy could be expected to diminish.

These factors, and a variety of others, have all contributed to the increase in congressional activity in foreign affairs. However, weighing the contributions of each differently leads to different conclusions regarding prospects for Congress' foreign policy role in the years ahead. For example, if broad transnational trends are at work, there is less expectation for short-term variation. The election of a Carter as opposed to a Reagan may not affect the level of Congress involvement in foreign policy. Alternatively, if the level of congressional involvement is tied to specific crises or specific presidents, short-term variation is to be expected--at least to the extent permitted by the intermediate range of structural factors. For example, a strong president would prevail except when existing foreign policy legislation mandates congressional involvement and Congress' structure permits individual members to push their own foreign policy priorities and interests.

There is disagreement over the significance of the congressional resurgence in foreign policy. Some maintain that Congress' reassertion constitutes something of a revolutionary change, with the result that we now have "foreign policy by Congress."[5] If foreign-policy making is perceived as a zero-sum situation, then a more active Congress must necessarily operate at the expense of the President. But it might be argued that, as the range of government activities has expanded, there are more foreign policy roles to play; if this is true, then an expanded congressional role need not necessarily be at the expense of the President, and Congress may have regained some of its lost power--but without really weakening the presidency.[6]

Complex Interaction

The policy studies in this volume suggest that the changes in Congress' role in foreign policy in the last decade have been dramatic but not revolutionary. Congress has become a more active and more visible participant in foreign policy than it was in the post-World War II period, but the executive retains key

prerogatives--especially in taking foreign policy initiatives and in implementing policy. What is new and
extremely important is that the executive has been compelled to consult Congress more regularly and, in some
cases, more formally on foreign policy questions. The
result is a complex pattern of interaction between the
executive and Congress.

The Constitution's shared powers create an "invitation to struggle" for control over foreign policy,[7] and
some foreign policy issues become the subject of institutional confrontation. But, dramatic confrontation
remains the exception, not the rule. What has evolved
over the last 15 years is a pattern of interaction that
usually facilitates the elaboration and implementation
of American foreign policy. Even on highly publicized
and politicized issues such as the Panama Canal Treaties, a President who is willing to consult with Congress has a good chance of achieving what he wants,
even where public support is weak. What Congress has
insisted on, and continues to insist on, is the right
to be consulted--before, during, and after the fact.

The preponderance of scholarly opinion seems to see
Congress as the weak link in the policy process,[8] the
part of the policy apparatus most in need of reform.[9]
Some analysts have called for restricting Congress'
foreign policy role because "the cost of conflict and
decentralization have become too great."[10] However,
other analysts have recognized the potential benefits
of increased congressional involvement in foreign policy. For example, Congress' involvement is seen as a
way of formulating a foreign policy that enjoys a
higher degree of public support and is therefore easier
to implement and more consistent over time. Consultation with Congress sometimes improves the quality of
foreign policy by airing the issues and alternatives.[11] Even institutional conflicts between the
executive and Congress can sometimes be turned to
diplomatic advantage. But these positive contributions
are outweighed or lessened in the estimation of many
observers by the negative consequences of a frequent
lack of coherence in U.S. foreign policy and an inability to carry through objectives--weaknesses that are
attributed at least in part to the congressional role.

Legitimacy and Efficacy

In judging whether Congress' foreign policy assertiveness is a good or bad development, there are two
interrelated dimensions that have to be dealt with:
the question of legitimacy and the issue of efficacy.
The legitimacy of Congress' involvement in foreign
policy has its foundation in the Constitution: constitutional provisions clearly establish foreign affairs

as a "shared power" between the executive and the legislative branches, with special responsibilities given to the Senate. Two-hundred years of precedents validate the notion that Congress has a right and a responsibility to participate in the making of American foreign policy. But the level and type of congressional participation has varied widely through history. Therefore, there is a second kind of legitimacy test that must be applied, one that relates to the climate of opinion of the times. Beginning in the 1960s, Congress' resurgence coincided with and was partly caused by a decline in the political consensus that had supported postwar American foreign policy,[13] a reaction fed by the perception that actions of successive presidents threatened the constitutional system. Congress' expanded role gained legitimacy from public support. A new foreign policy consensus has not emerged to replace the old, and concerns about the executive's abuse of power declined during the Carter presidency. Without the support of a clear public consensus on foreign policy, the responsibilities so assertively regained by Congress in the early 1970s have been exercised with circumspection through the early 1980s.

There are fewer questions about the legitimacy of Congress' deep involvement in foreign policy than there are about how well Congress performs its foreign policy responsibilities: efficacy is a bigger issue than legitimacy. The preoccupation with efficacy is not, however, a secondary concern. Efficacy complements legitimacy: unless Congress is able to fulfill the expectation that its participation in foreign policy is positive in impact, and helps the nation achieve its foreign goals, then the legitimacy of Congress' involvement in foreign policy will be open to question. A much more limited definition of the proper level and kind of congressional involvement in foreign affairs is likely to result. Those who prefer a high degree of congressional participation in foreign policy must be the first to be concerned about the effectiveness of that participation.

In the postwar period, the foreign policy challenges faced by the United States helped to consolidate the predominance of the executive branch over the Congress. Whereas the concentration of power in the executive had typically been dismantled in the wake of a war, after World War II it was decided that America's new world role would not allow a reversion to type, with the attendant danger of a return to interwar isolationism. The Cold War served to justify the maintenance of a President who alone could respond to crises in a period, by definition, of permanent threat to an America transformed into a global superpower. For example, it became part of the conventional wisdom that the nuclear age rendered anachronistic that part of the

Constitution that requires a declaration of war by Congress. A diverse body of 535 men and women, however well organized, could not be expected to act with the clarity of purpose and efficiency of a single individual, the President. The assumption that, by definition, the President is better equipped to make foreign policy has persisted even after the consensus on the wisdom of an American global role has evaporated.

Standards for Evaluation

How has foreign policy been judged? Standards for judging foreign policy have often been implicit rather than explicit, and are not usually treated systematically. For example, scholars and journalists often cite the need for leadership in foreign affairs, but rarely seek to analyze systematically either the nature of leadership or the circumstances which permit its successful exercise.[14] However, themes recur in analyses of foreign policy that provide some basis for evaluating the president's foreign policy performance.

First, the need for leadership is always stressed—the need to have a clearly defined policy, articulated unambiguously and implemented efficiently.[15] In foreign policy even more than in domestic policy, "there is no substitute for a capable, determined, and knowledgeable President."[16]

In principle, the need for leadership is difficult to challenge. Particularly in foreign affairs, where so much is beyond the direct control of any single government, the need for clarity of purpose and consistency of action is unarguable. The problem with leadership is less one of principle than of practice. In fact, for much of the last 20 years presidents have been unable to perform this foreign policy function well. With Lyndon Johnson and Richard Nixon, the nation had strong leaders. But Johnson was increasingly a leader without followers, persisting in the Vietnam War long after it would have been politically expedient for him to abandon the struggle. Nixon had relatively well-defined foreign policy goals, but he used his foreign policy to justify abuses of executive power in the name of "national security." The American people elected Jimmy Carter in part because he was not a "Washingtonian," but when he continued to behave as an outsider even after four years in the White House, his ability to lead the country was called into question. Confusion in his foreign policy contributed to this perception. Surprisingly, the Reagan Administration quickly followed the pattern of its predecessor, with foreign policy zig-zags that robbed the Reagan foreign policy of much coherence beyond rhetorical anti-communism. With recent experience in mind, the assumption that the president is, and should be, the central source of an effective foreign policy is open to question. Leadership in contemporary American politics is more of a problem that a policy panacea.

A second standard that is used to measure foreign policy performance is the degree to which the policy implements some recognizable national interest, a notoriously slippery concept. In principle, the President has a structural advantage over the Congress in defining national interest because he alone has a national constituency, whereas all other political authorities have much more limited geographical constituencies. A national constituency should incline the President to a national view of problems, just as the more limited constituencies of members of Congress should make them more prone to parochialism and to influence by special interests. With different terms of office as well as different constituencies, the political needs of the legislative and executive branches may often be at odds.[17]

The degree to which theory and practice corresponds with respect to the national interest is not clear. There are examples of presidents behaving in a manner consistent with a broad definition of national interest in foreign affairs in the face of parochial pressures from Congress (e.g., Nixon's 1974 Trade Act): there are as well examples of presidents bowing to parochial interests (Reagan's lifting of the grain embargo on Russia in 1981). Special interests and lobbies for foreign governments impact on the executive branch as well as the legislative branch.

It could be argued that the collective judgment of either or both of the two Houses is as representative of the U.S. national interest as the judgment of the President and a handful of advisors. Certainly, as long as the President is a politician he will be affected by electoral considerations. With a four-year term, presidents may be expected to be less craven than representatives with two-year terms but more than senators with six-year terms. For example, President Carter proposed to increase defense spending in order to improve the prospects for Senate approval of the SALT II Treaty. Having termed SALT "tragically flawed" in the campaign, in office, President Reagan chose to abide by the terms of the SALT II Treaty but not to ratify it. Politics, rather than the national interest, dictated presidential policy in both these examples.

A third standard for judging foreign policy performance is organizational competence--i.e., whether or not the institutional infrastructure is adequate to formulating and conducting an effective foreign policy.[18] Here, the executives' centralization and hierarchical structure are supposed to be great advantages

over the relatively decentralized and often anarchic
environment on Capitol Hill. But here, too, there are
considerations that call into question the executives'
supposed foreign policy effectiveness. First, the
executive foreign policy bureaucracy is both enormous
and complex, and often operates very differently from a
hierarchical flow-chart. The State Department and Defense Department are both independent entities reporting directly to the President on foreign policy matters. Formally, the intelligence community is supposed
to report through the President's national security advisor, but in fact both civilian and military intelligence agencies have fairly independent roles in the
policy community. The complexity of the executive foreign policy apparatus is such that there are more than
40 executive agencies with representatives abroad in
major American embassies; apparently, whatever centralization there is does not extend to overseas operations. Furthermore, the interplay of the executive
agencies to influence policy is often described in
terms of the "bureaucratic politics model" in which internal procedures and institutional rivalries may pre-
dominate in determining policy outcomes that have no
necessary relationship to rationally derived "policy,"
much less the "national interest." On the whole, what
emerges is a foreign policy establishment that differs
more in degree than in kind from Congress' foreign policy organization.

A <u>fourth</u> standard for judging foreign policy performance is the level of information and expertise that
is brought to bear on a problem.[19] In terms of information, the President has a natural advantage because
he is at the center of a worldwide network. Most members of Congress have competing demands on their time
and few incentives for deep or sustained involvement in
foreign policy issues. The Hill staff explosion has
reduced the gap between the information that Congress
can process, as opposed to the executive, but even this
cannot compensate for the volume and quality of foreign
policy expertise at the disposal of the president. Indeed, much of the foreign policy information available
to Congress continues to come from executive branch
sources.

Nevertheless, information must be analyzed and put
to use in order to have a policy impact. In the case
of Iran, for example, the intelligence and diplomatic
establishments did not anticipate the Shah's downfall,
nor were they prescient regarding the future of the
country in the hands of the mullahs. This kind of policy failure may reflect the pattern at the State
Department whereby the important decisions are taken by
the political appointees on the seventh floor, while
the people with the practical experience and county
expertise on the fifth and sixth floors are not always

included in the deliberations. Depth of knowledge in foreign policy has varied widely in the White House in recent years. Especially in the Reagan Administration, a lack of substantive knowledge or experience in foreign affairs has not been a bar to top foreign policy positions. William Clark was made Deputy Secretary of State in spite of his foreign policy ignorance and then served as National Security Advisor to the President because of his skill as a bureaucratic actor and close relationship with the President. Clearly, a lack of foreign policy expertise is not an exclusively congressional shortcoming.

It is necessary to articulate better, more systematic standards for judging the foreign policy performance of the President. The gap between the informal standards that are often used and presidential performance over the last decade raises the question whether the standards are unrealistic and, therefore, of questionable relevance if we are to describe accurately or prescribe presidential behavior. The observed shortcomings of the executive in the performance of his foreign policy responsibilities cannot excuse Congress' own shortcomings in this field. Rather, this discussion suggests that to use a presidential set of standards for evaluating Congress' performance may be misleading, first because the executive branch itself does not in practice live up to these standards, and second because the standards are intrinsic to executives and, by definition, could never be satisfactorily attained by a legislative body. What is needed is a set of standards that is both realistic, descriptively accurate of Congress' performance at its best, and appropriate to a legislative body. In other words, if we are to judge Congress, we need congressional standards for doing so.

Reflection on the peculiar demands of making foreign policy and on the particular circumstances of contemporary American politics suggests at least five standards for judging Congress' exercise of its foreign policy responsibilities.

1) <u>Legitimacy</u>. Both the role Congress plays in foreign policy and the manner in which the role is played should be a logical extension of Congress' constitutional responsibilities--to declare war, raise armies, approve treaties, confirm ambassadors, and more generally oversee the implementation of laws by the executive.

2) <u>Interest articulation and public information</u>. Congress should bring the views and interests of various groups in society to bear on foreign policy questions. Congress' consideration of an issue should raise the level of public debate on foreign affairs, helping to educate the public and to shape public opinion.

3) <u>Expeditious consideration</u>. Congress' participation in foreign policy should be neither hasty nor
dilatory. Circumstances will dictate the degree of
dispatch that is appropriate in a particular case, but
generally congressional action should not be so time
consuming as to damage substantial national interests.
Different standards would apply to an international
"crisis" than would apply to a more routine foreign
policy situation.

4) <u>Coherence</u>. The effect of Congress' participation should be greater coherence and consistency in
U.S. foreign policy, not greater confusion. There are
two dimensions to the coherence standard--between the
two branches and within Congress. Executive/legisla-
tive coherence exists when the President and Congress
agree on a foreign policy issue; agreement on the objective to be pursued but disagreement on the proper
means might still preserve the semblance of coherence.
Where there are fundamental differences between Congress and the President over both means and ends, then
properly Congress' should be responsive to public opinion, contributing to a basis for a coherent policy when
and if the executive changes course. Internal coherence exists when the Senate and the House agree on a
foreign policy issue. Disagreement between the two
Houses of Congress breeds policy confusion.

5) <u>Effectiveness</u>. The impact of Congress' actions
on U.S. foreign policy should achieve the intended purpose and not be counterproductive. While judging effectiveness can be highly subjective and speculative,
it is nonetheless a standard that must be considered.

Using these standards to evaluate Congress' foreign
policy performance in the policy studies in this volume
will provide a better basis for understanding U.S. foreign-policy making, and will provide a relevant basis
for prescriptive assessments as to what Congress should
and should not do in the foreign policy field.

NOTES

1. Arthur Schlesinger, Jr., <u>The Imperial Presi-
dency</u> (Boston: Houghton Mifflin, 1973); and Richard
Haass, <u>Congressional Power: Implications for American
Security</u>, Adelphi Papers, no. 153, 1979.
2. Bayless Manning, "Congress, the Executive, and
Intermestic Affairs," <u>Foreign Affairs</u> 55, January 1977.
3. I. M. Destler, "Trade Consensus and SALT
Stalemate" in Norman Ornstein and Thomas Mann, eds.,
<u>The New Congress</u> (Washington: American Enterprise
Institute, 1981), p.332.

4. Joseph Nogee, "Congress and the Presidency: Dilemmas of Policy-Making in a Democracy" in Nogee and John Spanier, eds., Congress, the Presidency, and American Foreign Policy (New York: Pergamon Press, 1981), pp.198-99; and Haass, op. cit., p.34.

5. Thomas M. Franck and Edward Weisband, Foreign Policy by Congress (New York: Oxford University Press, 1979).

6. Thomas P. Cronin, "A Resurgent Congress and the Imperial Presidency" Political Science Quarterly, summer 1980, vol. 95, no. 2.

7. Cecil V. Crabb, Jr. and Pat M. Holt, Invitation to Struggle: Congress, the President and Foreign Policy (Washington: Congressionaly Quarterly Press, 1980).

8. John Spanier, "Introduction," in Spanier, Nogee, p.x.

9. James Sundquist, "Congress the President, and the Crisis of Competence," in Larry Dodd and Bruce Oppenheimer, eds., Congress Reconsidered (Washington: Congressional Quarterly Press, 1981), pp.362-364.

10. I. M. Destler, "Executive-Congressional Conflict in Foreign Policy: Explaining It, Coping With It," in Dodd and Oppenheimer, eds., p.306.

11. Douglas J. Bennet, Jr., "Congress in Foreign Policy: Who Needs It?" Foreign Affairs 57, fall 1978, and Haass, Congressional Power, pp.31-32.

12. Destler, in Dodd and Oppenheimer, p.306.

13. See, for example, James Chace, "Is a Foreign Policy Consensus Possible?" Foreign Affairs 57, fall 1978.

14. Ryan J. Barilleaux, The Presidential Ordeal: Evaluating Presidential Performance in Foreign Affairs, Ph.D. Dissertation, University of Texas at Austin, August 1983.

15. Spanier, pp.xxvii-xxx; Nogee, pp.190-193; Destler in Ornstein and Mann, pp.354-55.

16. Nogee, p.199.

17. Destler, in Mann, Ornstein, pp.300-302; Spanier, pp.xxii-xxiii.

18. Sundquist, pp.362-364; Destler, in Dodd and Oppenheimer, pp.310-12.

19. Spanier, pp.xxvi-xxviii.

3
Tracing the Congressional Role: U.S. Foreign Policy and Turkey

Hoyt Purvis

On March 12, 1947, President Harry Truman addressed a joint session of Congress to recommend assistance to Greece and Turkey under what became known as the Truman Doctrine. The President spoke in grave terms about the threat to freedom in the two countries and described the matter as urgent because British officials had recently notified the United States that Britain could no longer fulfill its traditional commitments in Greece and Turkey.

Beginning with the Truman Doctrine and the immediate post-World War II era, Turkey has held a key position in the U.S. foreign policy perspective, with its strategic location giving it particular importance. The changing patterns of congressional involvement in foreign policy can be traced through U.S. policies toward Turkey. Indeed, focusing on Turkey provides a particularly instructive paradigm for examining the evolution of U.S. foreign policy since World War II, and the congressional role during that period.

Congress and the Truman Doctrine

President Truman, in his appeal to Congress, said, "As in the case of Greece, if Turkey is to have the assistance it needs, the United States must supply it. We are the only country able to provide that help. I am fully aware of the broad implications involved if the United States extends assistance to Greece and Turkey..."[1]

In his address, Truman noted that one of the primary objectives of U.S. foreign policy was "the creation of conditions in which we and other nations will be able to work out a way of life free from coercion."[2] Although the clear implication of Truman's message was that Turkey and Greece were threatened with the prospect of Soviet/communist domination, he did not make any

23

specific references to the Soviet Union. However, he was more explicit when he later recalled, in his memoirs, the factors that led to the U.S. commitment to Greece and Turkey:

> ...The alternative was the loss of Greece and the extension of the Iron Curtain across the eastern Mediterranean. If Greece was lost, Turkey would become an untenable outpost in a sea of communism. Similarly, if Turkey yielded to Soviet demands, the position of Greece would be endangered...Greece and Turkey were still free countries being challenged by communist threats both from within and without. These free people were now engaged in a valiant struggle to preserve their liberties and independence.
> America could not, and should not, let these free countries stand unaided...The ideals and the traditions of our nation demanded that we come to the aid of Greece and Turkey and that we put the world on notice that it would be our policy to support the cause of freedom wherever it was threatened.[3]

This was a major point of demarcation in American foreign policy, and one that has met with substantial criticism. The Truman Doctrine has been seen by some critics as having made the Cold War inevitable. Senator J. W. Fulbright, long a leading foreign policy figure in Congress, termed the doctrine a seminal development. Fulbright said this was true because President Truman based his appeal to Congress for support of Greece and Turkey not primarily on specific circumstances of those two countries at that time, but on sweeping ideological (anti-communist) grounds. Actually, Truman did focus on specific circumstances of Greece and Turkey, while acknowledging that broader implications were involved. Fulbright, who voted for the original Greek-Turkish aid package, concedes that the Truman Doctrine "may have made sense for its time and place,"[4] but says that it "came to be recognized as the basic rationale, from the American standpoint, for the Cold War."[5] According to Fulbright, regardless of the original merit of the Truman Doctrine, it served as the charter for 25 years of "global ideological warfare" and it was this "subsequent universal application" of the Truman Doctrine that Fulbright and others criticized.[6] Some of Truman's phraseology might have easily fit into a speech on Vietnam by American presidents in the 1960s.

Fulbright has written, "Sustained by an inert Congress, the policymakers of the forties, fifties, and early sixties were never compelled to re-examine the premises of the Truman Doctrine, or even to defend them in constructive adversary proceedings."[7]

Since the Greek-Turkish aid program and the Truman Doctrine were decisive turning points in U.S. foreign policy and set the tone for two decades--a period during which many viewed the congressional role as relatively minor--what role did Congress play in establishing the doctrine?

White House Initiative

On February 21, 1947, the British Government officially notified the United States that London could not provide the support needed by Greece and Turkey. On February 27, congressional leaders were summoned to the White House to be briefed on the matter by President Truman and Secretary of State George Marshall. Truman realized that with Republican control of Congress "the situation was more precarious than it would have been with a preponderantly Democratic Congress," and said it seemed desirable "to advise the congressional leadership as soon as possible of the gravity of the situation..."[8]

Also present at the meeting was Under Secretary of State Dean Acheson. Never noted for his modesty, Acheson later offered his recollection of that historic session:

> When we convened...in the White House to open the subject with our congressional masters, I knew we were met at Armageddon. We faced the 'leaders of Congress'--all the majority and minority potentates except Senator Taft, an accidental omission to which Senator Vandenberg swiftly drew the President's attention.[9]

Although Marshall had described the situation in stark terms, Acheson felt that the Secretary had "flubbed" his opening statement. Acheson recalled:

> In desperation I whispered to him a request to speak. This was my crisis. For a week I had nurtured it. These congressmen had no conception of what challenged them; it was my task to bring it home...Never have I spoken under such a pressing sense that the issue was up to me alone. No time was left for measured appraisal. In the past 18 months, I said, Soviet pressure on the Straits, on Iran, and on northern Greece had brought the Balkans to the point where a highly possible Soviet breakthrough might open three continents to Soviet penetration...The Soviet Union was

playing one of the greatest gambles in history
at minimal cost...We and we alone were in a
position to break up the play.[10]

According to Acheson's account, subsequently repeated by a number of authors, a long silence followed
his remarks. Then, according to Acheson, Senator
Arthur Vandenberg said solemnly, "Mr. President, if you
will say that to the Congress and the country, I will
support you and I believe that most of its members will
do the same."[11] In his differing description of the
meeting, Vandenberg said of the reaction of the congressional leadership, "We all made general comments
but no commitments. This was the extent of the 'bipartisan technique' in this instance. But it must be
remembered that the whole thing was precipitated upon
our government so suddenly that there really was very
little opportunity for preliminary consultations and
studies."[12]

Joseph Jones, who was a State Department official
at the time, and who later wrote The Fifteen Weeks, a
respected chronicle of this decisive period in U.S.
foreign policy, offered this account:

> Slowly and with gravity, Vandenberg said
> that he had been greatly impressed, even shak-
> en by what he had heard...He felt that it was
> absolutely necessary that any request of Con-
> gress for funds authority to aid Greece and
> Turkey should be accompanied by a message to
> Congress, and an explanation to the American
> people, in which the grim facts of the larger
> situation should be laid publicly on the line
> as they had been at their meeting there that
> day...
> Vandenberg wrote some time later that no
> commitments were made at this meeting. That
> is true. None had been asked. But the very
> definite impression was gained, and was con-
> veyed to the State Department staff the next
> day...that the congressional leaders would
> support whatever measures were necessary to
> save Greece and Turkey, on the condition, made
> by Senator Vandenberg and supported by others
> present, that the President should, in a mes-
> sage to Congress and in a radio address to the
> American people, explain the issue in the same
> frank terms and broad context in which it had
> been laid before them.[13]

However, Jones also makes clear that most of those
in the State Department, led by Acheson, were from the
beginning strong advocates of a tough approach on this
issue. In working on the Greek-Turkish aid program,

they "found release from the professional frustration of years." According to Jones "there was little dissent in the Department or anywhere in the government from the view that the boldest kind of confrontation was necessary."[14]

At a State Department meeting on February 24, 1947 --three days before the first meeting with congressional leaders--John Hickerson of the Office of European Affairs, had urged that the new program be presented to Congress "in such a fashion as to electrify the American people."[15]

A number of later accounts of the White House meeting on February 27 state that Senator Vandenberg told Truman that to gain approval for the proposal, he would have to "scare hell" out of the country. This is frequently cited as a reason for the strong tone of Truman's subsequent appeal to Congress. However, this rendition considerably overstates the accounts of the principals in their memoirs, certainly Vandenberg's own account, and is perhaps apocryphal. There are ample indications that the tone of Truman's approach may have owed as much or more to sentiments within the executive branch and views of key figures in the executive as to what would be necessary to gain public and congressional support than to the urging of Vandenberg or others in Congress.

(One of the earliest examples of this statement being attributed to Vandenberg is found in Eric F. Goldman's The Crucial Decade--And After, America, 1945-1960 (1956). Goldman wrote, "As Vandenberg left, he remarked to Truman: 'Mr. President, if that's what you want, there's only one way to get it. That is to make a personal appearance before Congress and scare hell out of the country.'" (p. 59). There is no documentation of the comment attributed to Vandenberg. Alexander DeConde in A History of American Foreign Policy (1963) used the same quote and the footnote said, "Quoted in Goldman, Crucial Decade." (p. 669, 2nd. ed.). In America, Russia, and the Cold War, 1945-1966 (1968), Walter Lafeber wrote, "Truman and his advisors ...went to some length to oversell the doctrine ideologically. As Vandenberg advised, the President 'scared hell out of the American people,' by painting in dark hues the 'totalitarian regimes' which threatened to snuff out freedom everywhere. (p. 45). There is no documentation of the comment attributed to Vandenberg. For similar accounts see: Arthur M. Schlesinger, Jr., The Imperial Presidency (1973), p. 128: "He (Truman) also paid a price: to get the policy he had to overcolor the crisis. Thus Senator Vandenberg told him that, if he wanted to enlist Congress behind aid to Greece and Turkey, he would have to scare hell out of the country. Truman therefore elevated a reasonable and limited program into a transcendent

principle."; also, Schlesinger's introduction to The
Dynamics of World Power--A Documentary History of
United States Foreign Policy, 1945-1973 (1973) p.xxxv:
"But, recalling the hard fight for a British loan in
1946, Truman feared that a conventional request for aid
would not pass the Congress. Accordingly he accepted
the counsel of Senator Vandenberg that he had to scare
the hell out of the country."; Robert A. Divine, Foreign Policy and U.S. Presidential Elections, 1940-1948
(1974), p. 170: "Urged by Senator Arthur Vandenberg to
'scare hell out of the American people,' the President
justified his proposals by sketching out a struggle
between the forces of good and evil..."; Dewey W.
Grantham, The United States Since 1945: The Ordeal of
Power (1976), p. 20: "Senator Vandenberg was later
quoted as saying..."Mr. President, if that's what you
want, there's only one way to get it. That is to make
a personal appearance before Congress and scare hell
out of the country."; also Garry Wills in excerpts from
his book, The Kennedy Imprisonment, in The Atlantic
Monthly, February 1982, p. 63: "Yet, in an extraordinary series of moves, President Truman followed Senator
Vandenberg's advice and scared hell out of the country. Solidifying new prerogatives from this sense of
crisis, he instituted the security system, established
the CIA, and opened a campaign to avoid 'losing' Turkey
and Greece as we were losing China." None of these
accounts provide any documentation of the statement
attributed to Vandenberg.)

Republican Vandenberg was a key congressional
figure, although he had been Chairman of the Senate
Foreign Relations Committee only since the beginning of
1947, when the Republicans gained a Senate majority for
the first time since 1932. (Republicans also took
control of the House in 1947, the first time since
1930.) Until World War II, Vandenberg had been a
leader of the isolationists in Congress. But, by the
end of the war, Vandenberg was a delegate, along with
Democratic Senator Tom Connally, to the early United
Nations and European peace conferences. By February
1947, Vandenberg had become "a veteran in bipartisan
internationalism--strong, dependable, indispensable to
the conduct of foreign relations."[16]

Vandenberg had known nothing of the Greek-Turkish
crisis until he was called to the White House. But he
was inclined to go along with the Administration's
request, having been impressed by Marshall's comment
that the American choice was "between acting with energy or losing by default."[17] Nonetheless, Vandenberg
had some doubts about both the process and aspects of
the policy being proposed. In his diary, Vandenberg
expressed his misgivings about the way the problem had
been raised:

The trouble is that the 'crises' never reach Congress until they have developed to a point where congressional discretion is pathetically restricted. When things finally reach a point where a President asks us to 'declare war' there is usually nothing left to do except to 'declare war.' In the present instance, the overriding fact is that the President has made a long-delayed statement regarding communism on-the-march which must be supported if there is any hope of ever impressing Moscow with the necessity of paying any sort of peaceful attention to us whatever. If we turned the President down--after his speech to the joint congressional session--we might as well either resign ourselves to a complete communist encirclement and infiltration or else get ready for World War No. Three.[18]

The Congressional Dilemma

Later, in opening Senate debate on the issue, Vandenberg emphasized this concern. "It is regrettable that policies of such magnitude could not have had more time for consideration. I knew nothing of this matter until we were called to the White House on February 27. I repeat, it is unfortunate when such important decisions have to be made on a crisis basis..."

"Congress does not have an unprejudiced chance to exercise truly independent and objective judgments in such circumstances as we here confront," said Vandenberg. He cited the dilemma which Congress often faces because of the nature of its role in foreign policy. "Congress does not enjoy original jurisdiction in foreign relations. That is the prerogative of the Chief Executive. We come in, usually, only at the eleventh hour, when our choice is the lesser of two evils--as in this instance, when we must decide which is the wiser 'calculated risk' for us."

As Vandenberg said, "...the fact is that by the time these issues reach us for ultimate conclusions, we are heavily precommitted by the very fact of the presidential request. I do not for an instant mean to say that among the paramount factors to which we dare not deny due weight is this: To repudiate the President of the United States at such an hour could display a divisive weakness which might involve far greater jeopardy that an sturdy display of united strength. We are not free to ignore the price of noncompliance."[19]

Vandenberg's statement summarized the predicament in which Congress frequently finds itself: wanting to exercise independent judgment, but, at the same time,

being careful not to undercut the authority of the
President and the position of the United States in the
world. Vandenberg's misgivings about the congressional
role when the executive confronted it with a "crisis"
situation were similar to those felt by congressional
leaders on other occasions. Fulbright, for example,
objected to such meetings at the White House being
called "consultations," when they were often merely
briefings to inform members of Congress about predetermined courses of action. The meetings were essentially
pro forma and, in Fulbright's view were on occasion in
the nature of "cheerleading" sessions to build support
for presidential policies. Fulbright noted that frequently the major decisions had already been reached
before the congressional leaders were summoned to the
White House, sometimes based on information that had
not been available to congressional leaders.[20] And
sometimes there were questions about whether a "crisis"
was real, or whether a crisis atmosphere was created in
order to make it difficult to oppose predetermined
presidential policies.

Congressional leaders are nomally reluctant to take
issue with executive decisions on "crisis" matters.
After President Truman's message to Congress on March
12, Vandenberg told the press, "In such a critical mo-
ment the President's hands must be upheld. Any other
course would be dangerously misunderstood. But Congress must carefully determine the methods and explore
the details in so momentous a departure from our previous policies."[21]

Congress grappled with this problem of executive-
legislative roles in the early 1970s in considering the
War Powers resolution. As finally enacted, over President Nixon's veto in 1973, Congress did establish a
procedural formula for a codeterminative role, but
still left broad leeway to the President, particularly
in the early stages of a crisis.

Bipartisanship

The executive can make effective use of appeals to
bipartisanship in cases of international crisis or potential crisis. And, although Vandenberg's name was to
become identified with the concept of bipartisanship,
Vandenberg wrote, "There is a great deal of misunder-
standing...regarding this whole subject of 'bipartisan
foreign policy.' Many people seem to think that I act
as sort of a Co-secretary of State in connection with
foreign policy decisions. This of course is totally
erroneous...Our 'bipartisan foreign policy' has been
quite definitely confined (1) to the evolution of the
United Nations and (2) to the peace treaties in
Europe."[22]

Truman considered the Greek-Turkish aid package to be a notable example of bipartisan policy, a policy that he traced back to his own tenure in the Senate during World War II, when Cordell Hull was Secretary of State.[23] And Vandenberg did become a staunch defender of bipartisanship, or nonpartisanship as he sometimes preferred, although always insisting that bipartisanship should not be presumed to cover all foreign policy issues. Vandenberg would later refer to the Greek-Turkish aid as having been a bipartisan action, and he said such bipartisan policy "permits our democracy to speak with a great degree of unity at moments when swift decision is vital and when we face totalitarian opponents who can command their own instant unity by... degree."[24]

Vandenberg also understood that if actions on foreign policy were perceived to be partisan, they could backfire politically. A "responsible" opposition usually seeks to steer a course between backing the President on critical foreign policy issues and avoiding what Vandenberg referred to as a slavish "me too" parroting of the Administration on foreign policy issues.[25]

More than 30 years later, another key Republican senator, Howard Baker, perhaps justifying his attacks on President Jimmy Carter, said, "The bipartisan foreign policy of World War II and the postwar era has been replaced by the rhetoric of human rights and the passivity of an unwilling actor on the world scene."[26] Baker strongly attacked Carter on the SALT II Treaty and other issues, yet backed the President on the Panama Canal Treaties and lifting the embargo on arms to Turkey in 1978.

As Vandenberg noted, bipartisanship becomes more simple when one party controls the executive and another controls the legislative branch, as was the case in 1947. "There has to be cooperation under such circumstances or America would be devoid of any foreign policy at all," Vandenberg said.[27]

In appealing for bipartisanship a President can make those who question his proposals or actions appear almost unpatriotic. For example, in 1981, President Ronald Reagan, advocating sale of Airborne Warning and Control Systems (AWACS) planes to Saudi Arabia, said those senators who opposed the sale "are not doing their country a service."[28]

Winning Congressional Approval

The Truman Administration, keenly aware of the need for bipartisan support, went to great lengths to give the appearance of congressional involvement, but to leave Congress little option to reject or redirect the Greek-Turkish policy. In her study of Truman and the

80th Congress, Susan Hartmann wrote, "In deciding not
to involve Republicans in the decision-making process,
the President may have chosen to avoid a premature re-
buff by confronting legislative leaders with the situation in such a way that they could not resist going
along. In any case, Truman had already made his decision when he called congressional leaders to the
White House on February 27."[29] This was a pattern that
would be frequently repeated in executive-legislative
relations.

After the February 27 meeting, the Administration
set out to win congressional approval, creating and
capitalizing on a crisis atmosphere. The primary focus
was on the President's planned March 12 speech to Congress. According to Acheson, "Like all presidential
messages, this one stimulated controversy within the
government. George Kennan thought it too strong, since
it took the line I had taken with the legislative
group, and feared that it might provoke the Soviet
Union to aggressive action."[30]

Several key figures in the Administration expressed
concern about the tone and ideological emphasis of the
speech drafts. Secretary Marshall, who was traveling
in Europe when he received the proposed text, thought
that there was "a little too much flamboyant anti-
Communism in the speech."[31] Marshall cabled back to
Washington, expressing his view that the case was being
overstated. He received a reply stating that it was
the opinion of the executive branch, including the
President, that the Senate would not approve the doctrine without the emphasis on the communist danger.[32]
Kennan objected to the "sweeping nature" of the Administration's proposal and "the commitments which it implied."[33] Kennan's reaction was somewhat ironic, since
he is often regarded as the mastermind of the policy of
containment. It was Kennan who, as the pseudonymous
Mr. X, authored an article titled "The Sources of
Soviet Conduct," in the July, 1947, Foreign Affairs.
The article has been viewed as the blueprint for
American Cold War policy, the intellectual/philosophi-
cal rationale for the Truman Doctrine.

Kennan's article has been subjected to a variety of
interpretations, and Kennan himself has expressed regret about some of the interpretations that were attached to the article, and particularly its linkage to
the Truman Doctrine.[34] The article was an outgrowth of
a cable (which became known as the "Long Telegram")
which Kennan sent to Washington in February, 1946,
while serving as charge d'affaires in Moscow. In the
X-Article, Kennan depicted Soviet policy as relentless-
ly expansionist, governed by Marxist evangelists who
saw communism in pseudoreligious terms and were spurred
by a long distrust of the West. According to Kennan,
the U.S. should engage in a "long-term, patient but

firm and vigilant containment of Russian expansive tendencies." There must be "adroit and vigilant application of counter-force at a series of constantly shifting geographical and political points." This would "increase enormously the strains under which Soviet policy must operate," and encourage changes within Russia leading to "either the breakup or the gradual mellowing of Soviet power."[35]

Later, in his memoirs, Kennan said perhaps the most serious of several deficiencies in the X-Article was the failure to make clear that his notion of the containment of Soviet power "was not the containment by military means of a military threat, but the political containment of a political threat."[36] It was Kennan's view that the U.S. should not resort to bluster and excessive reliance on military force in meeting the Soviet challenge. Indeed, Kennan was opposed to providing military aid to Turkey in 1947, and, in fact, the aid to Turkey was primarily military, not economic. Kennan said that he suspected "what had really happened was that the Pentagon had exploited a favorable set of circumstances in order to infiltrate a military aid program for Turkey into what was supposed to be primarily a political and economic aid program for Greece."[37]

Joseph Jones, who was involved in drafting Truman's speech, has acknowledged that "the treatment of Turkey and the strategic importance of the Middle East in the President's message was something less than the 'full and frank' presentation that Senator Vandenberg had wanted."[38] Jones said that the strategic significance of Turkey ranked high in discussions with congressional leaders, but this was consciously played down in public discussion. "Too much emphasis upon supplying military aid to Turkey might have been alarming to the point of defeating the proposed action."[39] Another concern was that supplying military aid to a country on the Soviet border might result in a Soviet reaction, and would lead to charges of provocation and encirclement by the Soviets. So, as Jones noted, "Military aid to Turkey was not concealed; but it was not emphasized."[40]

In his speech, Truman simply asked Congress "to provide authority for assistance to Greece and Turkey in the amount of $400 million for the period ending June 30, 1948," without being specific about the allocation or purpose of those funds.[41] Indeed, a careful reading of the speech leaves the impression that the aid to Turkey was for economic purposes. Truman said, "The British Government has informed us that...it can no longer extend financial or economic aid to Turkey. As in the case of Greece, if Turkey is to have the assistance it needs, the United States must supply it." Truman did say that, in addition to funds, he was asking Congress to authorize sending American civilian and military personnel to Greece and Turkey to assist in reconstruction, and to supervise the use of financial and material assistance.[42]

The aid to Turkey was really the beginning of the modern U.S. security assistance program. However, whereas the Truman Administration was reluctant to "sell" military assistance to a war-weary Congress in 1947, subsequent administrations found that "security" assistance (even if it was primarily economic aid) was easier to sell to Congress than pure economic assistance, which was viewed by many in Congress as the politically unpopular "foreign aid."

The Truman Administration's argument that aid to Turkey would enable that country to strengthen its security forces without overburdening its economy would be repeated by the Carter and Reagan Administrations more than 30 years later.

As work continued on President Truman's speech to Congress, the congressional leaders were invited to the White House again on March 10. However, Acheson said that the congressional group, despite Vandenberg's "earlier assurance," was cool and silent. Acheson wrote of the meeting: "In his matter-of-fact way, the President laid out the need for action and the action proposed...Vandenberg reiterated his insistence that the President put the crisis before Congress in its broadest setting. No one else said much. No commitments were made."[43]

Given the congressional role in foreign policy, and the frequent necessity to build public support for foreign policy initiatives, policy statements from the executive are often made with an eye on the politics of Congress. It is clear that when Truman went to Capitol Hill on March 12, his speech and the Administration's overall approach had been designed in a manner thought certain to win congressional support. Some, such as Richard Freeland, have suggested that the primary purpose of the speech was not to enunciate American foreign policy, but to assure congressional approval of the Greek-Turkish aid program. "In these terms," said Freeland, "the speech was a complete success, for its mere delivery made congressional rejection of the aid program impossible."[44]

The message confronted Congress with what author Susan Hartmann called "an inflexible either-or situation." By presenting its proposal as the only solution to a crisis, the Administration offered Congress "the choice of either approving it or repudiating the President and thereby crippling the United States internationally."[45]

Daniel Yergin, author of The Shattered Peace, which examines the origin of the Cold War, believes Truman's speech reflected the anticommunistic consensus that had emerged within the executive branch. "The Doctrine was not a cynical maneuver, as some writers have since argued. But it was deliberately written as a 'sales job.'"46

"The Administration exaggerated the extent of the crisis and bluntly portrayed its proposals in bold, crusading, ideological terms," Hartmann wrote. "In part, this endeavor was necessary to win approval from the Republican-controlled Congress. The anti-communist tone...would delight Republicans who had been pressing the Administration for a tougher approach to Russia. The crisis atmosphere might convince economy-oriented legislators that financial sacrifices were necessary. But the tone fo the proposal also faithfully portrayed the way in which most policy makers viewed the situation."47

Congressional Consideration

After Truman's speech, Congress moved quickly to begin its consideration of the proposal. On the morning of March 13, 1947, Vandenberg convened an executive session of the Foreign Relations Committee in the committee room in the Capitol. However, there was resistance--as there frequently is in Congress--to a deadline imposed by the executive. The first matter to come up in the committee's meeting was an objection to the Administration's March 31 deadline for action on the program. Vandenberg said, "...I am afraid that all of the detailed implications involved in implementing the President's programs are going to create such a division and debate in Congress, particularly in the Senate, that it may be just physically impossible to do business by March 31...particularly in view of the other congestion on the Senate calendar."48 The Administration probably recognized that the "deadline" was not realistic, especially for the Senate. (House rules often allow it to move more speedily.) The "deadline" may simply have been a tactic to help create a sense of urgency and maintain the crisis atmosphere. Part of the problem for those involved in foreign policy in the executive branch is that they sometimes forget that the congressional agenda contains many time-consuming domestic matters as well.

Among those representing the Administration at that executive session of the Foreign Relations Committee were Acheson, Secretary of War Robert Patterson, and Secretary of the Navy James Forrestal. Like Acheson, Forrestal had been a key figure within the Administration in moving toward the policies embodied in the Truman Doctrine. It was Forrestal who had done the most to call attention to Kennan's original "Long Telegram" from Moscow, distributing copies to others in Washington. It was at Forrestal's request that Kennan wrote a follow-up paper that eventually became the

X-Article.[49] Forrestal became the first Secretary of Defense when that position was established later in 1947.[50]

The Administration representatives encountered some initial skepticism from the committee members. Senator H. Alexander Smith, New Jersey Republican, commented, "Everybody who has talked to me about this has said, 'We are just going to give a blank check without knowing what the check is for.'"[51] That comment would be echoed at numerous congressional hearings through the years, as members of Congress expressed doubts about granting broad authority to the executive without having more specific information about how funds were going to be utilized. In later years Congress would often be more insistent about having such information.

Acheson told the committee that because of military requirements, there was "a very great strain on the Turkish economy" and that the Turkish Army was high in manpower and low in equipment.[52] These too were comments that would be repeated numerous times over the years at congressional hearings on requests for assistance to Turkey.

Chairman Vandenberg and Senator Smith raised a question that would come up often during congressional consideration of the Greek-Turkish aid program: Why wasn't the U.S. working through the United Nations to deal with the problem? But, Senator Walter George seemed to reflect the recognition by the committee that the U.N. would not be a productive channel for achieving Truman's aims. George said, "I do not see how you are ever going to get anywhere through the United Nations. I do not see how the President's speech...can be characterized as a mere plea for assistance to Greece and Turkey. If it were mere economic assistance it would be one thing, and easily done. But he put this nation squarely on the line against certain ideologies."[53]

Vandenberg said he had no illusions about the prospects for early United Nations action, but that he thought it important for the American people to understand that the U.N. did not have "any power that it could use in this situation."[54] Vandenberg's comments offered insight into his concept of the role of congressional hearings and the need to build public understanding: "I do not think they (the American people) understand it this morning much better than they did before the President delivered his message, and I think one of our major jobs is to make them understand it, and I do not believe they ever will unless we dramatize this thing in every possible way."[55]

During the hearings a number of senators expressed concern about the U.S. giving the impression that it was circumventing the U.N. and thus establishing a precedent in regard to the fledgling organization.

Senator Claude Pepper (D-Florida), who was not a Foreign Relations Committee member, appeared before the
committee and said, "Let us take the lead in...trying
to solve it through the United Nations. Then, if they
fail or if they refuse, we have clear justification
before our citizenry and the world in going in and
giving relief..."[56]

(Pepper had previously been a Foreign Relations
member, 1937-1946, but was dropped from the committee
due to the reduction in the number of members, as provided in the Legislative Reorganization Act of 1946.
Pepper returned when Democrats regained control of the
Senate in 1949. He was defeated for re-election in
1950, but later served a long tenure in the House,
beginning in 1962.)

Pepper referred to a Gallup poll which he said
indicated that the public generally approved Truman's
policy, but with the majority expressing regret that
the problem was not put to the United Nations in the
beginning. Also, the poll reported that the country
was opposed to any military involvement or sending
American military advisers to train the Greek and
Turkish armies.[57]

Senator Edwin Johnson of Colorado proposed amendments to the committee that would have reaffirmed U.S.
policy "to bring before the United Nations all...condi-
tions which may endanger the peace of the world" and
not to take unilateral action or intervene in the
internal affairs of foreign countries. Johnson also
proposed to strike all assistance to Turkey from the
bill because he was opposed to the military nature of
the aid.[58] Altogether, 22 amendments were considered
by the Senate committee, which conducted lengthy hearings, with testimony from executive branch witnesses,
senators who had introduced amendments, and 33 non-
governmental witnesses. Chairman Vandenberg invited
all senators to submit questions they might have with
respect to Greek-Turkish aid. More than 400 such
questions were received, and then consolidated so as to
avoid duplication, with a questionnaire of 110 items
ultimately submitted to the State Department. Both
questions and answers were published in what was at the
time a unique legislative document. It was a precedent
for the extensive background information which Congress
would come to expect in considering later foreign policy programs.

The committee approved five amendments, but none of
them seriously altered the original proposal. One
required that the chief of any mission appointed by the
president to head the assistance program to Greece or
Turkey must receive Senate confirmation--the Senate
protecting its role in confirming major presidential
appointments. Two of the amendments dealt with the
United Nations. One, sponsored by Vandenberg and

Connally, inserted a long preamble designed to identify
the Greek-Turkish aid more closely with the U.N. program and purposes. The second, offered by Vandenberg,
was the key amendment. It indicated the willingness of
the U.S. to withdraw its aid program if the U.N. General Assembly found that action taken by the U.N. would
make the continuation of such assistance unnecessary or
undesirable. The U.S. would waive its right of veto in
such a case.

Amendment Strategy

Neither of Johnson's amendments were approved, although portions of his U.N. amendment were incorporated
in the Vandenberg amendment. Vandenberg pushed hard
for his amendment, which was discussed at length by the
committee. Having played an active role in helping to
launch the U.N., and having led congressional support
for U.S. participation, Vandenberg was particularly
concerned about the Administration's neglect of the
U.N. on this issue. He saw this as the one major flaw
in Truman's plan. Vandenberg regarded the U.N. as "our
first reliance and our prime concern" and believed this
defect in Truman's plan must be corrected.[59]
The Administration initially resisted Vandenberg's
amendment, but, after much discussion and some compro-
mises on the language, the State Department "reluctant-
ly agreed" to accept the amendment.[60] "It was a cheap
price for Vandenberg's patronage," according to
Acheson, and the amendment "won over the bulk of the
doubters."[61]
To some extent, Vandenberg and administration
leaders were acting out roles in what came to be an
understood but unstated strategy. As Acheson later
described the process: "One of Vandenberg's stratagems
was to enact publicly his conversion to a proposal, his
change of attitude, a kind of political transubstanti-
ation. The method was to go through a period of public
doubt and skepticism; then find a comparatively minor
flaw in the proposal, pounce on it, and make much of
it; in due course a proposed change, always the
Vandenberg amendment. Then, and only then, could it be
given to his followers as a true doctrine worthy of all
men to be received."[62] As Acheson noted, Vandenberg
did this not only in connection with the Greek-Turkish
proposal, but with other major foreign policy initiatives, including the Marshall Plan. However, Acheson
acknowledged that the strength of this stratagem lay in
the genuineness of Vandenberg's belief in each step.
Through the years, other congressional leaders
utilized similar techniques. During his term as Senate
Majority Leader (1977-1980), Robert Byrd was a master
of this form of minuet. On a number of major foreign

policy issues Byrd offered amendments or extracted
pledges from the Carter Administration that in Byrd's
view strengthened various proposals and made them more
acceptable to Congress. This approach allowed the Senate to put its stamp on various foreign policy actions,
and, often, in return for support of Byrd and other key
congressional figures, the Administration was willing
to share credit. A notable example of this process
occurred during Senate consideration of the Panama
Canal Treaties in 1977, when the "leadership amendments" introduced by Byrd and Minority Leader Howard
Baker were instrumental in Senate passage of the
treaties. (See Chapter 4.) When the Senate voted to
lift the arms embargo on Turkey in 1978, Byrd added a
provision requiring the President to report to the Senate on progress toward settlement of the Cyprus issue,
and this helped the measure pass, just as Vandenberg's
amendment was a key element in congressional passage of
the original Greek-Turkish aid package.

The Congressional Debate

After the Foreign Relations Committee reported the
bill to the Senate, with amendments, on April 3, 1947,
debate began in the Senate. Even if the outcome seemed
preordained, it was not a pro forma debate. There was
a spirited and wide-ranging discussion centering on the
proper congressional role in foreign policy, as well as
conflict over the implications of the program Congress
was being asked to approve. Criticism focused on these
points: (1) bypassing the United Nations; (2) the un-
known costs of the venture the U.S. was undertaking;
(3) a precipitant and possibly irreversible worsening
of the strained relationship with Russia, an ally only
a short time before; (4) the setting of a dramatic new
course in U.S. foreign policy without thorough consideration of the ramifications.
Opponents tended to be clustered on the left or the
right, but even some of those who supported the legislation raised some fundamental questions. Senator Homer
Capehart, an Indiana Republican, chided the Truman Administration for being so slow to condem the Soviet
Union, which formerly was viewed as "that great liber-
ty-loving ally of ours."[63] Capehart also questioned
whether the U.S. had raised the Greek-Turkish issue
directly with the Soviets. Ironically, while the Senate debate was taking place, Secretary of State Marshall
was in Moscow for a meeting of the Council of Foreign
Ministers--yet Congress was debating what one senator,
Democrat Johnson of Colorado, referred to as an "un-
declared declaration of war" on Russia.[64]
Because Marshall was in Moscow, and not in Washington lobbying for the bill, there were suggestions that

he was not a strong supporter. Indeed, after Vandenberg expressed his concern to Acheson about this problem, the Acting Secretary sent a telegram to Marshall in Moscow April 18:

> I have just talked to Vandenberg who tells me that there has for some days been a whispering campaign to the effect that the Greek-Turkish aid program was formulated in your absence and you have not expressed yourself on it. Vandenberg says this campaign today came into the open in the introduction of a resolution by Senator Wiley to the effect that action on the bill should be deferred until you return and the Senate has had the benefit of your views. This resolution will be referred to the Foreign Relations Committee where it will be defeated but Vandenberg would like very much to close the debate...with a brief statement from you endorsing the bill in strong terms...[65]

Marshall responded by sending Vandenberg a strong statement of support, stating that he attached the "highest order of urgency to immediate passage of the Greek-Turkish aid legislation."[66] Vandenberg made effective use of Marshall's message during the debate.
Capehart wound up supporting the aid, as did Senator Homer Ferguson, Vandenberg's Republican colleague from Michigan, who said he viewed "the loan to Greece and Turkey...as a stopgap while the United Nations is being strengthened to take over the permanent job."[67] Senator Robert Taft (R-Ohio) also referred to the "Greek and Turkish loans," although they were not really loans. Taft, known as "Mr. Conservative" in the Senate, said he was in accord with the Vandenberg amendment, and that the U.S. should "in any event withdraw as soon as normal economic conditions are restored."[68] And Vandenberg insisted that, by enacting the legislation, the U.S. would be "holding the line" for the U.N. "until such times as the United Nations can progressively take over these responsibilities--and evolution which we not only crave but openly invite."[69]
However, Senator Harry Byrd, a conservative Virginia Democrat, said the "attempts to justify our by-passing of the United Nations" were "merely window dressing, a lot of pious words without effect or legal validity."[70] Byrd was also critical of efforts "to cloak the passage of this legislation with an atmosphere of a great impending crisis" while "nobody knows the cost of such a program."[71]
Another Republican, George Malone of Nevada, was similarly critical, saying, "I object on principle to a policy which seekd to stampede us into further huge

loans and gifts and actions which all agree will in all probability result in establishing a definite policy trend for this nation, about which no opportunity for the thorough investigation which is certainly justified..."[72]

Foreshadowing some future criticism of U.S. policies, Malone said, "If our action is, indeed, dictated by the danger of communism, then we must consider that any state which will shout this danger is in a position effective to blackmail the United States into supplying money and arms, even if such a state were fascist in character and devoted to objectives contrary to the entire spirit of freedom."[73]

Senator Kenneth Wherry of Nebraska posed the issue in dramatic terms when he said, "Never in the history of our nation have the American people and the United States Senate faced an issue more grave and far-reaching than confronts us here today in the proposed Greek and Turkish so-called loan. In making this statement I am not unmindful of the decisions leading up to the Civil War."[74]

"This is no financial arrangement or relief project," Wherry said. "It is a military adventure. This is a commitment...to an entirely new foreign policy of such magnitude and potentialities that every honest American man and woman is compelled to the deepest soul-searching in its consideration." Citing the warnings of Washington and Jefferson that America should "remain free from foreign entanglements"--warnings often recalled by those branded as congressional "isolationists"--Wherry said the Greek-Turkish aid request was only the "first of what will be many demands upon the United States Treasury."[75]

Wherry said such a policy would ultimately have a tremendous negative impact on the domestic economy, and would cause the U.S. "to employ imperialistic methods." He told his Senate colleagues, "If we intend by this method to stop the march of communism, let us say so frankly to the American people." Prophetically, he said that the public should understand that the $400 million was merely the first installment of billions of dollars to follow. "If we are going to organize and finance the world for American ideals and freedom, let us face frankly and realistically what the cost will be; what the potential dangers are; how we may become involved; and what may happen to us in the process. Let us not do it blindly or by subterfuge."[76]

Wherry repeatedly referred to Vandenberg's comments that Congress did not have "an unprejudiced chance to exercise truly independent and objective judgments" because it had been forced to deal with the issue on a crisis basis."[77] "The basic implication of the Truman Doctrine," said Wherry, "is that it will compel the return to and the perpetuation of wartime conditions and

controls." He cited the experience of U.S. entry into
the two World Wars when "we abandon our democratic
processes; we set up the presidency as a virtual dictatorship." He likened the Truman Doctrine to "requests
for declarations of war" and said it would lead to "a
perpetual state of war emergency and government by control and crisis."* [78]

Fulbright and the Congressional Role

Fulbright was a Senate member in 1947, and he also
referred to the decision on Greek-Turkish aid as "one
of the most important" decisions Congress had faced in
the nation's history.[79] In announcing his support,
Fulbright noted that the principal criticism of the
proposal had been allayed to a great extent by the
Vandenberg amendment. He said the amendment negated
the charge of imperialism "as well as the charge that
we would, by this unilateral action, scrap the United
Nations." Indeed, said Fulbright, in giving the organization "the right to disapprove our actions, I think
we would strengthen the United Nations."[80] Fulbright
shared Vandenberg's strong support for the U.N. In
1943, as a first-term member of the House of Representatives (where he served one term before being elected
to the Senate), Fulbright introduced a resolution which
laid the groundwork for U.S. participation in the
United Nations.** The Fulbright Resolution, as it
became known, was overwhelmingly approved by the House,
and a similar resolution by Senator Connally was approved by the Senate.

In his statement backing Greek-Turkish aid Fulbright

---

*Wherry later was to argue that President Truman
should have sought a declaration of war for the Korean
conflict (which, Wherry believed, Congress would have
granted). In 1951, Wherry touched off a "great debate"
with his Senate resolution seeking to force the President to secure the consent of Congress before sending
any more American troops to Europe. Instead, the Senate passed an innocuous substitute.

**The Fulbright Resolution was introduced April 31,
1943, and passed by a 360-29 vote on September 21,
1943. The resolution said: "Resolved, The the House
of Representatives hereby expresses itself as favoring
the creation of appropriate international machinery
with power adequate to establish and to maintain a just
and lasting peace among the nations of the world, and
as favoring participation of the United States therein
through its constitutional processes."

said, "With the information I now have, it is my intention to support the President's proposal." He commented, "Under our system of government, the President
has a particular responsibility in our foreign relations. He has access to information which, in the
nature of things, we cannot have, and he is in constant
touch with the members of the State Department who are
directly charged with conducting our affairs with foreign nations. The judgment of these men, and of the
President should prevail, in the absense of clear proof
to the contrary."[81]

In later years, Fulbright would take a differing
view of legislative-executive relations. It is interesting to notice the echoes of some of Wherry's 1947
comments in a Fulbright statement made 24 years later:

> Thirty years of war, cold war, and crisis
> have propelled the American political system
> far along the road to an executive despotism,
> at least in the conduct of foreign relations.
> So far has the process of expanding presiden-
> tial power advanced that, in the publicly
> recorded view of the Senate Committee on
> Foreign Relations, 'it is no longer accurate
> to characterize our government, in matters of
> foreign relations, as one of separated powers
> checked and balanced against each other.'[82]

Fulbright also became critical of what he called the
"cult of experts" and "tyranny of secret information,"
suggesting that the executive used these to preclude
Congress from involvement in major foreign policy
decisions when, in fact, the executive had no monopoly
on truth or wisdom. Fulbright liked to point to a
statement made by George Reedy, who served as President
Johnson's press secretary and special assistant: "On
sweeping policy decisions, which are, after all, relatively few, a President makes up his mind on the basis
of the same kind of information that is available to
the average citizen."[83]

The belief that Congress was at a disadvantage in
obtaining and analyzing information became a major factor in the congressional push to expand its staff and
resources in the 1970s, concurrent with the congressional drive to play a more active and independent role
in foreign policy. Fulbright was one of those who led
the effort for that stronger role, but he always maintained that it had to be kept in perspective. He believed that Congress must guard against abuses by the
executive, and in cases where legislators viewed executive actions as strongly misguided, it was their responsibility to oppose them. Speaking not long before
the Greek-Turkish aid legislation was enacted,
Fulbright said:

> Many Americans are impatient at the lack
> of vision and initiative of the Congress, but
> they should not forget that it is the Congress
> that stands between their liberties and the
> voracious instinct for power of the executive
> bureaucracy...An important responsibility of
> the legislature is to provide a check upon the
> tendency of the executive power of the state
> to become arbitrary and oppressive.[84]

Twenty-five years later, Fulbright said he felt confirmed in his earlier judgment. In a 1971 speech, Fulbright added, "Out of a well-intentioned but misconceived notion of what patriotism and responsibility require in the time of world crisis, Congress permitted the President to take over the two vital foreign policy powers which the Constitution vested in Congress: the power to initiate war and the Senate's power to consent or withhold consent from significant foreign commitments."[85] Indeed, Fulbright, who was at the center of the executive-legislative conflict over foreign policy, particularly during the Vietnam years, said that "the United States has joined the global mainstream; we have become, for purposes of foreign policy--especially for purposes of making war--a presidential dictatorship."[86]

In 1961, Fulbright made a speech in which he said, "It seems clear to me that in foreign affairs, a Senate cannot initiate or force large events, or substitute its judgment for that of the President, without seriously jeopardizing the ability of the nation to act consistently, and also without confusing the image and purpose of this country in the eyes of others."[87]

Fulbright critics would later recall the 1961 speech and contrast those views with his subsequent and seemingly contradictory views on the role of the President and the Senate. But, in a broad sense, Fulbright maintained that the 1961 speech was an accurate reflection of how he thought the system should work. In that speech, Fulbright commented, "The role of the Senate is also influenced by the nature of foreign policy as it exists at any given time." He added, "Today, the ability of the government to conduct its external affairs depends to a great extent upon its success in developing a consensus among the people regarding our purposes and responsibilities in the foreign field. While only the President can act, only the people can arm him to do so."[88]

In the 1961 speech, Fulbright emphasized that his contention that the Senate should normally play a supporting and not an initiating role in foreign policy "does not mean that the role of the Senate is confined to one of blind obeisance." To underline this point, he said, "When Vandenberg was cooperating with Truman and Acheson, neither he, nor his committee, nor the

Senate were without influence upon the course of events. He and his colleagues, by persuasion and by their example, exercised great influence upon the other members of the Senate as well as the executive. They were making judgments, essentially political, as to the 'art of the possible'--what could be done and how it could be done--but, always, I believe, from the standpoint of what had to be done. The determination of this last they left, pretty much, in the hands of the executive. Vandenberg and his colleagues found ways to do what had to be done."[89]

Although, as noted earlier, Fulbright would become critical of the pattern of foreign policy which had been set in motion by the Truman Doctrine, he supported the original concept as he understood it. He believed that the emphasis upon "freedom" at the time of the Greek-Turkish aid request later gave way to an entirely different emphasis--anticommunism.[90]

Looking back, Fulbright says, "The Truman Doctrine with its universal implications did create a climate conducive to intervention in later years. Aid just to Turkey and Greece would not have had the same effect. At the time, I was not on the Foreign Relations Committee and had no thoughts about its long-term significance. It took me several years and many bills before I recognized the danger of intervening all around the world on a bilateral basis."[91]

Senate Dissenters

Fulbright, often a Senate dissenter two decades later, was in the majority in supporting aid to Turkey and Greece in 1947. Dissent has, in principle at least, long been respected in the Senate, with its traditions of extended debate and discussion. Democrat Mike Mansfield, who served as Majority Leader, 1961-1976, said in 1968 that the right of dissent is "a right which I will uphold, as long as it is constructive, for every member of the Senate and for every American, because...it is the stuff of which democracy is made."[92]

Senator Albert Gore, a Tennessee Democrat and Foreign Relations Committee member, also speaking in 1968, said that a senator not only has a right to express dissent "but a duty to do so." Gore said, "It will be a lamentable day, indeed, when U.S. Senators refrain from criticizing or questioning the policies of our government because of the fear that to do so will bring upon them the opprobrium, the accusation, the insinuation...of being unpatriotic..."[93]

Many of the opponents of the Greek-Turkish aid believed that it was an extremely important issue and saw it their duty to speak out. Wherry was one of those who criticized from the right, while Pepper was a major spokesman for the left, and kept returning to the United Nations issue.

However, once the Vandenberg amendment had been accepted, according to one analyst, those who still charged that the U.S. was dealing a blow at the United Nations "such as Senators Pepper and Taylor in the Congress and Henry Wallace* outside of it" found themselves in the company of Soviet representatives Andrei Gromyko, who had little support at the U.N.[94] Sometimes congressional action can be influenced as much by who is against a proposal as by who favors it. As John Campbell wrote, "Intelligent criticism of the Truman proposals suffered from the reaction provoked by Wallace's reckless charges of 'ruthless American imperialism' and his picturing the Greek communists as sterling Democrats. When, early in April, he carried his campaign to Europe and denounced the Truman Doctrine... any remaining doubt that the Greek-Turkish aid bill would pass both Houses by thumping majorities was removed."[95]

Pepper said that although the Vandenberg amendment improved the bill, "I charge that this unilateral action on our part is a breach of our solemn covenant assumed to the United Nations organization."[96] On the final day of the debate, April 22, Pepper told the Senate he had wanted to support the bill, but he had been moved by a speech he had heard by a young World War II veteran, Cord Meyer. Pepper said Meyer spoke "of the necessity of preventing war by strengthening the United Nations organization." Pepper added, "I became convinced in my heart...that young man was pointing to the future, and that those who were advocating this measure were pointing to the past, to the old ways and to the old wars."[97]

Interestingly, Meyer later became a high-ranking official of the Central Intelligence Agency. Immediately after World War II, Meyer had been active in the American Veterans Committee and the United World

---

*Henry Wallace served as Vice President under Franklin D. Roosevelt, 1941-1945. He was replaced on the Democratic ticket in 1944 by Truman. He then served as Secretary of Commerce, until he was removed from that post after Truman became President. Wallace launched a "progressive" political movement. Among their goals, the Progressives favored accomodation with the Soviet Union, and they tolerated communists within their membership. Wallace was the Progressive Party presidential candidate in 1948, gaining 2.4 percent of the popular vote, slightly less than the total of States Rights candidate Strom Thurmond, who later served in the Senate.

Federalists, two groups with the stated goals of supporting international cooperation and world peace. But Meyer became disillusioned because of communist efforts to dominate the AVC and other organizations, and eventually joined the CIA in 1950.*

The McCarthy Era

Meanwhile, Pepper was defeated for re-election in 1950, at least partially because of his "internationalist" views. He lost in the Florida Democratic primary to George Smathers, who had earlier been a Pepper ally. Pepper was accused of being "soft" on communism, and much was made of a 1945 trip he made to Moscow, where he met with Joseph Stalin, the Soviet dictator.[98] By 1950, McCarthyism was becoming a strong force in the country, and accusations of being sympathetic to communism--or not sufficiently anti-communistic--could be highly damaging to public figures, even if the charges were unsubstanciated. Senator Joseph McCarthy, who had remained on the sidelines during the 1947 Truman Doctrine debate (although voting in favor of Greek-Turkish aid), launched his attack on alleged pro-communists in the U.S. early in 1950s. It was a difficult time for dissenters, and McCarthyism fed on the fears generated by the Cold War conflict between the U.S. and the Soviet Union.

In California a heated battle for election to the Senate was waged in 1950 by two House members--Republican Richard Nixon, who had supported Greek-Turkish aid in 1947 and Democrat Helen Gahagan Douglas, who had opposed the aid. Nixon played no role in the House debate on Greek-Turkish aid, but Mrs. Douglas took an active role and made several efforts to amend the bill. One of her unsuccessful amendments would have prohibited aid to Turkey until the President had first requested United Nations action on any threat to Turkey's national integrity. If the U.N. failed to act within one year, U.S. aid could then be provided. She said her amendment was motivated by her conviction that military assistance to Turkey was a problem for the U.N. and "not for the consideration of any single country or group of countries however unselfish and benevolent their intentions."[99] Douglas added, "Russia has no

---

*In another ironic twist, while Meyer was serving in the CIA in 1953, the FBI told the CIA they could not give Meyer a security clearance. Meyer was suspended from his duties, but successfully fought for reinstatement, overcoming the flimsy FBI charges. See Thomas Powers, The Man Who Kept the Secrets: Richard Helms and the CIA, New York: Knopf, 1979, pp.61-63.

right to bring the kind of pressure against Turkey to
maintain an army she cannot afford. If she is doing so
she should be called to account. And she should be
called to account for her actions before the nations of
the world."[100]

The proposed Douglas amendment gave way to a substitute amendment by Representative Jacob Javits of New
York. Republican Javits, who would later become a
leading member of the Senate Foreign Relations Committee, offered a harmless amendment that would simply require the president to bring to the attention of the
U.N. any situation which threatened the territorial
integrity of Turkey or other countries.[101]

In the 1950 California Democratic primary, Mrs.
Douglas, although she had a strong record of opposition
to communism, and had fought against Henry Wallace's
Progressive Party, was accused of having given "comfort
to the Soviet tyranny by voting against aid to Greece
and Turkey."[102] As Pepper was called "Red" in the campaign against him, she was dubbed the "Pink Lady." In
the general election campaign Nixon said her record in
Congress "discloses the truth about her soft attitude
toward communism."[103]

Some critics maintain that it was the Truman Doctrine that set the stage for the Cold War and for
McCarthyism. John Gaddis wrote, "By portraying the
Soviet-American conflict as a clash between mutually
irreconcilable ideologies, the president and his advisors managed to shock Congress and the public into
providing the support necessary to implement a tough
policy. But in the process they trapped themselves in
a new cycle of rhetoric and response which in years to
come would significantly restrict the administration's
flexibility in dealing with Moscow."[104]

Richard Freeland in The Truman Doctrine and the
Origins of McCarthyism develops the theme that the
Truman Administration exaggerated the crisis nature of
the Greek-Turkish aid request and over-emphasized the
communist threat in order to gain support for the proposal. Freeland maintains that Truman Administration
policies created an atmosphere which encouraged McCarthyism. "In fact, in 1947-1988 Truman and his advisors
employed all the political and programmatic techniques
that in later years were to become associated with the
broad phenomenon of McCarthyism. It was the Truman
Administration that developed the association of dissent with disloyalty and communism, which became a central element of McCarthyism."[105]

Robert Divine has written, "To some extent, the
Truman Administration...was to blame for the hysteria
over subversives. The overblown rhetoric that Truman
and Acheson used to describe the nature of the communist threat abroad created the feeling that the United
States was engaged in a crusade against evil."[106]

But a Truman defender, reacting to suggestions that the President's speech on Greek-Turkish aid gave rise to McCarthyism, argues that the virulent anticommunism was more related to "such non-Truman-connected occurrences" as developments in China, Korea, Soviet spies in the U.S., and "Senator McCarthy's rare gifts for invention and invective."[107]

McCarthyism plagued the Truman Administration through its final years in office. Even Acheson, who clearly played an important role in formulating the tough tone of the Truman Doctrine speech, came under attack, as did George Marshall. Richard Rovere wrote of McCarthy, "He was by no means the first man to use senatorial immunity or the investigative powers of Congress for selfish and unworthy ends, but he was surely the cleverest."[108] McCarthy continued to rail against what he called "appeasement" and a "cowardly" foreign policy, but by 1954, during the Eisenhower Administration, McCarthy had badly overplayed his hand and was rapidly losing credibility. In December 1954 the Senate voted to censure the Wisconsin Senator.

Despite the excesses which may have resulted from the Truman Doctrine, and despite the warnings--some of which seem to have been justified--by congressional opponents, the prevailing view was that the Truman Doctrine, beginning with aid to Turkey and Greece, was a reasonable and necessary response to challenging conditions. There was strong conviction in Congress that the U.S. had a responsibility to act.

Congressional Approval

The Senate passed the bill on April 22 by a 67-23 vote, with 35 Republicans and 32 Democrats in favor; 16 Republicans and 7 Democrats opposed. The Johnson amendment--to remove the military provisions--was defeated 68-22.

The legislation was considered for only three days on the House floor but the debate was intense. One of the strongest speeches in support of Greek-Turkish aid was delivered by House Democratic leader Sam Rayburn of Texas. Rayburn, who served as House Majority Leader, 1940-1946, and 1949-1961, did not speak often on the House floor. But on this occasion he spoke in stirring fashion, and said, "I trust that in our considerations here...that this thing called isolationism may not again crawl out of the shadows and defeat the hopes of men and again break the heart of the world."[109]

Opposing amendments to the bill, Rayburn said, "If Greece and Turkey need help, they need it now...If we do not accept our responsibility, if we do not move forward and extend a helping hand to people who need and want help, who are democracies or want to be, who

do not want to be smothered by communism; if we do
not...assume our place, God help us; God help this
world."110

On May 9, the House passed a bill substantially
similar to the Senate bill by a 287-108 vote, with 127
Republicans and 160 Democrats in favor. Among the supporters were Representatives Nixon, Lyndon B. Johnson,
and the 29-year-old John F. Kennedy. It was opposed by
94 Republicans, 13 Democrats, and 1 independent. A
conference committee quickly reconciled the differences
between the House and Senate versions, and both Houses
agreed to the conference report by voice votes on May
15. President Truman signed the bill into law on May
22, some 10 weeks after his speech to Congress.

Although the bill authorized the aid to Greece and
Turkey, the second stage of the congressional funding
process, appropriations, had to be completed as well,
and on July 26, 1947, a supplemental appropriations
bill which included $400 million for Greece and Turkey
was enacted.

Within a short time after Congress completed action
on Greek-Turkish aid, the administration was proposing
the Marshall Plan and in 1948 Congress gave its approval to the first installation of the multi-billion dol-
lar European Recovery Program.

The Truman Doctrine was a landmark in the history
of U.S. foreign policy. It was also the beginning in
the post-war era of a congressional habit of placing
broad, vaguely limited powers in the hands of the executive branch, which often made full use of that authority. In the case of Greek-Turkish aid, Congress had
taken some steps to assert a congressional role, but at
the same time it had essentially yielded broad power to
the executive, where it would largely remain for more
than 20 years, a period when Congress frequently played
a relatively minor role in foreign policy.

Through the years, Turkey has continued to be an
important element in the governing perception of United
States security interests. It became a member of NATO
in 1952. Along with its Mediterranean neighbor and co-
beneficiary of Truman Doctrine aid, Turkey has held up
the southern flank of NATO. However, Greece and Turkey
have often been at odds. Turkey's strategic location--
bordering the Soviet Union and astride the U.S.S.R.'s
maritime route from the Black Sea to the Mediterran-
ean--has given it particular importance.

Turkey has been a leading recipient of U.S. assistance, especially in terms of military aid, which began
in 1947, but also as the eighth-largest beneficiary of
Public Law 480 (Food for Peace) aid.111 Direct U.S.
military aid between 1950 and 1974 averaged about $165
million annually and in the 1980s Turkey has again
become a major recipient of U.S. aid. Since 1947,
total U.S. military assistance to Turkey has amounted

to substantially more that $4 billion in equipment,
supplies, facilities, and training.[112]

NATO and Turkey

Before Turkey and Greece were admitted to NATO, the
Department of State consulted informally with members
of the Senate Foreign Relations Committee on their
attitudes about the proposed admission. This was discussed in an executive session of the committee on September 17, 1951, and is an example of the long-standing
practice of informal consultations between the State
Department and the committee. In this case, the committee members discussed the proposal among themselves
and agreed that the committee staff should "communicate
to the State Department our offhand informal attitude"
in favor of admission.[113] In seeking this informal
opinion, Chairman Tom Connally told his colleagues,
"They (the Administration) want to know our attitude
before they act, because if they find a lot of opposition here there is no point in their acting."[114]
Senator Theodore F. Green said the U.S. representatives at a NATO meeting in Ottawa did not want to advocate admission "and be repudiated when they come
home."[115] Senator Fulbright had conferred with State
Department officials about the matter and they had
asked him to help determine "whether the committee
thought it was a good idea or not."[116] Fulbright said
he favored the plan, as did Republican Henry Cabot
Lodge, Jr., who said, "I think the Turks and Greeks are
two of the best bets we have had. I think Greek and
Turkish aid legislation has paid for itself many times
over."[117]
At the Ottawa meeting, the North Atlantic Council
invited Greece and Turkey to join NATO. This required
amendment of the North Atlantic Treaty and needed Senate approval. The Senate had approved the treaty in
1949 after lengthy consideration. In between the prolonged debate over the Treaty of Versailles in 1919-
1920 and the Panama Canal Treaties in 1978, the NATO
Treaty was probably the most protracted treaty debate.
Once again on the NATO Treaty, as in the case of
Greek-Turkish aid and the Marshall Plan, Vandenberg
played a key role. In June 1948, the Senate passed the
Vandenberg Resolution, which sanctioned U.S. participation in a regional security pact. The resolution was a
"sense of the Senate" resolution—not binding, but expressing the will of the Senate. It cleared the way
for U.S. participation in the North Atlantic negotiations. During the negotiations, Vandenberg and
Connally "were in fairly close touch with negotiations"
through consultations with the State Department.[118]
During this period Vandenberg and Connally insisted

upon two changes in the treaty "before isolationist senators had an opportunity to use them as rallying points for opposition to the treaty."[119]

The NATO Treaty was submitted to the Senate early in 1949. The Foreign Relations Committee conducted 16 days of hearings, although committee support had already been assured during the consultation process. The hearings were important in educating the public and in giving opponents an opportunity to be heard, but in this case the committee was already committed.[120]

A group of Republican senators, headed by Taft and Wherry, objected to the treaty. Opponents raised questions about foreign entanglements, loss of freedom of action, a threat to the Senate's war-declaring power, and the costs of implied defense expenditures. But the North Atlantic pact was approved by an 82-13 vote--far more than the necessary two-thirds--in July 1949. Some suggest that this series of major foreign policy actions--Greek-Turkish aid, the Marshall plan, President Truman's Point Four aid program to developing countries, and NATO--marked the end of a period of collaboration between executive and legislative policymakers. Over the following 20 years congressional influence in foreign relations declined.[121]

Certainly the Senate's consideration of the Greek-Turkish amendment to the NATO Treaty in 1951 was relatively minimal. Republicans did raise the issue of whether Congress might be losing control over actions that could lead to war. But, with only six members present, the Senate first approved the protocol on January 21, 1951, by a voice vote. Democratic Majority Leader Ernest McFarland (the Democrats regained control of Congress in the 1948 elections) said it had been a mistake to act with so few members present, and the Senate asked the President to return the treaty. When it was reconsidered on February 7, Senator Arthur Watkins, a Utah Republican, proposed a reservation to the treaty to the effect that U.S. forces in NATO should not be used "in a manner which would necessarily involve the United States in war, unless the Congress by act or joint resolution so provides." But Senator George assured Watkins that "all the provisions of the treaty must be implemented by the Congress," and Watkins withdrew his proposal.[122] The Senate then approved the protocol adding Turkey and Greece to NATO by a 73-2 vote.

The 1950s

The 1950s have been referred to as the "golden era" in U.S.-Turkish relations. Turkey proved to be a valuable ally of the U.S. during the Korean conflict. Turkey also cooperated in a variety of joint strategic

arrangements engineered by Secretary of State John
Foster Dulles.

In 1956, the Senate voted to create a Special Committee to Study the Foreign Aid Program, charged with
studying the extent to which foreign assistance "serves,
can be made to serve, or does not serve, the national
interest."[123] In addition to members of the Foreign
Relations Committee, the chairmen and ranking minority
members of the Appropriations and Armed Services Com-
mittees--both of those committees having obvious involvement in foreign policy matters--also served on the
Special Committee. An analysis of military assistance
programs up to that point called Turkey a bright spot
"in a military sense." The report said, "Communist
infiltration is insignificant and the Turkish citizenry
are aware of the dangers of Russian agression. At the
present time, Turkey is in the throes of severe economic difficulties, and defense support (i.e., economic
aid designed to strengthen a country's defense capability) promises to play an important role in helping
Turkey overcome it."[124] The statement about Turkey's
economic difficulties--first heard when the Truman Doctrine was launched--was a portent of even greater problems to come, as was the report's comment that Greek-
Turkish problems over Cyprus had "strained relations"
between the two NATO members.

The 1960s

By the 1960s, numerous problems plagued U.S.-
Turkish relations. There was a shift in Turkish attitudes toward the Soviet Union, due at least in part to
fallout from the Cuban missile crisis. U.S. willingness to remove its Jupiter missiles from Turkey, in exchange for Soviet removal of missiles from Cuba in the
1962 showdown, was seen by some Turkish leaders as evidence that the U.S. placed its security interests above
those of its allies. Once again Turkey became involved, through the missile pullout, in a major episode
in U.S. foreign policy. (Although there were lengthy
discussions within a small group in the executive
branch about how to handle the missile crisis, Congress
was not involved. Arthur Schlesinger, Jr., wrote:
"Congress played no role at all...It was only after he
had made his decision that Kennedy called in the congressional leaders. The object was not to consult them
but to inform them."[125] Fulbright later said, "President Kennedy's actions proved to be effective and responsible. Nonetheless the episode served to underline
the inadequacy of executive 'consultation' with the
legislative branch during crisis situations, a problem
that was greatly heightened during the following
years."[126]

Late in the 1960s, Turkey began to place some restrictions on U.S. military facilities in the country.
Economic cooperation with the Soviet Union gradually
increased, and Turkey experienced a brief period of
prosperity, which contributed to a more independent
attitude.

The Cyprus Problem

One issue has consistently haunted the triangular
relationship between the U.S., Turkey, and Greece: the
problem of Cyprus. The troubled history of that small
island nations stems from its strategic location between Europe and Asia, and the sharp difference between
two communities--Greek and Turkish--which constitute
almost the totality of the population, currently estimated at about 630,000.

Cyprus is only 40 miles south of Turkey, and about
600 miles southeast of Greece. With 3,572 square
miles, it is about three times the size of Rhode
Island. About 80 percent of the population are Greek-
speaking; 18 percent are Turkish. Cyprus became an
independent republic in 1960, after 82 years of British
rule. This followed a civil war between the Greek and
Turkish communities, which was finally concluded by an
agreement between Greece, Turkey, Cyprus, and Britain,
known as the Zurich Settlement.

There has been a continuing movement among elements
of the Greek community for enosis, or union with
Greece. However, when Cyprus became independent, it
agreed "not to participate, in whole or part, in any
political or economic union with any state whatsoever." But independence and the Zurich Settlement did
not bring an end to the internal conflict. Civil war
broke out again in 1963-1964, and a United Nations
force had to be stationed in Cyprus. Strife was renewed in 1967-1968. Matters grew even worse in 1974.
The Cypriot National Guard, led by Greek officers,
overthrew the Cyprus government, which had long been
headed by Archbishop Makarios. Turkey sought unsuccessfully to get British action to end the crisis; the
British were supposed to be the guarantor of the 1960
Zurich accord. The U.S. made an attempt to negotiate a
settlement, but could not hold off the threatened Turkish military intervention.

On July 20, 1974, the Turkish forces launched a sea
and airborne operation against the island. There was
heavy fighting, broken by several temporary cease-
fires. The U.S. Ambassador, Roger Davies, and his
secretary were killed during mob violence against the
embassy in the capital of Nicosia. When the fighting
finally ended, many Greek Cypriots had been driven from
their homes, and, in addition to the social upheaval

and economic stagnation, there were serious political
repercussions.

Congressional Response

The Turkish action on Cyprus set off a furor in
Congress. Turkey was, of course, a major recipient of
U.S. military assistance, and Turkey's use of U.S.-
supplied equipment for other than defensive purposes
was in contravention of U.S. arms transfer policies.
(The issue of whether recipient nations use U.S.-
supplied equipment for non-defensive purposes has been
a subject of recurring controversy and congressional
committee inquiries.)
Following the 1974 Turkish move on Cyprus, Repre-
sentative John Brademas introduced legislation in the
House to cut off military aid to Turkey. In the Senate
John Tunney, an ambitious first-term Democrat from
California, did the same. Brademas, from Indiana, was
of Greek heritage, and other members of Congress of
Greek origin, or with large Greek constituencies,
joined in standing ademantly against further aid to
Turkey. They had strong support from men such as
Benjamin Rosenthal in the House and Thomas Eagleton in
the Senate. However, the congressional leadership
stood almost completely united against an embargo on
arms to Turkey. Indeed, at an early stage in the
controversy, Senate Majority Leader Mike Mansfield
assured Secretary of State Henry Kissinger that there
was no substantial support in the Senate for such an
embargo.
Mansfield was able to manage a brief delay in Senate action. He even arranged for Kissinger to speak to
a meeting of the Senate Democratic caucus, an extraordinary occurence, particularly for a Republican Secretary of State. At a tense session behind the closed
doors of Room S-207* of the Capitol, Senator Eagleton
challenged the legality of continuing aid to Turkey.
Kissinger, although making a strong case for continued
aid, was unable to directly refute Eagleton's contention that further aid would be a violation of existing
law.
In previous years the combined support of the
administration and the congressional leadership would
normally have been sufficient to beat back almost any
challenge. But, in this case, the leadership could not
deliver--even for a compromise proposal. This was indicative of a significant change within Congress, and a

---

*Room S-207 was later renamed the Mansfield Room in
honor of the man who served as Senate Majority Leader
from 1961 through 1976.

trend frequently in evidence in subsequent years. Younger and less-experienced members, and members with no committee responsibilities in the foreign affairs area, were increasingly willing to speak out and play active roles on international questions, and to diverge from party leadership positions.

Secretary Kissinger was critical of what he considered to be an improper congressional intrusion into the foreign policy process and a violation of what he deemed to be the proper relationship between executive and legislative functions. But, as Lawrence Stern wrote in The Wrong Horse: "Brilliant as he was in the practice of private diplomacy and bureaucratic politics, Kissinger seriously misapprehended the temper of Congress on the Cyprus issue. He sought to deal through the traditional brokers of congressional consensus, the senior chairmen who held the established political franchises on Capitol Hill."[127]

The White House and Kissinger were slow to recognize the new realities in Congress. Congress was in an assertive mood, emboldened by the weakened presidency in the aftermath of Watergate, and it refused to go along with the Administration's pleadings. After twice votoing legislation which would have cut off military aid to Turkey, on December 30, 1974 President Ford signed into law the Foreign Assistance Act of 1974, requiring suspension of military assistance to Turkey until the president certified that "substantial progress" toward a Cyprus settlement had occurred. The embargo took effect on February 5, 1975.

Subsequently, some steps were taken to partially lift the embargo, but President Ford and Secretary Kissinger were unsuccessful in their continuing efforts to have it dropped altogether. Meanwhile, resentment built in Turkey, where the embargo was viewed as a humiliating slap at an old friend and as representing a pro-Greek bias. Kissinger, warning Congress that refusal to lift the embargo would have "disastrous" consequences for the U.S., blasted the "Greek Lobby" in Washington, which he credited for successfully pressing for continuation of the embargo. Turkey retaliated, as Kissinger predicted, by closing 26 U.S. installations in the country, including four key electronic-surveillance stations. Kissinger referred to this as a "Greek tragedy."[128]

Ethnic Politics

Later, looking back on these events, Senator Charles McC. Mathias, Jr., noted that "45,000 Americans of Turkish origin, most of them recent arrivals and not yet politically acculturated, were heavily outgunned by organizations claiming the support of three million

Greek Americans." As Mathias pointed out, "the Greek-
American organizations, spearheaded by the newly formed
and largely foreign-supported American Hellenic Institute (AHI), worked assiduously and successfully for the
arms embargo."[129]

This was one of the most obvious examples of ethnic
politics influencing American foreign policy. As
Mathias correctly states, "But for the activities of
Greek-Americans we might have overlooked, for larger
strategic reasons, the injustices suffered by the Greek
population of Cyprus."[130]

Another Republican senator, John Tower of Texas,
citing the example of the arms embargo, said, "In a society such as ours, with its heterogeneous mix of various national and ethnic groups, strong lobbies are inevitable." But, in Tower's view, to submit American
foreign policy to undue influence by these groups--
"often emotionally charged"--can impair a President's
ability to carry out a policy which reflects the overall national interest.[131]

Despite the strong role in support of the embargo,
however, the "Greek Lobby" is, as Mathias notes, "by
any objective measure of power and influence...'Number
Two,' and a fairly distant second" behind the Israeli
lobby in Washington.[132]

After the embargo on arms to Turkey was imposed,
and as continuing efforts were made to lift the embargo, "a Greek professional lobby emerged in Washington
somewhat self-consciously modeled on AIPAC."[133] (AIPAC
is the American Israel Public Affairs Committee, a
highly successful lobbying operation founded in
1951.)* For lobbying purposes, Greek business and
civic leaders established the American Hellenic Institute Public Affairs Committee (AHIPAC). The Greek lobby depended heavily on the network of American Hellenic
Educational Progressive Association (AHEPA) chapters
across the country.

Such lobbying groups can mobilize letters, phone
calls, or visits to members of Congress. They concen-
trate on senators and representatives with sizeable
blocs of ethnic voters in their constiuencies. Such
groups can also make important financial contributions
to campaigns. The Washington-based organizations keep
a close watch on congressional activities and maintain
contact with key staff members as well as members of
Congress.

Lifting the Embargo

When President Carter succeeded Ford in 1977, he
too determined that the embargo was not a wise policy,

---

*See Chapter 5 for more on the role of AIPAC.

and set about to end it. At the same time that Carter took office, Robert Byrd became the Democratic Majority Leader in the Senate. He was a strong ally of Carter on this and other major foreign policy issues, although he also spoke out against his party's President in some cases. Byrd had voted for the embargo in 1974, while serving as Senate Democratic Whip*, and was one of the few in leadership to do so. But he was convinced that the embargo had become counter-productive and had not contributed to progress in Cyprus.

Turkey was the linchpin of NATO's southern flank. Its strategic location between the Soviet Union and the Middle East had become all the more vital because of the importance and volatility of the Middle East. Yet the condition of the Turkish military, including NATO's second-largest contingent of ground troops, had badly deteriorated, and the economy was in even worse shape. The serious instability in Turkey made it ripe for terrorism and radicalism.

Early in the summer of 1978, Byrd traveled to Western Europe and met with European leaders and NATO officials. He reported back to his colleagues: "There was unanimity from everyone I met with in the NATO countries that the embargo on arms to Turkey should be lifted as soon as possible. The European leaders left no doubt about the overriding importance they attach to this matter."[134]

Senate Forces

The strong European sentiment increased Byrd's determination to see the embargo repealed. However, this meant overcoming the opposition of the Senate Foreign Relations Committee, which had already voted, on May 11, 1978, against lifting the embargo. Even in the era of reduced committee power, it is not often that committee votes are reversed on the floor. Opposition within the committee was led by Senator Paul Sarbanes, who, as a House member, had been an important figure in the successful effort to impose the embargo in 1974. Sarbanes argued that the Administration was seeking to put "law and the question of human rights and principle ... on the back burner" by lifting the embargo.[135] A representative of the American Hellenic Institute Public Affairs Committee (the Greek-American organization designed on the model of AIPAC) told the Foreign Relations Committee that Turkey should not receive "one dime of assistance" until Turkey "is in compliance with our laws and there is an agreed settlement on Cyprus."[136]

---

*The Whip is the party's assistant leader.

In the Senate, where actions are often influenced by personalities and personal relationships, Byrd was reluctant to oppose Sarbanes, a respected young member of his own party. Byrd and Sarbanes had only recently collaborated on the successful fight for the Panama Canal Treaties. Likewise, Senator Javits had recently traveled in the Mediterranean area and had concluded that the Turkish ban should be repealed. However, he was also reluctant to oppose Sarbanes, because of the prominent role Sarbanes had played in opposing the sale of jet aircraft to Saudi Arabia, a matter on which he had been allied with Javits.

Senator George McGovern also favored ending the embargo, and had so voted within the Foreign Relations Committee. When the security assistance bill was taken up on the Senate floor, McGovern planned to offer an amendment to repeal the embargo. However, Byrd arranged a meeting with McGovern, and when the South Dakotan learned of Byrd's plans for an amendment, McGovern deferred to the majority leader, recognizing that Byrd might be able to draw broader support. Byrd and McGovern were joined by Democrat Lloyd Bentsen (Texas) and Republican John Chafee (Rhode Island) in a disparate coalition sponsoring the amendment. Although the primary intent of the amendment was to end the embargo, it contained provisions for presidential reporting to Congress on progress toward resolution of the Cyprus issue, and provided equal amounts of military sales credit for Turkey and Greece.

Byrd and his co-sponsors made personal appeals to their colleagues, and Byrd organized a series of meetings in which members of the Joint Chiefs of Staff and top administration officials briefed senators and answered questions. He concentrated on newer members who had not been in Congress at the time of the earlier battles over Turkey. Meetings and briefings for staff members were also organized. Byrd repeatedly emphasized that his efforts were not anti-Greece or pro-Turkey, but in the best interests of both countries, of the U.S., NATO, and U.S. friends in the Middle East. After fierce debate, the Byrd amendment carried, 57-42.

The debate was even more difficult in the House, where the decisive vote to drop the embargo--on an amendment proposed by House Majority Leader Jim Wright --was by a narrow 208-205 margin.

More Battles on Turkey

The same issues tend to come up over and over in Congress, and such has been the case with Turkey. Although the embargo had been lifted, major fights over Turkish aid were still to come. Late in 1978, Byrd traveled to Turkey in his capacity as majority leader

and also as a special emissary of President Carter.
The visit to Turkey was part of a lengthy Byrd trip to
the Middle East and Iran. The trip was evidence of the
active role congressional leaders were playing in foreign policy and the importance the Administration attached to Byrd's role.

Upon his return, Byrd reported that there had been
a revitalization of U.S.-Turkish relations and noted
that Turkish Prime Minister Bulent Ecevit had allowed
reopening of the four U.S. intelligence monitoring
posts in Turkey. These facilities, which helped monitor Soviet military activities and weapons testing,
increased in importance early in 1979, following the
fall of the Shah and the loss of key monitoring facilities in Iran. While noting the improved U.S.-Turkish
relations, Byrd said, "After having visited Turkey...I
concluded that there has not been sufficient recognition of the scope and urgency of Turkey's economic and
military needs."[137]

Because of Turkey's severe economic difficulties,
and as part of a broader Western effort to assist Turkey, President Carter, in April 1979, asked Congress to
approve $50 million in military grants and $100 million
in economic grants for Turkey. This was a special request in addition to the $301.2 million for Turkey the
Administration had already requested, and the $227.5
million approved the previous year.

Once again the Senate Foreign Relations Committee
proved to be a stumbling block for the Administration.
The committee, led by Sarbanes, disapproved the military grant proposal, substituting $50 million in for-
eign military sales (FMS) credits instead, and adding
$42 million in FMS credits for Greece. Nonetheless,
the fact that the committee was willing to approve the
credits and the rest of the package was a substantial
change from previous years. Initially, the Administration was inclined to accept the committee's alternative
rather than wage still another battle over Turkish aid.
However, in early May 1979, Deputy Secretary of State
Warren Christopher visited Turkey to meet with Prime
Minister Ecevit. The Turkish leader, citing his country's economic woes, pushed hard for more aid. He
insisted that Turkey needed some grant assistance.
Credits--loans which can be used to purchase military
equipment from the U.S.--would merely add to Turkey's
debt burden. Evecit used the U.S. intelligence installations as leverage, recognizing that with the Carter
Administration soon to be pushing for the SALT II
Treaty, the U.S. needed Turkey's cooperation in monitoring Soviet treaty compliance.

Christopher returned to Washington convinced of the
importance of the grant aid. He recognized that in
addition to its actual value, the grant aid was a matter of prestige and symbolic significance for the

beleaguered Turkish military, and the military leaders were an important element in the uncertain Turkish political equation. For the Turkish military, it was also a matter of equity, since Greece had received grant funds the previous year and Turkey had not. Finally, the Turkish military officials pointed out that as a grant recipient, Turkey would be able to purchase excess U.S. military equipment at nominal cost.

One of Christopher's first stops upon his return was Byrd's office. Byrd had been awaiting word from the Administration on whether an effort should be made to restore the grant funds. Byrd was prepared to lead the fight again, but not without the Administration's backing. In their meeting on May 11, Christopher left Byrd with no doubt that the Carter Administration wanted to see the grant funds included in the bill.

Building Senate Support

Byrd went to work immediately, using the same tactics and strategy he had successfully applied in lifting the embargo and had subsequently refined in other foreign policy battles. Quickly he was joined by John Chafee on the Republican side. Byrd and Chafee then put together an impressive bipartisan coalition of co-sponsors: Democrats Bentsen, Sam Nunn, and Edmund Muskie, and Republicans Ted Stevens (the Minority Whip), John Tower, and Henry Bellmon.

On May 16, this group circulated a "Dear Colleague" letter to other senators, asking for support of the amendment. The next day, a group including Sarbanes and Claiborne Pell of the Foreign Relations Committee, plus four other Democrats--Eagleton, Edward Kennedy, Paul Tsongas, and Donald Riegle--circulated their own "Dear Colleague" letter. Their letter said, "In the belief that enough is enough, we ask you to oppose further revisions in the committee's recommendations." The authors of this letter said, "We think that $451 million in aid this year and $678 million over two years is generous help for an ally whose record of co-operation with NATO, on Cyprus, and with the United States is seriously flawed."[138]

The Byrd-Chafee group met in the Majority Leader's office and went down the Senate roll call list, dividing responsibility among themselves for contacting colleagues personally and urging support for the amendment. In some cases, key Administration officials were asked by the group to contact specific senators. On May 17, Byrd hosted a luncheon in the Lyndon B. Johnson Room in the Capitol, with Deputy Secretary Christopher, Air Force Chief of Staff Lewis Allen, and other Administration heavyweights joining Byrd in making a strong pitch to a group of senators. Allen was particularly

effective in speaking about Turkey's defense needs. A
similar luncheon was held in the Capitol's John F.
Kennedy Room on May 21, with Defense Secretary Harold
Brown among those in attendance. Byrd also emphasized
the importance of the amendment at his weekly press
conference on May 10, and the story received major
attention.

Meanwhile, the Administration provided information
packets to Senate offices and worked closely with the
Byrd group in building support. Edelman International
Corporation, a public relations firm hired by the Turkish Embassy, also provided information to Senate offices, including a copy of a May 14 column by Rowland
Evans and Robert Novak, which appeared in The Washington Post. The columnists wrote that Turkey's importance to the U.S. had reached new heights because of
the events in Iran, but that Moscow believed that Turkey was "ripe for destabilization." Evans and Novak
said the Soviets were using propaganda "to finish the
work insensibly started by the U.S. Congress with its
arms embargo and systematically reduce American ties
with Turkey."[139]

Paralleling the efforts of the Byrd-Chafee group
among senators was a similar operation at the staff
level. Staff members from the Senate Democratic Policy
Committee, which Byrd headed, canvassed the staff network and kept in close touch with the White House and
the State Department congressional liaison operations.

On May 22, the Senate took up the amendment. An
editorial in that morning's New York Times made a stong
case for the Byrd-Chafee amendment. Entitled, "Turkey
Needs a Hand, Not a Rod," the Times editorial supported
the grant funds: "There is no good reason to insist on
commercial loan terms except to revive the policy of
punishment. Senators who favor the Greek position on
Cyprus oppose the aid in that spirit."[140]

Going into the Senate debate, Byrd felt confident
of victory. His tally showed that he had 40 certain
votes, with only 18 definitely against. He counted at
least 16 senators leaning for the amendment. But Byrd
held these figures close to the vest and kept his
forces hard at work up to the time of the vote. The
Carter Administration lobbyists who worked with Byrd
were not sure as late as the night before the vote that
they had the votes to best the Foreign Relations Committee, the pro-Greek lobby, and others who opposed the
outright grant. The final vote was 64-32 for the
amendment, overriding the recommendation of the Foreign
Relations Committee.

As the Washington Post reported, "The question produced a rare example of intensely argued Senate debate
in which friends of Greece and austerity-conscious conservatives opposed the grant to Turkey while a bipartisan coalition of senators defended it as a necessary

symbol of concern for a troubled NATO ally."[141]

House Resentment

Although the Carter Administration had again won the Senate battle on Turkey, the House presented an even more formidable problem. On June 21, the House, by a lopsided 303-107 margin, voted to instruct its conferees in the House-Senate conference on the security assistance bill to insist on disagreement with the Senate amendment. It is a relatively rare occurrence for conferees to be so instructed. Conferees usually have the flexibility to negotiate.

In this case, more than opposition to the grant aid to Turkey was involved. Institutional pride and the belief that House prerogatives were being usurped undoubtedly influenced the House vote. As Representative Edward Derwinski (R-Illinois) noted when introducing his motion to instruct, the Carter Administration presented the request for additional Turkish aid, including the military grant, after the House had already completed action on the security assistance bill. "The Administration has thereby completely bypassed the House, alleging that an up-or-down vote on an eventual conference report is sufficient involvement for the House in this matter," Derwinski said.[142]

Representative Paul Findley, another Illinois Republican, argued vainly that Derwinski's motion "would not be a constructive development...it would be a needless and unfortunate slap at Turkey."[143]

There has often been resentment in the House of the more prominent role the Senate plays in foreign affairs, and in this case the White House tactic of requesting the additional aid after the House acted on the security assistance bill backfired. Contributing to the particularly intense House feelings about its proper role was the fact that earlier on the same day that the House had concluded its lengthy and highly contentious debate on legislation to implement the Panama Canal Treaties. The House had no role in considering the actual treaties, the advise and consent role being a Senate responsibility.

Many members of the House, including some who supported the treaties, believed that President Carter had circumvented the Constitution when he failed to seek House approval for the treaty-mandated transfers of property to Panama. (See Chapter 4.) During the debate on the implementing legislation which preceded the debate on Derwinski's motion on Turkish aid, Representative Don Clausen, a California Republican, said, "There is a growing body of opinion that the American people wanted and, indeed, expected the full Congress-- both the House and the Senate--to be involved in the

Panama issue. The American people resent an international negotiating process that relegates the U.S. House of Representatives to a followup role of having to vote to 'pay the bill' for a vital economic and national security package which was drafted by others and in which the House had no opportunity to participate."[144]

It was in this atmosphere of indignation about denial of the House's "rightful role" that consideration of the Derwinski motion occurred, and it undoubtedly contributed to the strong vote to instruct the conferees. That vote almost guaranteed a lengthy and difficult conference on the security assistance bill, and that is exactly what occurred.

Conference Deadlock

The deadlock lasted for more than three months. Meanwhile, the Administration was attempting to negotiate a Defense Cooperation Agreement with the troubled Turkish government. Such an agreement would govern the U.S. military and intelligence installations in Turkey, which were operating under a temporary agreement.

Initially, the conferees hoped to have the conference concluded by the July 4 recess, but neither side budged on the Turkey issue. The Senate conferees were anxious to finish the conference, because on July 9 the Foreign Relations Committee would begin its lengthy SALT II hearings. Chairman Frank Church and Jacob Javits, the ranking Republican on the Senate Committee, had voted for the credits rather than the grant; indeed, Javits had proposed the alternative. But Church and Javits had pledged Majority Leader Byrd to stand firmly behind the Senate position in favor of the grant.

Soon the conferees reached agreement on all items in the security assistance bill except Turkish aid. The House conferees would not agree to any grant military aid. The Administration signaled that it would hold firm in support of grant funds. With all other issues in the bill resolved, and with the Senate members of the conference committee preoccupied with SALT II, the conferees ceased to meet. Responsible staff members from Senate Foreign Relations, House Foreign Affairs, and the Senate Democratic Policy Committees met periodically to consider means of breaking the stalemate. Such a meeting occurred on August 1, when the staff group met with Matthew Nimetz, State Department Counselor, representing the administration. The House staff reported an unyielding attitude on the part of key figures in the House. Byrd insisted on holding out for some direct military aid to Turkey. One proposal considered was to grant Turkey a $50 million FMS loan, with the provision that the president could determine

the terms--and the president might decide to make the
loan on a "forgiveness" basis, as had been the case
with some loans to Israel. This approach would also
have allowed Turkey special access to excess defense
articles. But, like several others, this proposal did
not prove acceptable to all the major actors.

On September 6, Byrd met with Turkish Ambassador
Sukru Elekdag to discuss the issue. Elekdag stressed
the importance to the Turkish military of grant funds.
Byrd had seen a copy of a State Department cable reporting that Prime Minister Ecevit had told Representative Steven Solarz of New York, who had been in Turkey
during the August recess, that he might be able to convince the military to go along with a compromise. Such
a compromise would make the $50 million an economic
rather than a military grant, and would have specific
provision making Turkey eligible for excess military
equipment. But Elekdag gave no indication of a changed
attitude in Turkey, simply emphasizing that Turkey was
in desperate need for both economic and military aid.
Meanwhile, the political situation in Turkey was growing more precarious.

The next development in the effort to find a solution to the conference stalemate was a proposal put
forward by Deputy Secretary Christopher in mid-Septem-
ber. He visited all the key figures to suggest a compromise which would have replaced the $50 million mili-
tary grant with $30 million in economic grants and $20
million in grants for excess defense articles at current market rates. Even though this would not have involved any direct military grants to Turkey, the principal figures in the House balked. Part of their opposition may have been related to Christopher personally.
He was seen by some of the House activists on the issue
as having become too closely identified with Turkey.

Byrd and the Senate conferees were operating at a
disadvantage. If a conference committee is unable to
reach agreement on a funding issue, then the normal
procedure is to allow programs to operate under a "continuing resolution" with funding authorized at the same
level as for the previous year. In that case, Turkey
would have received much less than under the 1979
proposals.

Reaching Agreement

Finally, on September 19, a meeting occurred in
Byrd's office in room S-208 in the Capitol that set the
stage for an agreement. House Foreign Affairs Committee Chairman Clement Zablocki made the trip across the
Capitol to meet the Senate Majority Leader. Capitol
Hill often attaches great importance to such gestures,
and Zablocki's gesture in going to Byrd was important.

In this case, it made it easier for Byrd to give some ground on the Senate position. Zablocki was genuinely concerned about Turkey: He favored increased aid. However, he knew that he had an adamant group of House members to deal with and that restricted his flexibility.

Representing the Administration was Brian Atwood, Assistant Secretary of State for Congressional Relations, who had worked with top staff aides to Byrd and Zablocki to arrange the meeting.[145] Atwood's presence was ironic because in 1974, as an aide to Senate Thomas Eagleton, he had played a key role in helping to impose the embargo. Now he was working hard in favor of aid to Turkey.

In an atmosphere thick with cigar smoke, Zablocki and Byrd reached agreement. The two were old acquaintances, having served together in the House when Byrd was a representative, and these personal ties counted. Both wanted to see the issue resolved, and in a short time they arrived at an acceptable compromise. Turkey would receive $250 million in FMS credits; of this, $50 million would be on special repayment terms, similar to terms of loans to Egypt and Israel. As a recipient of FMS credits, Turkey would be eligible to purchase excess U.S. defense articles at fair market value--a matter of great importance from the Turkish viewpoint. Of the $198 million in economic aid, $75 million would be in grant form. There would also be a $2 million military training grant. The overall total of $450 million would make Turkey the third largest recipient of U.S. assistance, after Israel and Egypt. Therefore, although there was not direct military assistance grant in the package, the Senate could take some satisfaction in having obtained a $75 million economic grant and the $450 million total.

As Byrd said later, "If there had been another card in the deck, we could have played for Turkey in this conference. I would have been for playing it. But there would have been nothing left."[146]

With Byrd and Zablocki having sealed the deal, the conference committee officially approved it on September 26, ending the three-month deadlock. On October 4, 1979, more than four and one-half months after the Senate had acted on Turkish aid, the Senate took up the conference report. Byrd, Javits, and Chafee spoke in support of it. Byrd said the aid package for Turkey "while not fully satisfactory...would nonetheless provide substantial aid."[147]

More Hurdles

Ironically, after the long struggle to gain approval for the authorization of aid to Turkey, the

proponents of such aid were partially thwarted once
more when Congress failed to enact a foreign aid appropriations bill. Aid legislation had become so complex
and so politically unpopular, with very few members
willing to take the lead in supporting it, that aid
appropriations were allowed to languish. (When Congress passed a $11.5-billion foreign aid bill in Decem-
ber 1981, it was the first foreign aid appropriations
bill in three years. The aid bill passed during the
Reagan Administration's first year in office, and with
a strong push from the Administration, despite the fact
that many Reagan supporters in Congress had previously
been among those most critical of aid programs. But by
the next year aid was once again funded through a continuing resolution.)

Congress had authorized $250 million in FMS credits
for fiscal year 1980 for Turkey and nearly $2 million
for military education and training as part of the
overall aid package. However, as Secretary of State
Edmund Muskie informed Byrd in September 1980, "in the
absence of appropriations legislation, we shall be able
to disburse only $200 million and $1.4 million respect-
ively." Muskie said, "Our inability to provide the
full authorized amount has been a major disappointment
to the Turks, because of their critical need...and because the $250 million FMS amount was seen by them as
good faith by the Administration and the authorizing
committees to meet our commitment under the new Defense
and Economic Cooperation Agreement."[148] Muskie referred to the agreement between Turkey and the United
States which was signed on March 29, 1980. The five-
year agreement clearly would not have been possible
without the congressional action to end the arms embargo and to approve the 1979 aid authorization.

When a State Department official testified at a
hearing on the agreement before House Foreign Affairs
Subcommittee on Europe and the Middle East in May 1980,
Subcommittee Chairman Lee Hamilton opened the questioning this way: "The first question is how much is it
going to cost us?" Hamilton said he wanted to explore
"the linkage between the agreement and the money."[149]
The subcommittee was told that, although it was an
"executive agreement," containing no pledge of specific
economic or military assistance, the U.S. pledged to
continue to try to provide assistance in the range of
$450 million per year for Turkey, with possible larger
amounts in future years. In return, the U.S. received
authorization to maintain forces and carry out military
activities at specified installations in Turkey, including three intelligence-gathering installations.

Congress accepted the "executive agreement," not
requiring formal congressional approval, without much
fuss. This could be seen as evidence of both a more
relaxed congressional attitude toward the executive

than had been the case in the 1970s, and a recognition
that Congress still controlled the purse strings--the
funding being an integral if unstated part of the
agreement.

A Library of Congress study for the House Foreign
Affairs Committee in 1980 said, "In view of the significant problems facing Turkey, it seems clear that, for
the foreseeable future, Congress will be confronted
with requests for substantial economic and military assistance to help restore Turkey's military readiness
and economic viability...The position that Congress
takes on aid requests is likely to have a profound effect on further United States-Turkish relations and
U.S. interests in the eastern Mediterranean."[150]

A staff report issued by the Senate Foreign Relations Committee in March 1980 said, "Turkey's political
situation is critical. More than 10 years of coalition
governments, political polarization, urban terrorism,
renewed Kurdish nationalism, and fundamental socio-
economic problems give rise to a threat of anarchy or
military rule."[151] The detailed staff report was one
of a number of such reports issued by the foreign
affairs committees in recent years. Until Chairman
Fulbright of the Senate Foreign Relations Committee
began dispatching staff members to conduct overseas
studies and investigations in the late sixties and
early seventies, such reports had been rare. But the
increase in congressional staff and the more active
role of the congressional committees made such reports
more possible and more in demand. It gave the committees some independent sources of information and made
them less reliant on the executive for information,
even though the assistance of executive branch officials was often essential to the success of such studies and investigations. In the case of the 1980 report to the Senate Foreign Relations Committee, Chairman Frank Church asked staff members Hans Binnendijk
and Alfred Friendly, Jr., to visit the region and pre-
pare the report to assist the committee in its consideration of aid requests from the executive branch. The
report proved to be on the mark in several important
respects.

Turkey's Problems

On September 6, 1980 the Turkish military took over
the government in an attempt to bring order to the
highly troubled nation. The military leaders promised
to restore democracy after bringing the nation's turmoil under control. But the Turks found themselves
still in conflict with Greece within the NATO alliance,
and the European members of NATO criticized Turkey for
failing to restore democracy quickly. The Council of

Europe pressured the military government to end its banning of political parties, "human rights violations," and muzzling of the press. This estrangement from its European allies served to push Turkey closer to the U.S., where little had been heard in Congress in criticism of the military rule. In December 1981, Secretary of Defense Caspar Weiberger said the U.S. and Turkey had agreed to establish a high-level joint defense group to "enlarge and improve defense cooperation between the two nations."[152]

Parlimentary elections were held in November 1983, although only certain parties and candidates were allowed to participate. Even though the military did not back the winning party, former General Kenan Evren remained as president as a result of Turkey's new military-sponsored constitution, approved in 1982.

Under the Reagan Administration, Turkey continued to rank high among the U.S. aid recipients. In recent years, it has been at congressional insistence that a 7:10 ratio has been maintained in U.S. military assistance to Greece and Turkey. While executive branch officials have tried to steer away from such formula, Congress has adamantly retained the ratio, tying aid to Greece and Turkey. For fiscal year 1984, for example, with a strong push from supporters of Greece, congressional committees cut proposed aid to Turkey, and helped bring up the amount to Greece so as to maintain the 7:10 ratio.

A Focal Point

Turkey continues to be an important factor in United States foreign policy and international security arrangements. Even though Turkey might seem to many Americans to be at the periphery of American interests, it has, during the period since World War II, frequently figured in important United States foreign policy trends and developments.

Looking at U.S. relations with Turkey and U.S. policies toward that country during the post-World War II period provides a panoramic view of the evolution of American foreign policy, beginning with the Greek-Turkish aid program and the Truman Doctrine. The Truman Doctrine set the pattern for subsequent American policy and for the American outlook on the world. It had important implications at home too. Turkey managed to figure in a number of other key events in U.S. international relations--the building of the NATO alliance, the Korean War, and the Cuban missile crisis, in which the U.S. agreed to remove missiles from Turkey after the Soviets removed their missiles from Cuba.

Tracing the Congressional Role

If the position of Turkey in the U.S. foreign policy perspective is a useful way to examine the evolution of U.S. policy, it is also a means of examining the evolution of the congressional role during that same period. Congress played a relatively active role in considering Greek-Turkish aid in 1947, but it was also beginning a pattern of allowing broad discretion to the executive when a "crisis" was invoked.

Turkey was also at the center of events when Congress, during a particularly tumultuous period in its relations with the executive in the 1970s, reasserted itself in foreign policy. U.S. relations with Turkey became entangled in this congressional reassertion. In addition to being a case of Congress playing a decisive role on major foreign policy issue, the recent history of congressional action on Turkey provides notable examples of intra-congressional as well as congressional-executive struggles over foreign policy. It also illustrates the changing nature and influence of congressional leadership, the role of committees, and the importance of procedure and personalities in congressional action--this last factor being one that is too often overlooked in analyses of the congressional role. Finally, congressional consideration of U.S. policies toward Turkey (and its neighbor, Greece) provides a vivid demonstration of the role of ethnic politics and ethnic lobbies in influencing U.S. foreign policy.

There are many positive features to a more active congressional role in foreign policy, but there can be dangerous consequences, particularly if Congress tends to overlook the longer-term and strategic consequences of its actions and takes steps that, although perhaps politically popular at home, can be counterproductive to overall U.S. foreign policy interests and coherence. Recent events have shown Congress in what would appear to be a more responsible and balanced role in acting on policy toward Turkey, but a role that reflects congressional determination to remain actively involved in foreign policy.

NOTES

1. "Address of the President of the United States --Greece, Turkey, and the Middle East," Congressional Record, House, March 12, 1947, p.1981. (Also, "Recommendations on Greece and Turkey," message of the President to the 80th Cong., 1st sess., March 12, 1947, U.S. Department of State, Bulletin, supplement of May 4, 1947, p.832; "Recommendation for Assistance to Greece and Turkey," Address of the President of the United States, March 12, 1947, U.S. House of Representatives, 80th Cong., 1st sess., Doc. 171; "Recommendations on Greece and Turkey," Message of the President to Congress, March 12, 1947, A Decade of American Foreign Policy, Basic Documents, 1941-1949, U.S. Senate Foreign Relations Committee, Washington, 1950, p.1255.

2. Ibid.

3. Harry S. Truman, Memoirs, Volume II: Years of Trial and Hope (Garden City: Doubleday, 1956), pp. 100-101.

4. J. William Fulbright, The Crippled Giant (New York: Random House, 1972), p.22.

5. Ibid., p.17.

6. Ibid., p.19.

7. Ibid.

8. Truman, Memoirs, vol.II, pp.103.

9. Dean Acheson, President at the Creation (New York: Norton, 1969), p.219.

10. Ibid.

11. Ibid.

12. Arthur H. Vandenberg, Jr., ed., The Private Papers of Senator Vandenberg (Boston: Houghton Mifflin, 1952), p.339.

13. Joseph M. Jones, The Fifteen Weeks (New York: Viking, 1955), p.142.

14. Ibid., p.149.

15. U.S. Department of State, Foreign Relations of the United States, 1947, Volume V: The Near East and Africa (Washington: Government Printing Office, 1971), p.47.

16. Jones, The Fifteen Weeks, pp.123-124

17. Vandenberg, Private Papers, p.339.

18. Ibid., p.342.

19. U.S. Senate, Congressional Record, April 8, 1947, p.3198.

20. See Fulbright's comments, Congressional Record, December 10, 1973, pp.40352-40354.

21. Vandenberg, Private Papers, p.343.

22. Ibid., p.339

23. Ibid., p.558 (Letter from President Harry Truman to Vandenberg, March 12, 1949).

24. Ibid., pp.450-451.

25. Ibid., p.550.

26. Howard Baker, No Margin for Error (New York: Times Books, 1979), p.155.
27. Vandenberg, Private Papers, p.562.
28. Dallas Times Herald, October 25, 1981.
29. Susan Hartmann, Truman and the 80th Congress (Columbia: University of Missouri Press, 1971), p.57.
30. Acheson, President at the Creation, p.221. For a detailed account of the drafting of the Truman Doctrine, see Jones, The Fifteen Weeks, pp.148-170.
31. Charles E. Bohlen, Witness to History, 1929-1969 (New York: Norton, 1973), p.261.
32. Ibid.
33. George F. Kennan, Memoirs, 1925-1950 (Boston: Little, Brown, 1967), pp.319-320.
34. Ibid., pp.357-367.
35. X, "The Sources of Soviet Conduct," Foreign Affairs 25, July 1947, pp.575-576,582.
36. Kennan, Memoirs, p.358.
37. Ibid., p.317.
38. Jones, Fifteen Days, p.162.
39. Ibid.
40. Ibid.
41. Message of the President to the Congress, March 12, 1947, Basic Documents, p.1256.
42. Ibid., p.1257.
43. Acheson, Present at the Creation, pp.221-222.
44. Richard M. Freeland, The Truman Doctrine and the Origins of McCarthyism (New York: Knopf, 1972), p. 102.
45. Hartmann, Truman and the 80th Congress, p.60.
46. Daniel Yergin, Shattered Peace (Boston: Houghton Mifflin, 1977), p.283.
47. Hartmann, Truman and the 80th Congress, p.58.
48. U.S. Congress, Senate. Legislative Origins of the Truman Doctrine, Hearings Held in Executive Session on S.938, 80th Cong., 1st sess., 1947. Historical Series, 1973, pp.1-2.
49. Kennan, Memoirs, pp.354-355.
50. Forrestal resigned as Secretary of Defense in 1949. Suffering from severe depression and fatigue, he plunged to his death at Bethesda Naval Hospital two months later.
51. Legislative Origins, Hearings, p.6.
52. Ibid., p.9.
53. Ibid., p.15.
54. Ibid.
55. Ibid.
56. Ibid., p.115.
57. Ibid., p.107.
58. Ibid., p.101.
59. Vandenberg, Private Papers, p.345.
60. Foreign Relations, 1947, p.137.
61. Acheson, Present at the Creation, p.224.
62. Ibid., p.222.

63. Congressional Record, Senate, April 21, 1947, p.3727.
64. Ibid., pp.3752 (April 21, 1947) and 3773 (April 22, 1947).
65. Foreign Relations, 1947, p.147.
66. Ibid., p.148.
67. Congressional Record, Senate, April 21, 1947, p.3728.
68. Ibid., April 22, 1947, p.3786.
69. Ibid., p.3773.
70. Ibid., p.3777.
71. Ibid., p.3773.
72. Ibid., April 21, 1947, p.3729.
73. Ibid., p.3730.
74. Ibid., p.3737
75. Ibid.
76. Ibid., pp.3737-3738.
77. Ibid., p.3838.
78. Ibid.
79. Ibid., April 7, 1947, p.3137.
80. Ibid.
81. Ibid.
82. J. William Fulbright and John C. Stennis, The Role of Congress in Foreign Policy (Washington: American Enterprise Institute, 1971), pp.35-36; see also, U.S. Congress, Senate, National Commitments, Senate Foreign Relations Committee, Senate Report No.129, 91st Cong., 1st sess., 1969, p.7.
83. Fulbright, The Crippled Giant, p.213; see also Congressional Record, Senate, vol.117, no.51, 92nd Cong., 1st sess., April 14, 1971, S4784; and George Reedy, The Twilight of the Presidency (New York: World, 1970), p.27.
84. Congressional Record, Appendix, March 12, 1946, p.A1283 (text of an address, "The Legislator," delivered at the University of Chicago, February 10, 1946); see also, Karl E. Meyer, ed., Fulbright of Arkansas: The Public Positions of a Private Thinker (Washington: Luce, 1963), p.248.
85. "Presidential Dictatorship," Congressional Record, Senate, February 5, 1967.
86. Ibid.
87. J. William Fulbright, "American Foreign Policy in the 20th Century under an 18th Century Constitution," 47 Cornell Law Quarterly, no.1, pp.1-13 (an address delivered at Cornell University, May 5, 1961); see also Meyer, Fulbright of Arkansas, p.268.
88. Meyer, Fulbright of Arkansas, p.269.
89. Ibid., p.268.
90. handwritten memorandum, J. William Fulbright to author, 1973.
91. Letter, J. William Fulbright to author, April 1, 1982.

92. Congressional Record, Senate, March 7, 1968, p.5660.

93. Ibid., p.5666.

94. John C. Campbell (Council on Foreign Relations), The United States in World Affairs, 1947-1948 (New York: Harper, 1948), p.46.

95. Ibid.

96. Congressional Record, Senate, April 22, 1947, p.3786.

97. Ibid.

98. See Donald R. Mattews, U.S. Senators and Their World (New York: Random House, Vintage (paper), 1960), p.70; Robert Sherrill, Gothic Politics in the Deep South (New York: Ballantine (paper), 1969), p.162; Marjorie Hunter, "At 77, Florida's Pepper, a New Deal Veteran, Is Still Going Like '38," The New York Times, September 9, 1977.

99. Congressional Record, House, May 8, 1947, p.4809.

100. Ibid.

101. Ibid., p.4810.

102. Earl Mazo, Richard Nixon: A Political and Personal Portrait (New York: Harper, 1959), p.75.

103. Ibid., p.79.

104. John Lewis Gaddis, The United States and the Origins of the Cold War, 1941-1947 (New York: Columbia University Press, 1972), pp.317-318.

105. Freeland, The Truman Doctrine and the Origins of McCarthyism, p.359.

106. Robert A. Divine, Since 1945--Politics and Diplomacy in Recent American History (New York: Wiley, 1975), p.31.

107. Robert H. Ferrell, "Truman Foreign Policy--A Traditionalist View," in Richard S. Kirkendall, ed., The Truman Period as a Research Field (Columbia: University of Missouri Press, 1974), p.42.

108. Richard Rovere, Senator Joe McCarthy (London: Methuen, 1959), p.15.

109. Congressional Record, House, May 7, 1947, p.4741.

110. Ibid., p.4742.

111. Soviet Policy and the United States Response in the Third World, report prepared for the Committee on Foreign Affairs, U.S. House of Representatives, 97th Cong., 1st sess., by the Congressional Research Service, Library of Congress, March 1981, pp.175-176.

112. Turkey, Greece, and NATO: The Strained Alliance, staff report to the Committee on Foreign Affairs, U.S. House of Representatives, 96th Cong., 2d sess., March 1980, p.17; Soviet Policy and the United States Response, pp.216-218; "Basic Information on Turkey," document prepared by American Embassy, Ankara, Turkey, December 1978, p.10.

113. U.S. Congress, Senate, Executive Sessions of the Senate Foreign Relations Committee, Historical Series, vol.III, part 2, 82nd Cong., 1st sess., 1951, published 1976, p.380.
114. Ibid.
115. Ibid.
116. Ibid., p.377.
117. Ibid., p.378.
118. Vandenberg, Private Papers, p.476.
119. Ibid.
120. David N. Farnsworth, The Senate Committee on Foreign Relations (Urbana: University of Illinois Press, 1961), pp.75-76.
121. Cecil V. Crabb, Jr., and Pat M. Holt, Invitation to Struggle: Congress the President and Foreign Policy (Washington: Congressional Quarterly Press, 80), pp.33-34.
122. Congress and the Nation--1945-1964, vol.1 (Washington: Congressional Quarterly, 1965), p.108.
123. Foreign Aid Program, compilation of studies and surveys prepared under the direction of the Special Committee to Study the Foreign Aid Program, U.S. Senate, 85th Cong., 1st sess., July 1957, p.iv.
124. Ibid., p.1008.
125. Arthur M. Schlesinger, Jr., The Imperial Presidency (Boston: Houghton Mifflin, 1973), pp.174-175.
126. Congressional Record, Senate, December 10, 1973, p.40353.
127. Lawrence Stern, The Wrong Horse (New York: Times Books, 1977), p.142.
128. "Turkey: Blind Spots," Newsweek, August 11, 1975, p.37.
129. Charles McC. Mathias, Jr., "Ethnic Groups and Foreign Policy," Foreign Affairs 49, summer 1981, p.988.
130. Ibid., p.996.
131. John G. Tower, "Congress Versus the President: The Formulation and Implementation of American Foreign Policy," Foreign Affairs 60, winter 1981/82, p.237.
132. Mathias, "Ethnic Groups and Foreign Policy," p.990.
133. Thomas M. Franck and Edward Weisband, Foreign Policy by Congress (New York: Oxford University Press, 1979), p.192.
134. Congressional Record, Senate, July 20, 1978, p.S11233.
135. U.S. Congress, Senate, International Security Assistance Programs, Hearings before the Subcommittee on Foreign Assistance, Committee on Foreign Relations, on S.2846, 95th Cong., 2d sess., 1978, p.186.
136. Ibid., pp.192-205.
137. Robert C. Byrd, "Turkey is the Buckle on the Belt of Instability," Washington Star, April 8, 1979.

138. "Dear Colleague" letter, dated May 17, 1979, signed by Senators Claiborne Pell, Paul Sarbanes, Thomas Eagleton, Paul Tsongas, Edward Kennedy, and Donald Riegle, Jr.

139. Rowland Evans and Robert Novak, "Consigning Turkey to the Junkyard," Washington Post, May 14, 1979.

140. "Turkey Needs a Hand, Not a Rod," (editorial), The New York Times, May 22, 1979.

141. Robert G. Kaiser, "Senate Backs Intensely Debated Grant to Turkey," Washington Post, May 23, 1979.

142. Congressional Record, House, June 21, 1979, p.H490-.

143. Ibid., p.H4908.

144. Ibid., p.H4875.

145. Arranging and attending the meeting with Zablocki and Byrd were Atwood; Jack Brady, staff director of the House Foreign Affairs Committee; and Hoyt Purvis, foreign/defense policy advisor to the Majority Leader.

146. Congressional Record, Senate, October 4, 1979, p.S14139.

147. Ibid., p.S14139.

148. Letter from Secretary of State Edmund S. Muskie to Senate Majority Leader Robert C. Byrd, September 2, 1980.

149. U.S. Congress, House, United States-Turkey Defense and Economic Cooperation Agreement, 1980, Hearing before the Subcommittee on Europe and the Middle East, Committee on Foreign Affairs, 96th Cong., 2d sess., May 7, 1980, p.13.

150. Turkey's Problems and Prospects: Implications for U.S. Interests, Report prepared for the Committee on Foreign Affairs, U.S. House of Representation by the Congressional Research Service, Library of Congress, 96th Cong., 2nd sess., March 3, 1980, p.56.

151. Turkey, Greece, and NATO: The Strained Alliance, staff report to the Committee on Foreign Relations, United States Senate, 96th Cong., 2d sess., 1980, p.30.

152. Marvine Howe, "U.S. and the Turks Agree to Create Joint Defense Unit," The New York Times, December 6, 1981.

4
The Panama Canal Treaties: Legislative Strategy for Advice and Consent

John Opperman

Article 2, Section 2 of the U.S. Constitution states that the president has the power "by and with the Advice and Consent of the Senate, to make treaties, provided two-thirds of the Senators present concur."

The delegation of treaty responsibilities has always been the source of controversy, and subject to interpretation. Historically, the executive branch has negotiated treaties and then submitted them to the Senate for acceptance or rejection. Over the past 30 years, senators have occasionally been given the opportunity to participate in treaty negotiations, but the executive branch has always maintained ultimate responsibility for treaty-making.[1]

The congressional assertiveness since the Vietnam War that has changed the overall relationship between the executive and legislative branches has also effected treaty-making. The Panama Canal Treaties of 1977 are a case in point. These treaties were negotiated over a 13-year period by four different administrations. These negotiations included periodic consultations with Congress. Yet when the negotiations were completed in the summer of 1977, congressional and public questioning of and opposition to the treaties was so strong that several points in the treaties had to be "renegotiated," either by the Carter Administration, or, in some instances, by direct discussions between Panamanian leaders and members of the Senate.

Background

The original 1903 Panama Canal Treaty had long been considered inadequate in the context of United States-Panamanian relations. Certain aspects of that treaty were renegotiated in 1936 and 1955, but the central question of Panamanian sovereignty over the canal remained unresolved. The presence of the U.S. military

77

in the Canal Zone and U.S. control of Panama's major
economic resource were factors that kept the issue
alive over decades.

The Panamanian "flag riots" of 1964 resulted in a
temporary break in relations between the U.S. and Panama. Part of the agreement to normalize relations between the two countries thereafter was the reopening of
negotiations for a new canal treaty. Draft treaties
were completed as early as 1967, but domestic considerations in both countries prevented submission for ratification. After seven additional years of inconclusive
negotiations, a significant breakthrough was made in
February 1974 with the signing of a statement of agreed
principles by Secretary of State Henry Kissinger and
Panamanian Foreign Minister Juan Antonio Tack. This
statement reiterated the commitment of both nations to
negotiate a new agreement, but no significant progress
was to occur until 1977. Growing concern about the
vulnerability of the canal, considered vital to U.S.
economic and security interests, gave impetus to the
U.S. willingness to pursue the negotiations. There was
particular concern about the difficulty of protecting
and defending the canal if Panama was hostile and unfriendly to the U.S.

On January 12, 1977, President-elect Jimmy Carter
and Secretary of State-designate Cyrus Vance officially
committed the new administration to pursuing negotiations for a new Panama Canal Treaty. President Carter
indicated a desire to resolve the remaining issues
promptly, and noted his expectation that a new treaty
might be completed as early as June 1977.[2]

Negotiations by the Carter Administration proceeded
well, although the June deadline was not met--due at
least in part to congressional concerns. The New Panama Canal Treaties were finally completed in August, and
officially signed by President Carter and Panamanian
leader General Omar Torrijos on September 7, 1977.

Two treaties were actually negotiated. The first,
the Canal Treaty, provided for U.S. control and the
right to defend the canal until the year 2000. On the
effective date of the treaty, Panama would assume territorial jurisdiction over the Canal Zone, would use
parts of the areas not needed for operation or defense
of the canal, and would receive up to $70 million a
year from canal revenues.

Under a separate treaty (Treaty Concerning the Permanent Neutrality and Operation of the Panama Canal),
the U.S. would have the right to insure the neutrality
of the canal from any threat for an indefinite period.

Pre-Debate Period--The White House

The Carter Administration considered ratification

of the Panama Canal Treaties its first major foreign policy test in dealing with the Congress. Some Administration officials believed that too much political capital would be spent to secure ratification of the treaties. Nevertheless, President Carter considered the treaties a major foreign policy objective, and pressed forward. The Administration thought that approval of the treaties would have a major impact on gaining congressional support for other foreign policy initiatives on such issues as human rights, southern Africa, and SALT.[3] The President had already drawn strong criticism from Republicans for an "incompetent and incoherent" foreign policy, and failure to get Senate approval for the Panama Canal Treaties would definitely embolden opposition to Administration policies.

Encouraged by the progress of the negotiations, treaty negotiators Ellsworth Bunker and Sol Linowitz met with congressional leaders in late May 1977 to map out the legislative strategy. The Administration's plan was to submit the treaties by the August recess and have them acted upon before the fall adjournment. The White House hoped to avoid carrying the vote over into the spring since 1978 was an election year.

Pressures on General Torrijos by Panamanian leftists and nationalists and U.S. congressional concerns over some of the details of the treaties threatened to prolong negotiations. President Carter sent a confidential letter to Torrijos in August acknowledging that the terms agreed to so far "may be less than you expected or wished, but I hope you will understand that they represent the most we could undertake to do, based on our consultations with Congress."[4]

The following week, President Carter notified all members of Congress by telegram that negotiations would soon be completed, and asked that they reserve judgment until they had read the treaties. The White House strategy began to unfold soon thereafter. After solidifying support of members of the Cabinet and the Joint Chiefs of Staff, a campaign to inform the public was to commmence. It was vital for the treaties to be seen as a bipartisan issue. As a result, the White House pushed hard for support from Republican officials, in and out of office. These efforts received a big boost in mid-August when former President Gerald Ford and former Secretary of State Henry Kissinger publicly announced support for the treaties. Republican Senators Mark Hatfield of Oregon and Lowell Weicker of Connecticut chimed in with their support.

The White House campaign maintained a brisk pace through the final weeks of August. President Carter met with political and business leaders from various states at the White House to brief them on the importance of the treaties. General George Brown, Chairman of the Joint Chiefs of Staff, met with a group of retired generals and admirals to explain the Joint Chiefs' support. House Majority Leader Jim Wright (D-Texas) notified each member of the House that he supported the treaties, and asked that they keep an "open mind" on the issue.[5] In addition, President Carter announced the formation of a special task force to be headed by presidential advisor Hamilton Jordan that would be responsible for obtaining congressional and public approval for the treaties.

Although the Administration had hoped for Senate approval of the treaties before the fall adjournment, Senate Majority Leader Robert Byrd (D-West Virginia) warned that public opinion was not ready for it. Senator Byrd also cited the need to clear energy legislation through the Senate before the treaty debate could begin. After discussing the treaty problems with Byrd, President Carter decided to let the Majority Leader handle the timetable for the treaties.[6] The President showed great confidence in Byrd, considering that the senator was uncommitted on the treaties at the time.

The September 7 signing ceremony at the Organization of American States (OAS) headquarters in Washington, D.C., was also part of the strategy to generate support for the treaties. The guests included 26 Western Hemisphere leaders as well as scores of prominent Americans. Carter had breakfast with business leaders that morning to explain the pacts, then finished the day with a state dinner for Western Hemisphere leaders and 25 senators. The next day former President Ford lobbied Republican congressional leaders for support.

Following the hoopla of the signing ceremony, the White House involvement in the treaty campaign diminished considerably. Part of the strategy was to have State Department officials take the lead in briefing members of Congress, while the President continued to meet informally with political and business leaders from many states at the White House. However, through September and October the President became increasingly preoccupied with the problems of his Budget Director, Bert Lance. (Lance ultimately had to resign because of personal financial problems and the failure to fully inform the Senate about those problems.) As a result of the White House preoccupation with the Lance affair, much of the momentum that had been gained up through the signing ceremony was beginning to dwindle.[7]

On October 11, Carter, Vance, and National Security Advisor Zbigniew Brzezinski met with eight prominent senators, including Byrd and Senate Minority Leader Howard Baker (R-Tennesee), to clarify some of the points of the treaties. Many senators had expressed concern that the treaty was ambiguous with respect to U.S. rights to protect the neutrality of the canal, and the right of U.S. ships to "go to the head of the line"

during an emergency. The group of senators warned the
President that chances for approval of the treaties
seemed remote without some clarifications. As a result
of this session, President Carter arranged to meet with
General Torrijos a few days later to discuss the senators' concerns. Carter and Torrijos then agreed to a
Statement of Understanding which clarified the interpretations of the U.S. right of intervention and "head-
of-the-line" priority. The language in this statement
had been cleared with Majority Leader Byrd, but Byrd
remained uncommitted on the treaties even though he
favored the principles of the statement.[8] Although the
Statement of Understanding was made public, neither
leader signed it, presumably because of the political
repercussions that Torrijos might encounter for assuring such rights for the United States.

The Statement of Understanding helped the White
House regain some of the momentum that had been lost.
Senator Byrd then told the White House that the treaties would be the first major item of business when Congress reconvened in January 1978. Indeed, Byrd warned
White House officials that delaying the treaties beyond
that time could kill them because of the 1978 congressional elections.

The final stage of the Administration's pre-debate
strategy was an all-out effort to garner the greatest
momentum possible going into the Senate floor debate.
Public opinion polls were showing less opposition by
late December, and it was believed that the final push
for treaty support could make a big difference for
those senators who were uncommitted or leaning toward
approval. This final push became known as the "January
blitz." The key elements of the "blitz" were a speaking tour by Secretary of State Vance and a "fireside
chat" by President Carter. Vance made appearances in
West Virginia, Kentucky, and Louisiana, all states with
critical Senate votes. Carter appealed to the national
television audience to support the treaties, saying
that "...when the full terms of the agreement are
known, most people are convinced that the national
interests of our country will be best served by ratify-
ing the treaties."[9]

Senate Leadership

It is safe to say that passage of the Panama Canal
treaties would not have been possible had it not been
for the support and effective leadership of the Senate
Majority Leader Byrd and Minority Leader Baker. Although both Byrd and Baker remained uncommitted
throughout most of the pre-debate period, both made
significant contributions to securing passage of the
treaties. In previous years, both of the Senate

leaders had supported resolutions offered by Senator Strom Thurmond (R-South Carolina) that recommended that no treaty with Panama include "surrendering U.S. sovereignty" over the canal. But when confronted with an actual treaty in 1977, both Baker and Byrd discounted the Thurmond resolution as a "spring ritual" that really did not mean anything in the face of a new negotiated treaty.[10]

As far as the White House was concerned, the key actor in building support for the treaties in the Senate would ultimately have to be Senator Byrd. As a member of the President's party and the Senate leader, his support was essential. Although Byrd was uncommitted on the treaties at the outset, he still worked closely with Administration officials in mapping out the strategy for ratification. Byrd may have been leaning toward supporting the treaties from the beginning, but he did have serious questions about certain passages in the treaties. He discussed these issues with Administration officials on several occasions, and then publicly announced in late September that he expected that some reservations and understandings would have to be added to the pacts. Up to that point, the State Department had maintained the position that no alterations of the treaties should be made since that might require reopening the negotiations.[11] Nevertheless, President Carter admitted the following week that ratification was in doubt, and heeded advice given by Senate leaders on October 11 to secure the Statement of Understanding with General Torrijos.

On November 9 Senator Byrd and six other Democratic senators embarked on a four-day fact-finding tour of Panama. This trip played an important role in convincing Byrd that the treaties were indeed in the best interests of the United States. During the tour the senators engaged in frank discussions with General Torrijos regarding issues of particular concern. Most importantly, they wanted to be assured of the General's commitment to, and the Panamanian poeple's interpretation of, the principles of the Statement of Understanding. But much of the discussion also centered around the internal affairs of Panama. Among the issues discussed were the human rights situation, the right of due process, freedom of the press, and Panama's relations with Cuba and the Soviet Union.[12] Torrijos pledged to the senators that he would take action to improve human rights conditions and press freedom, and Byrd termed this "a positive step." On December 3, Torrijos wrote to Byrd informing him that action had been taken to restore constitutional guarantees on due process and strengthen press freedom. He concluded his message to Byrd by saying, "I am keeping my word. Please convey this to your colleagues..."[13]

Another important factor in influencing the

senators was a tour of the canal itself with Lt. General Dennis McAuliffe, Commander in Chief of the U.S. Southern Command (SOUTHCOM), headquartered in Panama. General McAuliffe pointed out the difficulties in defending the canal against terrorist acts and the extent of manpower needed to protect it. His point was that if the treaties were not ratified, defending the canal woule be more difficult than if they were.

Following the trip, three of the senators announced support for the treaties, and two others offered qualified support. Only Senator James Sasser (D-Tennessee) and Byrd remained uncommitted.

The week after the Panama trip, Senator Byrd noted that the chances for ratification had improved significantly. He believed the most influential factors for improved prospects were the White House public information campaign, increased editorial support, and General Torrijos' agreement to the Statement of Understanding.[14]

Byrd finally announced his own support for the treaties in the midst of the "January blitz." Byrd said that he would work hard for ratification, but only if the principles of the Statement of Understanding were somehow incorporated in the treaties.

During those final days prior to the Senate debate, Byrd was instrumental in two developments that played a major part in securing Senate approval. The first of these resulted from discussions between Byrd and members of the Senate Foreign Relations Committee. The committee had held hearings on the canal pacts since September, and was expected to report out the treaties in late January. Normally, the committee would have reported the treaty with what ever amendments or reservations its members thought appropriate. However, in this case Byrd intervened to ask the committee not to take any formal action on changes in the treaty. Byrd was convinced that there were only a few amendments that could be approved without endangering treaty ratification. These few beneficial amendments would draw widespread support from senators, and Byrd believed that more political mileage could be gained by giving all senators the opportunity to co-sponsor such amendments, rather than just having a vote to approve or disapprove actions already taken in committee. Thus, in an exceptional move, the Foreign Relations Committee agreed to Byrd's request and made only recommendations on amendments and reservations rather than taking formal action within the committee.

The second and related action engineered by Byrd was to incorporate the Statement of Understanding into the pacts. The two principles embodied in the statement (right of U.S. to guarantee the neutrality of the canal and "head-of-the-line" passage during crises) were among those few beneficial provisions that could be added to the treaties without threatening ratification.

This strategy was originally considered in discussions among staff members from the Foreign Relations Committee and Senate Democratic Policy Committee. Robert Dockery of the Foreign Relations staff suggested it as a means of helping to satisfy Senate concerns without jeopardizing the treaty. Staff members then refined the proposal and presented it to the Majority and Minority Leaders. Discussions between Byrd and Baker led to the recommendations that the principles of the Statement of Understanding be the basis for amending Articles IV and VI of the Neutrality Treaty. Upon agreement of Senators John Sparkman (D-Alabama) and Clifford Case (R-New Jersey), ranking members of the Foreign Relations Committee, all senators would be given the opportunity to co-sponsor these "leadership amendments." Thus senators were able to put their names on amendments that improved the treaties, and this would perhaps make it easier for uncommitted senators to vote for the treaties. Senators Byrd and Baker sent letters to all senators on February 2, 1978, explaining the proposed amendments and inviting co-sponsorship, and 76 senators agreed to co-sponsor the amendments.[15]

Although Minority Leader Baker was not as visible in the pre-debate strategy as Senator Byrd, Baker's role was nonetheless critical to the success of the treaties. As Republican leader in the Senate, Baker was in a particularly difficult political position. Several prominent Republican spokesmen and the Republican National Committee had come out strongly against the treaties. Since Senator Baker was considered a presidential hopeful in 1980, it was difficult for him to cross blades with treaty opponents. Baker remained uncommitted until just prior to the opening of the floor debate, and in the interim was under constant pressure from opponents of the treaties. He was a special target of conservative political action groups that saturated his home state of Tennessee with anti-treaty advertising. These groups pointed to the significance of Baker's role by telling his constiuents that he alone could decide the fate of the treaties.[16] Meanwhile, Senators Robert Dole (R-Kansas) and Paul Laxalt (R-Nevada) warned Baker that no Republican voting for the treaties could expect to win the 1980 presidential nomination.[17]

As in the case of Senator Byrd, Baker was heavily influenced by a trip to Panama. In early January 1978, Baker traveled to Panama with Senators Jake Garn (R-Utah), a treaty opponent, and John Chafee (R-Rhode Island), a treaty supporter. As in the Byrd expedition, it was frank discussions with General Torrijos that influenced Baker most. Prior to the trip, Baker and Byrd had discussed with President Carter the importance

of including the Statement of Understanding in the
treaty.[18] Rather than discuss this proposal with the
Panamanians through Administration channels, Carter
chose to allow Baker to carry this message to Torrijos
directly. In this way Torrijos would be confronted
head-on with the problems in the Senate; in addition,
Senator Baker, an influential leader in the Senate,
would be playing an active role in improving the treaties. President Carter's decision to handle the affair
in this manner proved beneficial in that Torrijos ac-
ceded to Baker's proposals, and Baker ultimately decided to vote for the treaties.

Another significant move on which Baker and Byrd
collaborated was the decision to have the Senate consider the Neutrality Treaty first, ahead of the Panama
Canal Treaty. This did not violate Senate treaty procedure but was unusual because, technically, the Panama
Canal Treaty was negotiated and submitted first. (In
fact, the two treaties were submitted to the Senate
simultaneously.) The general assumption had been that
the Panama Canal Treaty would be taken up first. But
Byrd believed reversing the order to be vital, given
the significance of the "leadership amendments," and
the fact that these amendments applied to the Neutrality Treaty. Such strategic moves in regard to timing
and order of consideration can be critical in congressional debate. The ability of a majority leader to
control such matters is a major source of his power
within the Senate.

By taking up the Neutrality Treaty first, the leadership amendments could be considered early, thus providing a strong start toward Senate approval. With
approval of the Neutrality Treaty, proponents could
argue that protection of the canal was assured.

Senate Committees

The primary responsibility for treaties among Senate committees belongs to the Foreign Relations Committee. In the case of the Panama Canal Treaties, several
jurisdictional disputes developed among committees.
Initially, the major dispute involved committees in the
House of Representatives which claimed the authority to
determine the transfer of U.S. property (as outlined in
Article IV, Section 3 of the U.S. Constitution). However, the Administration followed normal treaty procedure by submitting the treaties for advice and consent
of the Senate and leaving claims by the House to be
decided by the courts, which ultimately ruled in favor
of the Administration. (Once the treaties were approved by the Senate, both Houses of Congress had to
pass legislation to implement various aspects of the
treaties.)

With the treaties submitted to the Senate, Senator
Strom Thurmond pushed for joint jurisdiction by the
Foreign Relations and Armed Services Committees. Members of the Foreign Relations Committee and the Senate
leadership strongly opposed such an arrangement, and
committee responsibility for the treaties remained with
Foreign Relations.[19] However, while Foreign Relations
prepared for treaty hearings, the Armed Services and
Judiciary Committees took the opportunity to get in on
the action. The day after the Carter-Torrijos signing
ceremony at the OAS, treaty opponent Ronald Reagan appeared before the Judiciary Subcommittee on Separation
of Powers. Senator James Allen (D-Alabama), a treaty
opponent, chaired this subcommittee. Allen had called
hearings to consider the legality of transferring U.S.
property by treaty, but the lineup of witnesses suggested that it was more a partisan effort to have the
voices of treaty opponents heard. The Armed Services
Committee also began a series of hearings, focusing on
the military-defense and economic aspects of the
treaties.

Foreign Relations held the most comprehensive hearings on the pacts. The first series of witnesses were
Administration representatives who explained the content of the treaties and the importance of ratification. These witnesses included officials from the
Departments of State, Defense, Justice, and Transport-
ation. The second series of witnesses included nongov-
ernment officials with political, religious, and
academic backgrounds. The final series of hearings
included historians, legal scholars, and business
leaders. Although a number of treaty opponents appeared, the preponderance of witnesses were treaty
supporters. This was in line with the strategy of
Administration and Senate leaders, who saw the hearings
as an important part of the public education process.

An appearance by Majority Leader Byrd in support of
the treaties--with the principles of the Statement of
Understanding incorporated--completed the Foreign Relations hearings, and the markup process began. The original plan was that the principles of the Statement of
Understanding would be included as a separate article
at the end of the Neutrality Treaty. The committee approved this proposal by a 13-1 vote. Although General
Torrijos had agreed to include these principles in the
treaty, there had been no determination made as to how
this should be done. The Panamanian leaders exhibited
great concern over the committee's plan. General Torrijos expressed this concern to a group of senators who
were visiting Panama at the time. Torrijos warned that
such an addition to the treaty would require a second
Panamanian plebiscite. Senator Alan Cranston (D-Cali-
fornia), one of the senators visiting Panama, forwarded
that message to Senate colleagues. The result was a

reversal of the original committee decision: a new proposal was made to amend the existing language in Articles IV and VI of the Neutrality Treaty to include the principles of the Statement of Understanding.[20] Then, according to the procedure recommended by Byrd, the Foreign Relations Committee referred the amendments to the entire Senate so that a large number of senators would have the opportunity for co-sponsorship.

Opposition

Opponents of any new Panama Canal treaty had found ways to make their presence felt since the early 1960s. In the Senate, Senator Strom Thurmond's "ritual" of proposing that the government be prohibited from "surrendering" the canal to Panama was typical of efforts to mobilize opposition. However, these proposals received little public attention, and were not taken too seriously by most senators.

The first significant step to generate public opposition to a new treaty occurred in the 1976 presidential primaries. Ronald Reagan, then a candidate for the Republican nomination, brought up the issue and found strong public opposition to the suggestion that the U.S. might sign a new treaty turning over the canal to Panama. Reagan admitted later that even he was surprised by the reaction, as his campaign advisors had not considered the Panama Canal to be an issue.[21] Nevertheless, Reagan was able to gain significant political mileage from it.

After President Carter announced that a new canal treaty would be forthcoming, the initial opposition was led by Senators Strom Thurmond and Jesse Helms. Public reaction to these two Southern conservatives was not appreciable. As a result, the two senators looked to alternative means of stopping the treaties. It was believed that treaty opposition was much stronger in the House than in the Senate and some House members resented not having a voice in the treaty debate. Thurmond and Helms, working with a group of House members, sought to have any transfer of the canal be made subject to approval by both the House and the Senate. Part of this effort was a lawsuit brought by Thurmond and Helms to stop the transfer of the canal by treaty. The two senators also sent a letter to President Carter in June 1977 that was signed by four former Chiefs of Naval Operations encouraging the President to insure that any new treaty "retain full sovereign control for the U.S. over the Panama Canal and...the U.S. Canal Zone."[22]

A month-and-a-half later, after Carter had announced that a new treaty had been negotiated, Thurmond and Helms traveled to Panama on a fact-finding mission. Upon their return, the two appeared on NBC's "Meet the Press" declaring their opposition to the treaties. They predicted that the treaties would be defeated in the Senate, by filibuster in necessary.

After treaty negotiations were completed in August 1977, Reagan began his own crusade in opposition to the treaties, and treaty opponents quickly rallied behind him. As the opposition began to organize, a consensus began to develop for a strategy to defeat the treaties. The lawsuit brought by Thurmond and Helms would be discounted, since most believed it would inevitably fail. Instead, the focus of the opponents' campaign was to be a media blitz aimed at arousing public opposition in key states. Since only 34 votes would be needed to defeat the treaties, and many senators were already committed to the opposition, only 10 to 12 additional votes would be needed. As a result, the media blitz was to be concentrated in the South in an effort to swing the votes of 12 to 15 southern Democrats. This "southern strategy" was to be coupled with efforts to try to influence two other key senators, Clifford Case and Edward Zorinsky (D-Nebraska).[23] Case supported the treaties, but Zorinsky did join the opposition.

Anti-Treaty Campaign

Another aspect of the strategy was to initate a nationwide write-in campaign. The intention was to flood the Senate and White House with anti-treaty mail. This campaign was so successful in the early stages that Senator Baker estimated his mail to be "about 10,000 to 6" against the treaty.

In September 1977 the Emergency Coalition to Save the Panama Canal was formed. This coalition was made up predominantly of a dozen conservative groups. Joining these groups were the Veterans of Foreign Wars and the American Legion. The 2.7 million member American Legion pledged to write letters to senators who intended to vote for the treaties or who were uncommitted. John Wasylik, national commander of the VFW, promised to "go to the wall on this senseless act of self-mutilation."[24]

As the anti-treaty rhetoric became more inflamed, some of the treaty opponents feared that the lack of substantive alternatives would prove counter-productive in the long run. Therefore, suggestions were made that any new treaty should also include provisions to satisfy the Panamanians. Among the suggested alternatives were: raising canal tolls and giving the money to Panama, opening the Canal Zone to agricultural development and shipyards, and placing more Panamanians into management of the canal.[25]

Still, emotional rhetoric dominated the campaign.

Most of the rhetoric centered around the concept of the U.S. "giving away" the canal, and was highlighted by Senator S. I. Hayakawa's (R-California) statement, "we stole it fair and square." This rhetoric seemed to be effective in the early stages in generating public op-posiiton to the treaties. The opposition was able to raise 10 times as much money as the proponents: the average donatation was $14. As the treaties neared Senate debate, these contributions diminished. This was partly a reflection of a shift in public opinion (from 70 percent opposed in August 1977 to 42 percent in February 1978 according to Gallup Poll figures).[26] However, the anti-treaty fund-raising was also dealt a blow by a rift between Ronald Reagan and the Republican National Committee. The Committee had come out with a solid refutation of the treaties in October 1977, and Reagan agreed to lend his name to fund-raising efforts conducted by the Committee for treaty opposition. But Reagan later discovered that the money was being used to fund Republican campaigns for the 1978 elections, and had his name withdrawn.[27]

The final stage of the opponents' strategy to acti-vate public opposition involved the formation of so-called "truth squads." The purpose of these squads was to counter the public information efforts of the Admin-istration. The "truth squads" conducted their own blitz in an effort to head off any momentum that pro-treaty forces might be gaining so soon before the floor debate. Led by Senator Paul Laxalt, the squads toured states of senators who held key votes, speaking before enthusiastic crowds of anti-treaty groups. Despite these efforts, however, the polls indicated a continued decline in public opposition to the treaties.

With the anti-treaty media campaign in full swing, the strategy for opposing the treaties on the Senate floor was not yet developed. Two senators were soon to emerge as key actors in handling this aspect of the op-position. Senator James Allen was one of these. Allen had initially used his chairmanship of the Judiciary Subcommittee on Separation of Powers to promote treaty opposition. Prior to the floor debate, Allen and other opponents of the treaties decided to forego the option of a filibuster. This was partly because treaty proce-dures made such a maneuver questionable, and also be-cause opponents believed they could block the treaties in an "up-or-down" vote.[28] A filibuster could have led to charges that the opponents were afraid to let the treaties come to a vote.

Allen and the opponents planned to defeat the treaties through the introduction and acceptance of "killer amendments." The intention was to add amend-ments that would substantively change the treaties, thereby resulting in rejection by the Administration and/or Panama. This was similar to the strategy that

some senators used during the prolonged consideration
of the Treaty of Versailles following World War I. In
that case the Senate and President Woodrow Wilson became bogged down in controversy over Senate-approved
reservations and the treaty never received the necessary two-thirds approval.

Another treaty opponent who played a key role was
Robert Dole. Ironically, Dole was originally considered
a possible treaty supporter by the Administration. The
reasoning was that Dole had been President Ford's Vice-
Presidential running mate in the 1976 election, and had
supported Ford's policies. However, Dole soon let the
Administration know in not uncertain terms that he opposed the treaties, and he let it be known that presidential ambitions for 1980 played a part in his decision.[29] Senator Dole riled Administration officials in
October 1977 by releasing a classified State Department
cable which indicated sharp differences between the U.S.
and Panama over the interpretation of intervention
rights. President Carter sought to head off the repercussions from this incident by meeting with Senate leaders the following week and that led to the October 14
Statement of Understanding. Dole followed this with accusations that General Torrijos' brother was involved in
drug trafficking. Attorney General Griffin Bell answered
those charges, asserting that General Torrijos had no
involvement in the drug business, and that his brother
had only been remotely involved in a single minor
incident.

Dole also offered a packet of treaty amendments to
the Foreign Relations Committee in an attempt to alter
some provisions that he considered too favorable to the
Panamanians. Although all of these amendments were rejected, this served as a clear indication of Dole's intentions once the Senate debate began.

White House Efforts

As the Senate floor debate commenced on February 8,
the White House expressed guarded optimism for approval
of the treaties. During the "January blitz" several
previously uncommitted senators came out in support of
the treaties. The White House decided to let Majority
Leader Byrd handle the debate strategy and provide him
with whatever support was needed. As part of that support, Byrd and the White House officials agreed to establish an "operations center" in the Capitol to coordinate the floor debate. The center provided senators
and staff with information on issues pertaining to the
treaties and served as a focal point for developing and
coordinating pro-treaty strategy.

The operations center was manned by officials from
the White House, and the Departments of State and

Defense, working most closely with the staffs of Majority Leader Byrd and the Foreign Relations Committee.
Among the Administration officials, Ambler Moss and
Douglas Bennet of the State Department coordinated in-
formation-gathering so that questions raised during the
debate could be quickly answered. More importantly,
Moss, Bennet, Robert Beckel, and other members of the
liaison team were available to senators throughout much
of the debate period and were able to help keep supporters in line while encouraging uncommitted senators
to back the treaties.

Overall, the information provided by the Administration was important in countering the arguments of
the opposition in the debate. However, some tactical
errors were made in the information process that set
back pro-treaty efforts. The most prominent of these
errors occurred in the first weeks of the floor debate. The Administration had argued that the payments
to Panama for the canal up to the year 2000 would be
paid for by canal tolls, and, therefore, U.S. taxpayers
would pay nothing. During the first week of floor debate, Senator John Stennis (D-Mississippi), Chairman of
the Armed Services Committee, argued that his committee
estimated that the taxpayers' costs could run as high
as $1.02 billion.[30] Technically, the argument the Ad-
ministration was making might have been correct. However, the costs of the implementing legislation and
transfer of the canal were not accounted for. This was
seen by many as an effort to delude the Senate and the
public on the real costs of the treaties. Byrd had
warned the Administration that this would be a troublesome issue, and the situation was defused only after a
thorough explanation of the costs of the treaties by
Byrd and Edmund Muskie, Chairman of the Senate Budget
Committee, on the Senate floor.

As the final vote on the Neutrality Treaty neared,
the White House stepped up efforts to persuade the few
remaining uncommitted senators to support the treaties.
President Carter and Deputy Secretary of State Warren
Christopher were particulary active on this front.
Treaty opponents claimed throughout the final week before the vote that the Administration was placing undue
pressure on some senators. And one treaty supporter
stated after the vote that President Carter had been
"heavy-handed" in his dealings with senators.[31] However, other senators claimed that the President was
simply not that effective in his efforts at persuading
senators.

Two key votes were those of Senators Sam Nunn and
Herman Talmadge, both Georgia Democrats. Nunn was particularly important because of his influence in the Senate on defense issues. Administration officials met
with the two senators throughout the week of March 6-10
in an effort to secure their votes.[32] Nunn and Talmadge

asserted at that time that they could not vote for the treaties without some alterations. These meetings laid the groundwork for later discussions by Senator Byrd with Nunn and Talmadge that subsequently secured their support.

A Critical Obstacle

The Administration pursued a similar course for winning the vote of Senator Dennis DeConcini (D-Arizona). DeConcini also believed that some alteration or improvement would be necessary for his support. He met with Christopher on several occasions to discuss a proposed reservation to the Neutrality Treaty. DeConcini was concerned about U.S. rights to keep the canal open in the event of an internal crisis in Panama, e.g., a strike. The Administration considered the proposal unacceptable, but felt compromise language could be developed so as not to lose the DeConcini vote. However, no suitable language was forthcoming. The White House decided to put off DeConcini, a first-term senator, thinking that he would abandon his position once the treaty was on the line.[33]

On March 15, the day before the vote on the Neutrality Treaty, DeConcini was still hinging his vote on the acceptance of his proposed reservation. With the outcome of the vote too close to call, President Carter finally relented and approved the DeConcini reservation.[34] The language of the reservation provided that either the U.S. or Panama could independently "take such steps as it deems necessary...including the use of military force in Panama, to reopen the Canal or restore the operation of the Canal, as the case may be."[35]

When DeConcini submitted his reservation to the Senate on March 16, many senators were hesitant to support the reservation and turned to Senator Byrd for counsel. Byrd was preoccupied with vote counting and the floor debate, however, and looked to the Administration for a cue in responding to the proposal.[36] As word circulated that the White House had approved the reservation, concern largely subsided. The reservation was then approved by a vote of 75-23. Later that evening the Senate voted 68-32 for advice and consent to ratification of the Neutrality Treaty.

Approval of the Neutrality Treaty cleared what Administration officials considered to be their most difficult obstacle. As long as no crisis developed or blunders were made, approval of the Panama Canal Treaty was well within reach. Unfortunately, a crisis did develop, and the fate of the treaties once more hung in the balance. On April 5, Panamanian Ambassador Gabriel Lewis warned Frank Moore, Chief of Congressional Liaison for the White House, that the White House and Senate were not sufficiently aware of Panamanian dissatisfaction with the DeConcini reservation. Lewis urged that the Senate take measures to mitigate the implications of the reservation. The following day General Torrijos sent letters to Latin American heads of state and certain United Nations' officials regarding the concerns of Panama over the DeCocini reservation.[37]

The White House seemed surprised by the extent of the Panamanian dissatisfaction. Presidential aide Hamilton Jordan called General Torrijos and chided him for distributing the letters. Jordan warned the General that Senate approval could be in danger unless an official statement was made reiterating Panama's policy of making no comments on the treaties until the Senate was finished debating.[38] Torrijos, who had developed a warm friendship with Jordan, issued such a statement later that day.

On April 8 Administration officials met with DeConcini to discuss the need to alter the reservation. DeConcini refused to budge, suggesting that the Panamanians were bluffing, and later told newsmen that Panamanian dissatisfaction was a problem for President Carter and the State Department.[39]

As Panamanian reaction to the reservation grew more antagonistic, there was concern that the stability of the Torrijos government was threatened. The White House considered it imperative to find a way to reassure Panama that the U.S. did not intend to intervene in its internal affairs, but at the same time maintain the essence of the reservation. When efforts to negotiate a compromise with DeConcini failed, the White House turned to the Senate leadership to help resolve the problem.

While the leadership worked with DeConcini, the Administration turned its attention to Panama. Acceptance of the DeConcini reservation had damaged the trust established between Carter and Torrijos. As a result, Warren Christopher suggested that an intermediary might help restore relations between U.S. and Panamanian officials to a sound footing. The man Christopher had in mind was William D. Rogers, a Washington lawyer and former Assistant Secretary of State for Inter-American Affairs. Rogers knew Torrijos personally, and, in fact, had already been contacted by the Panamanians for advice on the implications of the DeConcini reservation. In addition, Rogers had Republican connections, which could make Senate approval of the arrangement easier.

The strategy to get a DeConcini compromise was to have Christopher work with Senate leaders in discussions with DeConcini, while Rogers worked with Ambassador Lewis to determine language that would be acceptable to the Panamanians. This arrangement finally succeeded with the formulation of Reservation No. 1 to the Panama Canal Treaty. This reservation was jointly submitted for Senate approval by nine senators, including

DeConcini, and was approved by a 73-27 vote. The new language provided that any action taken by the United States in the exercise of its treaty rights "shall be only for the purpose of assuring that the Canal shall remain open, neutral, secure, and accessible, and shall not have as its purpose nor be interpreted as a right of intervention in the internal affairs of the Republic of Panama or interference with its political independence or sovereign integrity."[40]

Last-Minute Threats

Once the DeConcini problem was taken care of, the White House had only to wait for the debate to wind down, or so it thought. However, going into the final day of debate, three senators who had voted for the Neutrality Treaty threatened to vote against the Panama Canal Treaty. One of these, Howard Cannon (D-Nevada), was holding out for acceptance of a proposed reservation dealing with interest payments by the Panama Canal Commission. The reservation was a minor matter and was subsequently approved by the Senate.

For Senators S. I. Hayakawa and James Abourezk (D-South Dakota), the stakes were much higher. Hayakawa complained that President Carter's foreign policy decisions were making the U.S. "look like a weak nation," and demanded some reassurances from the White House that that trend would not continue. The Senator claimed later that in exchange for his vote for the treaty, the White House agreed to consult with him on foreign policy matters on a regular basis. This report was denied by the White House.

Abourezk was upset not about the treaties, but about natural gas deregulation legislation that was under consideration by a House-Senate conference committee. It was a vivid example of how foreign policy and domestic legislative interests can become entangled. Abourezk, a strong foe of deregulation, was incensed because the conferees were meeting behind closed doors and he said that the conferees and the Administration were "selling out" to the gas industry. He threatened to vote 'no' to protest the secret meetings. Finally, however, as one of the last speakers in the lengthy treaty debate, Abourezk announced that he would vote for the treaty since he had received assurances that the White House would encourage "an open, democratic process" to resolve the natural gas issue.[41]

Even with Cannon, Hayakawa, and Abourezk in line, the outcome of the Panama Canal Treaty was in suspense until the final vote when it was approved 68-32.

Senate Proponents

During the week before the Senate floor debate began, Administration officials had worked out an arrangement with Majority Leader Byrd for debate strategy. It was agreed that any amendments to the treaties beyond the leadership amendments could jeopardize ratification. Therefore, the position maintained by Senator Byrd thoughout the floor debate was that no additional amendments were acceptable. Reservations and understandings might be approved, but only after careful scrutiny by Senate leaders, Administration officials, and Panamanian representatives. All parties agreed that Byrd would orchestrate the pro-treaty strategy.

The brunt of pro-treaty organization fell on the staffs of Senator Byrd (Democratic Policy Committee) and the Foreign Relations Committee. Throughout January 1978 these staff members pulled together the staffs of other Senate Democrats and pro-treaty Republicans in an effort to develop a "team approach" to the floor debate. The result was a five-point plan of pro-treaty strategy:

1) To assure the presence of pro-treaty senators on the floor during debate
2) To control or influence the course of the debate forcing the opposition to react rather than carry the fight.
3) Because of the radio audience, pro-treaty arguments and rebuttals to anti-treay arguments must be readily available.
4) Public and media perception would not only be influenced by substantive points, but also by the number and effectiveness of individual senators.
5) To track the opponents' statements to determine who was identifiable with certain issues.[42]

Pro-treaty forces decided that Senators Frank Church (D-Idaho) and Paul Sarbanes (D-Maryland) of the Foreign Relations Committee would be floor managers during the debate. Along with Byrd, these two played prominent roles in securing Senate approval of the treaties. They agreed that it would be most effective to have various senators argue particular aspects of the treaties. For example, defense and security aspects of the treaties would be debated by Senators Clifford Case (ranking Republican on the Foreign Relations Committee) and John Glenn (a respected Democrat on defense issues).[43] Coordinated with the staffs of pro-treaty senators, this floor debate strategy proved to be a success.

Part of the strategy to win support from uncommitted senators was to allow certain reservations or understandings to be approved that would not adversely affect ratification. In this way senators would be able to say that they had improved the language or substance of the treaty. Throughout the debate Senator Byrd worked with several senators to formulate the necessary language for acceptable reservations. Senators Jennings Randolph (D-West Virginia), Russell Long (D-Louisiana), Nunn, and Talmadge were among those who submitted reservations in this manner and won Senate approval.

When the debate began on February 8, the Senate leadership counted 62 senators probably for the treaties, and 28 against. Picking up the needed final five votes proved to be difficult. On March 10, with the vote on the Neutrality Treaty only a week a way, Senator Byrd was still short by at least 3-4 votes. In the final days before the vote, Byrd and Warren Christopher met several times with six uncommitted senators. This group included Senators Nunn, Talmadge, Long, DeConcini, Randolph, and Wendell Ford (D-Kentucky). Reservations were subsequently worked out for Nunn and Talmadge, Long, and Randolph to win their support. But Randolph was facing re-election in 1978 and was not considered a "safe" vote. Senator Ford seemed the least impressed by the arguments of Byrd and Christopher, so DeConcini's vote became critical.

While Byrd was ironing out the Nunn/Talmadge reservation, Senator DeConcini was trying to get White House approval for his own reservation. Although the White House had agreed to clear any additions to the treaty through Byrd, approval of the DeConcini reservation appeared to circumvent him. This seemed to be more a result of the pressure that the Administration and Senate leaders were under at the time, rather than a purposeful oversight.

After the Neutrality Treaty was approved, the goal of the proponents was to hold senators in line for the vote on the Panama Canal Treaty, and avoid conflict as much as possible. Trouble erupted, however, when news broke of Torrijos letters to the United Nations. It was evident that the impact of the DeConcini reservation in Panama had been misjudged. Initially, Senator Byrd warned against over-reacting to the Panamanian outcry, and suggested that it might blow over. But he soon realized that this was not the case. Byrd worked with Church and Sarbanes on a plan to defuse the issue as quickly as possible. The plan was to have DeConcini make a public statement disclaiming any U.S. intent to interfere with Panama's internal affairs, and follow this with a similar statement by Senators Byrd and

Baker on the day of the vote.[44] However, discussions with Ambassador Gabriel Lewis made it clear that this would not be sufficient to satisfy Panama.

Because of the interventionist implications of the DeConcini reservation, several Senate liberals threatened to vote against the treaty. Senator Byrd quickly formed a bipartisan team to keep the liberals in line while a means of softening the DeConcini language was found. Byrd's intent was "to develop language that would not be directed at the DeConcini reservation but at the same time enunciate nonintervention principles."[45]

The Senate leadership had suggested to DeConcini that a new reservation to the second treaty might be submitted that would clarify the intent of his original reservation. On April 15, DeConcini presented to Byrd a draft of a new reservation that he considered acceptable. Using this draft, Byrd entered discussions with Senators Church and Sarbanes, Deputy Secretary Christopher, and Ambassador Lewis. On Sunday, April 16, just two days before the final vote, the language for the new reservation was approved. It clarified U.S. adherence to the policy of nonintervention. Ambassasor Lewis proclaimed the measure "a dignified solution to a difficult problem."[46]

Although the DeConcini problem had been resolved, treaty proponents were unsure of its potential impact on the final vote. With the threatened defections of Senators Cannon, Hayakawa, and Abourezk, the outcome of the vote could not be predicted. Even Senator Byrd, who had kept close tabs on all Senate votes, was not certain how it would turn out. Fittingly, it was Senator Robert Byrd who cast the decisive 67th vote.

Senate Opponents

After public opinion became more favorable to the treaties during January 1978, treaty opponents sought to regain the initiative in their efforts to defeat the treaties. Conservative political action groups continued to take the lead in persuading the public, and mass mail-ins remained the primary technique for exerting outside pressure on senators.

Within the Senate itself, treaty opponents began to organize their strategy. The key opposition leader was James Allen. He had already made his presence known by using his Subcommittee of the Separation of Powers as a forum for treaty opponents. His relentless role in leading Senate opposition in the floor debate was to make a lasting impression, a performance that fell just short of legendary. He died within weeks after the Senate had completed the treaty debate.

Allen worked most closely with Senators Helms,

Thurmond, and Robert Griffin (R-Michigan). Their
efforts centered on the attempt to get approval of
"killer amendments." Since Majority Leader Byrd and
the Administration had made it clear that the only
amendments that would be accepted were the leadership
amendments, treaty opponents had to find a way to circumvent the leadership. The result was an effort to
amend ambiguous or controversial passages in the treaties with language that senators would find difficult to
turn down.

During the first 10 days of the debate, opponents
submitted amendment after amendment. Senator Allen led
this barrage with 11 proposed amendments. But the Senate leadership succeeded in having these amendments
"tabled," rather than forcing senators to cast an "up-
or-down" vote, on the amendments themselves. This procedure was important because it made it easier for uncommitted senators to turn down such amendments and
kept treaty proponents from having to vote against what
appeared on the surface to be very desirable amendments. This practice continued throughout the floor
debate, and at one point spurred criticism from Senator
Edward Brooke (R-Massachusetts), who was considered to
be a treaty supporter. Brooke argued that some of the
proposed amendments were "substantive" and should not
be subjected to tabling. Senator Byrd replied that he
would be willing to consider all remaining amendments
for an up-or-down vote if treaty opponents agreed to a
showdown vote on the treaties in just three days. That
offer was quickly rejected.[47]

One of the first efforts by the opponents was to
have the treaties submitted for debate in the order in
which they were negotiated, i.e., the Panama Canal
Treaty first, then the Neutrality Treaty. Senator
Allen was aware of Byrd's purpose in having switched
the order, and assumed defeat of the treaties would be
easier if it were reversed. But Allen's proposal was
rejected by a vote of 67-30. This was considered the
first "test vote" on the treaties' chances of Senate
approval.

After the Neutrality Treaty was approved, the opponents' hopes for defeating the treaties were severly
undercut. Two developments during the Panama Canal
Treaty debate, however, revived the possibility of
rejection.

The first of these was a proposed amendment by Senator Orrin Hatch (R-Utah). The Hatch amendment proposed that the treaty would not enter into force until
the Congress had disposed of, or had authorized disposition of, all U.S. property in the Canal Zone. This
would have had the effect of including the House of Representatives in the transfer of the canal to Panama.
The Senate debated the amendment for three full days,
and treaty opponents claimed they would garner at least

45 votes in favor of the amendment. However, the amendment was finally tabled by a 58-37 vote. This was a setback for treaty opponents, although Hatch noted that the 37 "no" votes were three more than would be needed to defeat the treaty.[53]

The second development that encouraged treaty opposition was the DeConcini controversy. Treaty opponents considered the Torrijos letter to U.N. officials an attempt to pressure the Senate to strike the DeConcini reservation and ratify the treaties as they were. They also used the controversy to point to the problems of interpretation that the treaties would create if ratified. Senator Laxalt claimed that the DeConcini affair would have enough impact to cause at least five senators to switch their voting position. He predicted that the Panama Canal Treaty would be defeated with as many as 38-39 opposition votes.[49] But it turned out to be just another storm weathered by treaty proponents. On the day of the final vote, 10 amendments were proposed in a last-ditch effort to kill the treaties; all were tabled.

Executive-Legislative Interaction

Advice and consent to ratification of the Panama Canal Treaties was formally approved on April 18, 1978, with Senate passage of the second of the two treaties. Securing Senate approval for the treaties was a result of extensive executive-legislative interaction cooperation. Despite that success, however, the process had serious defects. By identifying those defects along with the areas of success, the lessons for future executive-legislative interaction on foreign policy issues may be better understood.

The Carter Administration was particularly successful on two fronts. In its efforts to influence public opinion, the Administration concentrated on persuading "opinion-makers." This group was made up of local officials, editorialist, educators, labor leaders, and political activists. Although the success in influencing public opinion was uneven at times, it proved to be vitally important, given the emotional nature of the Panama Canal issue.

The second area that was handled well by the Administration was the network of cooperation established among the White House, the State Department, and Senate leadership. This was especially evident during the floor debate. In particular, State Department and Senate staff played key roles in maintaining communication and implementing the pre-planned strategy. But it was the ability to resolve unexpected crises (e.g., cost of treaties, DeConcini reservation) that made this effort extraordinary.

The decision by President Carter to let Senator Byrd handle the Senate debate may well have been his most important decision on the Canal Treaties. The Carter White House was often seen as insensitive to the pressure on members of the Senate, and allowing Byrd to conduct the pro-treaty efforts helped to get around this problem. The reliance on Byrd became more acute as the vote on the treaties neared. It was Byrd who played the lead role in winning support from Senators Nunn, Talmadge, and DeConcini after the White House had failed to do do. Senator Byrd recognized the concern of many senators over the interpretation of some of the ambiguous passages of the treaty. He accepted the fact that adoption of some reservations and understandings might be necessary. As a result, Byrd took the role of prodding the Administration to consider the problems in the Senate and show a willingness to compromise. Like-wise, he worked at persuading senators to recognize the problems faced by the Administration and Panama.

The trips to Panama by Senators Byrd and Baker were dramatic examples of the Senate's active role in the treaty process. The direct discussions and "negotia-tions" with the Panamanians were a significant factor in winning Senate approval. The discussions by Byrd and Baker with Torrijos helped to impress upon him the difficulty of securing Senate approval. At the same time, the senators became more familiar with the issues, which contributed to their support of the treaties.

The opposition forces lacked the power of the White House and the Senate leadership, but gained substantial mileage from the emotional nature of the issue. Their lobbying effort was concentrated at "grass-roots" lev-els, and was dominated by well-organized conservative groups. However, these groups tended to operate on their own, and, as a result, the opposition movement lacked the unity of overall organization. Neverthe-less, treaty opponents in the Senate almost succeeded in defeating the treaties.

Among the more serious defects of the Canal Treaty process was the extensive political capital that the Carter Administration was required to expend to win Senate approval. President Carter could not afford to lose the ratification fight because of the encumbering effect it would have on his ability to execute the du-ties of his office. But the case of the Panama Canal Treaties proved that the cost of winning can also be high. The highly emotional Panama Canal issue rallied political conservatives in opposition to the Carter Presidency, and was a significant factor in advancing the candidacy of Ronald Reagan for the 1980 election. Even many of the treaty supporters could not be counted on once the treaty debate was over. They had gone out on a limb for the President, and were reluctant to do so again.

A major issue during the Senate debate was whether senators should vote in support of what they perceived to be the national interest, even if they knew it was contrary to the sentiments of the majority of their constiuents. Senator Byrd praised the courage of his colleagues who, in his view, put the national interest above political popularity.

Support for the Canal Treaties became an issue in many subsequent senatorial campaigns and was a contributing factor in defeating some senators, particulary Thomas McIntyre of New Hampshire in 1978, and was used against several Democratic treaty supporters who lost in 1980. By the 1982 elections, the issue seemed to have diminished. Efforts to use the issue against such treaty supporters as Byrd and Lloyd Bentsen (D-Texas) were unsuccessful in 1982.

The controversy over the DeConcini reservation points to an even more serious problem in the treaty process. In this case, a junior senator with little political clout was able to surmount the authoity of the White House mainly because of the closeness of the treaty vote. Mishandling by the Carter Administration may also be partly to blame, but the point remains a potential problem for future treaty consideration. (See Chapter 7.)

Another aspect of the DeConcini reservation that caused problems was the failure of the White House, the State Department, and the Senate to anticipate the extent of Panamanian reaction to the reservation. If the Senate is going to alter a treaty, whether by amendment, reservation, or understanding, treaty advocates must be sure that the treaty will not be rejected in the process. The DeConcini reservation was aggravated by what General Torrijos described as the "steady flow of criticism" from treaty opponents.[50] This criticism, coupled with the interventionist nature of the reservation, antagonized the Panamanians and helped to detract from the original purpose of the treaties, i.e., better United States-Panamanian relations.

Conclusion

The treaty process is one of the few areas of foreign policy in which the Constitution specifically authorized the executive and legislative branches to share responsibilities. Since the legislative branch has played an increasingly assertive role in that process in recent years, the executive branch must find ways to better accommodate this more active congressional role.

In the case of the Panama Canal Treaties, it is evident from the Senate's actions that the Senate was intent on playing a major role. The Carter Administration had negotiated what it believed to be the best possible treaty for the United States that would still have been acceptable to Panama. Nevertheless, the Senate was in a position to demand what amounted to renegotiation of certain aspects of the treaties. These Senate changes required additional concessions by Panama. Under the circumstances, the Panamanians were faced with accepting the Senate revisions up to a point, or having the treaties rejected altogether. As the experience with the DeConcini reservation clearly indicates, there was a fine line between what was considered desirable by the U.S. domestic interests--and what was considered acceptable to Panamanian domestic interests.

The consultation process is one area where the executive branch could promote cooperation with the Congress in treaty-making. For example, the Panama Canal Treaties were negotiated over a 13-year period during which consultation with the Congress amounted to little more than "briefings" on the progress of the negotiations. President Carter made the decision to pursue the treaties with Panama before he was even inaugurated, and his consultations with Congress during those early months of negotiations were not extensive. Had the President consulted Congress more carefully, he might have better understood the opposition the treaties were facing, and some of the Senate's objections to certain aspects of the treaties.

In fairness to the successive administrations that negotiated the treaties, a consistent, in-depth consultation would have been difficult under any circumstances because of the very length of the negotiations, and the significant anti-treaty sentiment in the Congress throughout that period. As far as the Carter Administration is concerned, even if President Carter had been more aware of public and congressional opposition earlier, he might have chosen to go through with the treaties anyway, because of foreign policy considerations. In any case, consultation during negotiations might not help avoid Senate objections to aspects of a treaty. The fact remains that there will be cases when the Senate will want to formally put its mark on a treaty, and a clear way of doing this is by making alterations. In such instances, the executive branch will not be able to foresee all the contingencies, and can only try to minimize any changes.

It is worth noting that developing cooperation between the executive and legislative branches in treaty-making is not a new problem. Indeed, even President George Washington was frustrated by the process. In one instance, President Washington personally carried a negotiated treaty to the Senate, and remained through-out the debate to answer questions and make

clarifications. But by the time the Senate was through
debating and making alterations, the President was so
perturbed, according to Vice-President John Adams, that
he left the Senate chamber saying, "he would be damned
if he ever went there again."[51]
   The Panama Canal Treaties were yet another step in
developing the treaty-making process, and an experience
that could lead to a more effective, consistent, and
workable treaty-making relationship between the executive and legislative branches. The lessons of the
Panama Canal Treaties suggest that the executive branch
must expect an active Senate role on major treaties,
and that the consultation process must be used to the
fullest extent possible. Even with that consultation,
the Senate may insist on putting its mark on a treaty.

NOTES

   1. Cecil V. Crabb, Jr., and Pat M. Holt, Invitation to Struggle: Congress, the President, and Foreign
Policy (Washington: Congressional Quarterly Press,
1980), pp.65-67.
   2. U.S. Congress, House, Committee on International Relations, Chronologies of Major Developments in
Selected Areas of International Relations, 95th Cong.,
1st sess., 1977, p.1.
   3. Hedrick Smith, "White House Opens Drive to Win
Senate Approval of Canal Accord," The New York Times,
August 12, 1977, p.1.
   4. Chronologies, International Relations Committee, 1977, p.141.
   5. Marjorie Hunter, "White House is Lobbying Un-
usually Hard on Canal Pacts," The New York Times,
September 1, 1977, p.2.
   6. Interview with Hoyt Purvis, former Foreign
Policy Advisor to Senator Robert Byrd, March 5, 1982.
   7. Congressional Quarterly, vol.35, no.30,
September 24, 1977, pp.2033-2034; see also, "Picking Up
the Pieces," Newsweek, October 3, 1977, pp.22-27.
   8. Chronologies, International Relations Committee, 1977, p.151.
   9. Congressional Quarterly, vol.36, February 4,
1978, pp.316-317.
   10. Interview with Hoyt Purvis, March 5, 1982.
   11. "Byrd Expects Reservations to be Added to
Pacts," The New York Times, September 25, 1977, p.8.
   12. U.S. Congress, Senate, Report of the Senatorial Delegation to the Republic of Panama, November
9-12, 1977, Senate Document 95-79, 95th Cong., 2d
sess., pp.15-16, 1978.

104

13. Letter from General Omar Torrijos H., Chief of State, Panama, to Robert Byrd, Majority Leader, U.S. Senate, December 3, 1977.

14. C. L. Sulzberger, "Panama and U.S. Policy," The New York Times, November 9, 1977, p.25.

15. Letter from Office of the Majority Leader, U.S. Senate, to all Senators, February 2, 1978.

16. Joseph Lelyveld, "The Path to 1980," The New York Times, October 2, 1977, p.110.

17. Adam Clymer, "Baker Says Senate Won't Approve Canal Pacts Without Changes," The New York Times, January 5, 1978, p.10.

18. Interview with Hoyt Purvis, March 5, 1982.

19. Ibid.

20. Congressional Quarterly, February 4, 1978, pp.316-317.

21. Lelyveld, The New York Times, October 2, 1977, p.110.

22. Chronologies, International Relations Committee, 1977, p.140.

23. Adam Clymer, "Conservatives Map Drive Against the Canal Treaty," The New York Times, August 16, 1977, p.7.

24. Congressional Quarterly, vol.35, September 10, 1977, pp.1922-1923.

25. Adam Clymer, The New York Times, August 16, 1977, p.7.

26. Library of Congress, Congressional Research Service, Panama Canal Treaties: Consideration by the Congress, Issue Brief 1B 78026, July 28, 1978, p.38.

27. Adam Clymer, The New York Times, January 5, 1978, p.10.

28. Congressionaly Quarterly, September 24, 1977, pp.2033-2034.

29. Lelyveld, The New York Times, October 2, 1977, p.110.

30. "Carter Wins With 'Good Old Boys,'" Washington Star, March 17, 1978, p.1.

31. Ibid.

32. Congressional Quarterly Almanac, 1978, pp.393-394.

33. Robert Kaiser, "Panama Raises Challenge to Treaty," Washington Post, April 7, 1978, p.1.

34. Congressional Quarterly Almanac, 1978, p.393-394.

35. Elaine Adams, ed., American Foreign Relations: 1978, (New York: NYU Press, 1979), p.83.

36. Interview with Hoyt Purvis, April 13, 1982.

37. Chronologies, International Relations Committee, 1978, p.235.

38. "The Engineering Feat Behind the Canal Treaties Began on a Bleak Day," Washington Post, April 24, 1978, p.1.

39. "Canal Showdown," <u>Newsweek</u>, April 24, 1978, p.27.

40. <u>American Foreign Relations: 1978</u>, p.85.

41. Robert Kaiser, "Senate Approves Final Canal Treaty," <u>Washington Post</u>, April 19, 1978, pp.1,23.

42. Memorandum: Mary Jane Checchi, Aide to Senator Robert Byrd, to Hoyt Purvis, February 17, 1978.

43. Ibid.

44. "Canal Showdown," <u>Newsweek</u>, April 24, 1978, p.27.

45. <u>Congressional Quarterly Almanac</u>, 1978, p.396.

46. <u>Congressional Quarterly Almanac</u>, 1978, p.396.

47. <u>Chronologies</u>, 1978, p.234.

48. <u>Congressional Quarterly Almanac</u>, 1978, p.394.

49. <u>Newsweek</u>, April 24, 1978, p.28

50. Letter: General Omar Torrijos to Senator Robert Byrd, April 22, 1978.

51. U.S. Congress, Senate, Committee on Foreign Relations, <u>The Role of the Senate in Treaty Ratification</u>, 95th Cong., 1st sess., 1977, p.34.

5
Congress, Country X, and Arms Sales

Hoyt Purvis
John Opperman
Tura Campanella

During the past two decades arms sales have become an increasingly significant element of United States foreign policy, and Congress has gradually staked out for itself a role in which it can be influential on arms sales policies.

Arms sales, as Andrew J. Pierre has written, have become a crucial dimension of world politics. "Arms sales are far more than an economic occurence, a military relationship, or an arms control challenge--arms sales are foreign policy writ large."[1]

The nature of U.S. arms transfers began to shift from grants to sales in the 1960s. Before the Kennedy Administration, most American weapons transfers to developing countries were in the form of grant aid. The sales push began in the early 1960s, with Iran becoming a major customer. In fiscal year 1958, the U.S. gave away $1.96 billion and sold $230 million worth of weapons; by fiscal year 1968, grant aid was down to $466 million, while sales were up to $1.5 billion.[2] This switch from aid to sales was strongly urged by many in Congress. Those arguing for the shift believed that the U.S. could no longer afford to "give away" large quantities of weapons. But, as the shift occurred, Congress found itself largely excluded from participation in arms sales to particular countries. Over a period of years Congress made a number of efforts to attempt to increase its role in the arms sales decision process. The best known of these was the landmark Nelson-Bingham amendment of 1974, and the International Security Assistance and Arms Export Control Act of 1976, which did assure a stronger role for Congress in arms transfer policies.

Origins of Congressional Involvement

The first significant instance of a congressional

attempt to limit the executive domination of the arms
sales field occurred in 1967. It followed a Senate
Foreign Relations Committee staff study which disclosed
that the Department of Defense and the Export-Import
Bank (Eximbank) had developed an intricate procedure
for financing arms exports that was circumventing Congress.[3] When this practice came to light, it stirred
strong congressional opposition. The Eximbank had been
lending to the Department of Defense, which then used
the loans to finance arms sales to developing countries
to which Eximbank was not otherwise prepared to extend
credit. In this way the Eximbank provided the finance
but did not deal with the buyer or even know the buyer's identity. Hence the loans were called "Country X
Loans." The loans were not publicized, and before
their "discovery" in 1967, the role of the Eximbank in
arms sales was mentioned only in an occasional phrase
in the Department of Defense mutual aid statements.
From 1965-1967, the Country X program financed more
than $600 million in military equipment to 14 develop-
ing countries.[4]

The Foreign Relations Committee's staff report revealed that overall arms sales had been rising at a
rapid rate and that an ever-increasing revolving account, originally authorized by the Mutual Security Act
of 1957, was permitting the Department of Defense to
put the guarantee of the U.S. government behind more
than a billion dollars in military credits. The pattern suggested by the committee staff analysis was
symptomatic of the broader trend in post-World War II
foreign policy. Gradually, the executive was exercising more and more authority, with relatively little
congressional involvement and oversight. The study indicated that legislation regarding the regulation of
arms sales (the Export Control Act of 1949 and the
Mutual Security Act of 1954 and amendments to these
acts) was not being adhered to by the executive.[5] However, at the time the Department of Defense was not
even required by Congress to submit comprehensive reports on export sales, nor to indicate how the military
assistance credit account was being used.

Background to Country X

Executive branch officials were eager to maintain
American influence and protect what they perceived to
be American security interests by using foreign assistance as an element of U.S. security policy. But they
were faced with growing congressional resistance to
foreign assistance, even if it was primarily military
or "security" assistance. During the Kennedy and Johnson Administrations, Secretary of Defense Robert
McNamara believed that the Military Assistance Program

(MAP) was suffering from its identification with foreign aid. (Years later, as President of the World
Bank, McNamara was a staunch advocate of international
economic assistance.) He wanted to transfer the military assistance program to the Department of Defense
budget and away from the State Department.

Congressional leaders opposed the switch, however.
Thomas E. Morgan (D-Pennsylvania), Chairman of the
House Committee on Foreign Affairs, responding to a
request from McNamara for his opinion of the proposal,
informed the Defense Secretary: "A separation of the
military aid program from economic assistance would, in
my judgment, result in a drastic curtailment of economic aid...I do not regard this proposal as sound and I
would regard its acceptance by the executive and the
Congress as creating major, and perhaps insuperable,
problems in the implementation of our foreign policy."[6]

Having failed in this effort, Defense officials
sought alternative means of accomplishing their goal of
expanding military assistance. The result was an
amendment to the Foreign Assistance Act of 1964, which
allowed the Department of Defense to use the revolving
fund to guarantee credit extended by any "individual,
corporation, partnership, or other association doing
business in the United States" for the purchase of
military equipment.[7]

The new provisions for financing credit sales gave
birth to Exim's Country X loans. In fiscal year 1965,
Exim provided just $9 million in credit to developing
countries for arms purchases, while private banks extended almost $49 million. This appeared to be in line
with what the Johnson Administration set out to achieve
--to have private banks finance arms credit sales to
the fullest extent possible. However, by year's end
the money market situation had grown so tight that commercial banks were unwilling to finance arms sales.
Exim was the alternative, and an increasingly attract-
ive one because of its lower-than-market interest rates.

While the guarantee authority allowed more participation by Exim in foreign arms sales, the volume of
such loans did not increase significantly. Discussions
between Department of Defense and Exim led to another
proposal for inclusion in the foreign aid legislation
of 1965.[8] Because of the revolving fund limits, the
Department of Defense sought to expand the guarantee
authority by requiring that only 25 percent of any
credit extended by Exim or other banks be guaranteed by
the Department of Defense. In other words, a $10 mil-
lion Exim loan would require the Department of Defense
to provide a guarantee of just $2.5 million instead of
the full $10 million. This could have the effect of
increasing the guaranteed credit sales fourfold, without an increase in appropriations. In fact, after Congress approved the authority, credit sales increased

from $68 million in fiscal year 1965 to $289 million in
fiscal year 1966. For Exim, credit arms sales increased from $9 million in fiscal year 1965 to $281
million in fiscal year 1966.

Congressional Involvement

Although Congress had provided the legislative
authority for the Country X loans, the program remained
veiled from the legislative branch. In 1967, when the
program became publicly controversial, President Harold
Linder of the Eximbank asserted that he had consulted
with the chairmen of the House and Senate Banking and
Currency Committees before Exim had begun financing the
arms sales.[9] However, both of those chairmen had left
office by 1967, and, in any case, neither of those committees was involved with foreign policy.

The first inkling of congressional opposition to
Exim's involvement in arms sales came in 1966 during
consideration of foreign aid appropriations. Senator
Allen Ellender of Louisiana strongly questioned the
Exim financing. Actually, Ellender's questioning was
spurred by the Kashmir conflict between India and Pakistan and an escalating arms race in Latin America. At
that time he did not know the extent of Exim financing
of sales to developing countries, but considered any
such financing to be improper within the context of the
bank's charter. In defending the financing policies,
McNamara pointed to the congressional insistence on
moving from arms grants to arms sales. He also
stressed the political risks to private banks in financing arms sales, and, as a result, the need for Exim
financing.[10]

In late 1966, Linder expressed his concern to the
White House about possible problems facing legislation
which would extend the life of the bank. But the White
House assured Linder that Exim legislation was not in
jeopardy, and when President Johnson sent the Exim bill
to Congress in January 1967, the role of the bank in
financing arms was not expected to be a problem.[11]

However, the Senate Foreign Relations Committee's
staff report in January 1967, flagged the issue of arms
sales and heightened the committee's concern. The
study, written by committee consultant William B.
Bader, called for a reappraisal of the adequacy of the
machinery of policy control and legislative oversight
governing the sale of arms.[12] Bader, who later served
as the committee's staff director under Senator Frank
Church, 1979-1980, recalled that at the time the 1967
report was written the committee has only a small
staff, and he drafted the report which was then re-
viewed only by the staff director, Carl Marcy, and by
Chairman Fulbright. Meanwhile, the executive branch

had large numbers of people working on arms transfer issues.[13]

The Arab-Israeli War in June 1967 (the Six Days War) was another factor contributing to congressional concern about arms sales. The U.S. had supplied weapons to both sides in the conflict. (In the case of Israel, the U.S. did not begin selling it arms until 1962, but after 1967 became almost the sole external arms source for Israel. In some cases Congress urged the executive to go beyond what it planned to sell Israel, and the sales frequently were made on highly favorable "forgiveness" terms.)

In examining the U.S. role in regional arms races in 1967, congressional committees began to scrutinize the Country X loan program. The program came under fire on three counts: the circumvention of Congress; the impact on regional arms races; and the concern that developing countries were diverting capital from economic development in order to purchase military equipment. With some members of Congress outraged at the "backdoor" aspects of arms financing, the legislation extending the life of the Export-Import Bank and increasing its lending authority became the subject of controversy. The House and Senate Banking Committees had approved the bill in the spring of 1967, but the legislation was delayed after arms sales became a hot issue. The Senate committee held further hearings on the legislation and reported the bill with an amendment expressing the sense of Congress that the bank should not be involved in Country X loans. The committee report asserted that there was no explicit authority for Exim financing of arms sales in its charter or legislative history.[14]

Another concern of some members of Congress was that major arms sales policy decisions were being made at middle levels of government. Senator Stuart Symington (D-Missouri) was the first to raise this matter, questioning the role of the Department of Defense's Henry Kuss, Deputy Secretary of Defense for International Logistics Negotiations. Kuss was in charge of all arms sales negotiations for the Department of Defense, and his role in the booming arms trade business was being widely publicized. He was described in new articles as the Pentagon's "super-salesman," and was quoted as saying that U.S. arms sales would soon reach $2 billion as year.[15]

Members of Congress were concerned that the Defense Department had become too involved with arms manufacturers, and that the two were combining to direct arms sales policy. Although supervision of arms transfers was supposed to be under the Secretary of State's authority, the words and actions of Administration officials left strong doubt that this was the case. In July 1967 the Foreign Relations Committee was told that

arms sales were coordinated by a "Senior Interdepartmental Group." This group was made up of officials
from Departments of State and Defense, with occasional
attendance by officials from the Agency for International Development (AID), Treasury, the Arms Control
and Disarmament Agency (ACDA), and the Bureau of the
Budget (BOB). When Senator Albert Gore (D-Tennessee)
questioned the role of the Interdepartmental Group in
specific Country X sales to Iran, Morocco, Argentina,
and Jordan, it was found that the group met on only one
of these sales (Morroco), and that representatives from
Treasury, the Arms Control and Disarmament Agency, and
the Bureau of the Budget did not meet with the group at
that instance.[16]

The chairman of the Interdepartmental Group, Jef-
frey Kitchen, Deputy Assistant Secretary of State for
Politico-Military Affairs, indicated that his job was
to coordinate arms sales with the Department of Defense
and insure that all sales were made with State Department "leadership and guidance." Nonetheless, upon
questioning by Symington, Kitchen admitted that he knew
little about Country X loans, and, in fact, seemed to
know less than the staff of the Senate Foreign Relations Committee. Secretary McNamara tried to clear up
the confusion in his testimony before the committee.
He explained that the Department of Defense had the
primary responsibility for arms sales decisions and
that the Department of State was often "less informed"
on those matters as a result.[17] This was contradictory
to the 1963 directive by President Johnson that the
Secretary of State be responsible for all arms transfers, a position that the President had reiterated in a
1966 message to Congress on foreign policy.[18] McNamara
also said that the Exim Bank could deny any request
made for financing by the Department of Defense. However, he acknowledged that Exim had never turned down
such a request. Harold Linder of Exim said that his
understanding was that all Country X loan requests required a presidential determination.[19]

The Legislative Struggle

With Congress questioning Administration procedures
and Senator Frank Church of the Foreign Relations Committee making a speech attacking the Administration's
arms sales policies, some Johnson White House officials
wanted to counter the charges. There was a particular
concern about Church's claim that balance-of-payments
considerations were overriding foreign policy. White
House officials began working on a reply, and received
help from Kuss' office at the Department of Defense.
The initial reply was rejected by presidential aides
when it was discovered that State Department officials

had not been involved in the drafting.[20] Later, a formal statement on arms sales policy was forwarded to the
President, with the support of the Departments of State
and Defense and several presidential aides.[21] The only
definite voice of dissent was the President's National
Security Adviser, Walt Rostow. He advised the President no to make a statement at that time because of the
continuing sensitivity of the Middle East situation.
Rostow's argument won out, and no statement was made.

But the controversy continued in Congress. After
more hearings, the Senate took up the Exim legislation
in August 1967 and there were efforts to attach amendments to tighten the "sense-of-Congress" provision approved by the Banking Committee. An amendment by Senators Ellender and Joseph Clark (D-Pennsylvania) to
flatly prohibit the bank from financing arms sales to
developing countries was defeated 49-40, leaving the
committee's language intact.

The companion bill in the House originally contained no restrictions on arms sales. However, the
growing congressional concern over the issue resulted
in an effort in the House Banking Committee, led by
Representatives William Widnall (R-New York) and Henry
Reuss (D-Wisconsin), to prevent the Country X loans.
Committee Chairman Wright Patman (D-Texas), a strong
Administration backer, headed the opposition to these
efforts. As a compromise, a Reuss amendment, which included an important presidential waiver, was accepted
by the committee. The amendment called for discontinu-
ation of Exim financing of arms sales to less-developed
countries, but it also empowered the President to approve such financing if it was necessary for "national
security."[22]

Final action on the Exim bill was delayed, however,
as the prolonged controversy spilled over into other
legislative debates. This is a typical pattern in Congress. When an issue generates major interest, members
often find a variety of vehicles for debating and acting on that issue. Congress gets at least two cracks
at many issues because of the dual process of authorization and appropriations bills. (For example, the
Senate Foreign Relations Committee and House Foreign
Affairs Committee consider foreign aid authorizing legislation before it goes to the Senate or House floor;
similarly, the House and Senate Appropriations Committees act on the funding bills for foreign aid and forward them to the full House and Senate for final action. In some cases, there is still a further opportunity for action in the conference committees and on
conference reports.)

In this case, both the foreign aid authorization
and appropriations bills, as well as the Exim Bank extension bill, contained arms sales provisions and dealt
with the Country X revolving fund.

Already facing severe reductions in its foreign aid
proposals, with Congress cutting the authorization level to the lowest in the 20-year history of U.S. aid,
the Administration was forced to defer its efforts to
secure passage of the Exim bill because of problems
surrounding the aid bill. The aid bill reported to the
Senate by the Foreign Relations Committee included an
amendment by Frank Church to repeal at the end of 1967
the Pentagon's authority to maintain a revolving fund.
A strong lobbying effort was mounted by the Administration as the Senate neared action on the aid legislation. Administration officials argued that elimination
of the Country X loans would threatened the security of
Israel, and several members of Congress acknowledged
that they were lobbied by American Jewish organizations
to support the Country X program.[23] In addition, the
Chairman of the Joint Chiefs of Staff, General Earle
Wheeler, warned the Senate Armed Services Committee
that cuts in military assistance would invite Soviet
and Chinese aggression.

On the day of the Senate vote, key senators met
with Administration officials who were attempting to
enlist support for an amendment by Senators Henry Jackson (D-Washington) and John Tower (R-Texas). The Administration was represented at the meetings in Majority Leader Mike Manfield's office by Paul Nitze, Deputy
Secretary of Defense; William Gaud, Administrator of
the Agency for International Development (AID); and
Nicholas Katzenbach, Under Secretary of State. During
the discussion, senators discovered that there was a
provision in the proposed amendment that, in effect,
not only kept the Department of Defense revolving fund
intact, but allowed it to be replenished through a dis-
counting mechanism with Exim. Several senators saw
this as an attempt by the Administration to mislead
them, and angrily left Mansfield's office. Senators
Fulbright and Symington, increasingly at odds with the
Administration over Vietnam and other issues, charged
that there had been a effort to dupe Congress through a
lobbying effort as intense as they had seen in their
years in Washington. Some senators said they switched
their votes as a result of the episode in Manfield's
office. Fulbright said the Country X program "had been
very successfully concealed from Congress,"[24] and Symington referred to "the indiscriminate selling of arms,
at times clearly without the knowledge, let alone approval of the Congress."[25]

During the Senate debate, Senator Wayne Morse of
Oregon, who had been one of only two senators voting
against the 1964 Gulf of Tonkin resolution, charged
that the Jackson-Tower amendment was "another of the
many instances where the Pentagon seeks blank-check
powers from Congress."[26] However, Jackson maintained
that a President "needs flexibility--freedom to deal

with each individual request for arms and equipment on
its merit in the light of the developing situation at
the time."[27] And Republican Whip Thomas Kuchel supporting Jackson and Tower said, "I am not going to
place the man in the White House in a straitjacket."[28]
He quoted a Los Angeles Times editorial stating that
Congress seemed determined to "hamstring the executive
branch in its handling of delicate foreign policy
situations."[29]

But Church said the real issue was whether the Foreign Relations Committee and Congress were going to
"reestablish adequate congressional surveillance and
control" over military assistance. Opposing efforts to
simply require that Congress be informed after the fact
about arms sales, Church said, "Closer congressional
supervision requires that they first tell us how they
plan to disburse the arms, where they are to be placed,
whether by sale or grant. Only then will we be in a
position to know whether we want to give or continuing
approval to the program or make changes in it."[30]

The Senate Foreign Relations Committee had become a
stronghold of opposition to Johnson Administration foreign policy. Another member of that committee was Eugene McCarthy, who took issue with suggestions that by
placing a measure of congressional control over arms
sales the Senate would somehow be undermining national
security. McCarthy said the Senate was simply seeking
a share in decision-making instead of leaving every-
thing to those in the Pentagon on the assumption that
"they are so wise and all-knowing that we should not
question the procedure."[31] (Later in 1967 McCarthy announced his candidacy for the Democratic presidential
nomination. Although his candidacy was not successful,
many believed it was a factor in Johnson's 1968 decision not to seek re-election.)

With the group of activist Democrats from the Foreign Relations Committee leading the way, the Senate
rejected the Jackson-Tower amendment 50-43. Tower then
proposed a similar amendment, still restoring the revolving fund, but on a more restricted basis. Tower's
amendment was defeated by one vote, 46-45.[32]

Congressional Restrictions

The bill reported by the House Foreign Affairs Committee contained no restrictions on the revolving fund.
Indeed, the bill approved by that committee included an
Administration-backed provision which would have enabled the Defense Department to buy promissory notes being held by U.S. arms manufacturers who sold weapons to
foreign governments. As was also provided in the unsuccessful Tower amendment, such notes would then be
sold to U.S. financial institutions. When the measure

went to the House floor, Widnall was successful in amending the bill to eliminate the promissory note provision, overriding the lobbying efforts of both the Johnson Administration and the arms manufacturers.

The Conference Committee charged with resolving the differences between the House and Senate versions remained deadlocked from September 14 until November 2, 1967, because of the controversy over the arms sales provisions. The Administration suggested transferring the loan authority from the Defense Department to the President. House conferees were willing to go along, but Senate conferees balked, insisting that the proposal would change nothing. Meanwhile, the House proceeded to act on the foreign aid appropriations bill. The House Appropriations Committee attached language proposed by Representative Silvio Conte (R-Massachusetts) that would prevent the sale of sophisticated weapons to all developing countries except Greece, Turkey, Iran, Israel, Nationalist China (Taiwan), South Korea, and the Philippines. Working through Committee Chairman George Mahon (D-Texas), the Administration attempted to block this restriction too, claiming that Conte's amendment would tie the President's hand in carrying out foreign policy.[33] But when the Mahon effort failed, Administration officials argued that Conte's restrictions should satisfy the Senate and that the authorization bill should thus be approved by the conferees without the restrictions approved earlier by the Senate. Nonetheless, the Senate conferees held firm, and were given renewed impetus by reports of an Administration decision to offer F-5 supersonic fighter aircraft to several Latin American nations. The Conference Committee finally agreed on a provision to abolish the Country X revolving fund as of June 30, 1968, and to limit the amount of arms purchase loans that could be guaranteed during fiscal 1968 to $190 million.

President Johnson was reluctant to sign the bill, and AID Administrator Gaud urged a veto. Gaud warned that U.S. influence would decline as a result of the congressional cuts and restrictions and said that developing countries would be forced to pay cash for military equipment, which would increase demands for economic assistance.[34] (Congress had also approved a Symington amendment requiring the President to terminate development loans and food aid to any nation diverting such assistance to military expenditures, or diverting their own resources to "unnecessary military spending to a degree which materially interferes" with their own development.[35] As passed by the Senate, the amendment would have applied to all foreign aid, but it was toned down in the Conference Committee.) When Johnson signed the bill, which not only cut his aid proposals but tied the executive's hand on the dispatch of arms to developing nations, the President said,

"I believe the money cuts and other restrictions in this act will seriously inhibit the government's efforts to assure and enlarge the security of the free world."[36]

The foreign aid appropriations bill was finally approved in mid-December, and it reflected the same pattern of funding cuts and policy restrictions. The bill prohibited any use of military assistance funds or the Department of Defense revolving fund to finance the sale of sophisticated weapons to developing countries except those which had been specified by the House Appropriations Committee. There was, however, a provision for a presidential waiver if the President determined that such a transaction was vital to the U.S. national security and so reported to Congress within 30 days of his determination. Such waivers have often been attached to legislation so as to leave a measure of flexibility for the President in matters of urgency.

Final action on the Exim Bank legislation did not come until March 1968, and only after further fierce battling in the House. Representative Widnall attempted to flatly prohibit any Exim financing of arms sales to developing countries and to drop the President's waiver authority. He said this would be consistent with the action taken by Congress in 1967 setting a mid-1968 termination date for the Country X fund.

In a rare speech on the House floor, aging Speaker John McCormack (D-Massachusetts) strongly attacked Republican Widnall's proposal. "If ever an amendment was against the national interests of our country, it is this amendment," McCormack argued.[37]

Other supporters of the Johnson Administration criticized Widnall's amendment as a partisan effort. Ed Edmondson (D-Oklahoma) argued for using the "arsenal of democracy for democracy" and said the arms financing was needed.[38] Widnall's amendment was defeated and when the bill went to conference, the House version was accepted. As finally enacted in March 1968, the bill prohibited Exim credits for sales of military equipment to developing countries unless the President declared that such sales were in the national interest and gave Congress 30 days notice.

Efforts at Congressional Assertion

Thus, Congress had moved in a piecemeal fashion, through three separate legislative measures and after prolonged debate, to place restrictions on credit sales of military equipment to foreign countries. Congress had begun to assert some control over the executive's role in arms sales, which had previously been loosely restricted and had allowed considerable executive flexibility in how arms sales were negotiated and financed. At times, both the country seeking American arms and elements within the executive involved in arms sales were in agreement that the potential congressional check on arms sales was a troublesome obstacle. In the interest of preserving arms sales relationships and initiating new ones, special arrangements to circumvent congressional oversight, such as the Country X loans, were created and flourished until detected by Congress.

In 1968, Congress moved to consolidate the arms sales provisions, in modified form, into one bill--the Foreign Military Sales Act. This first effort by Congress at comprehensive arms sales legislation was a major foundation statute of what later became, in 1976, the Arms Export Control Act.

The congressional action on arms sales in 1967-1968 constituted an important step on the path toward increased congressional involvement in international security affairs, and was one of the first signs of the more assertive congressional role. During the same period there were other signs of a more active Congress.

Questioning National "Commitments"

In July 1967, President Johnson dispatched three transport planes to the Congo (later known as Zaire) to aid Congolese President Joseph Mobutu in putting down a rebellion.[39] (About 150 American military personnel were involved.) The decision was taken without any congressional participation, and resulted in strong criticism from Capitol Hill. The criticism came from both supporters and opponents of the Johnson Administration's Vietnam policy, and the broad range of opposition was seen as a demostration of the growing concern about U.S. involvement overseas. Especially significant was the role of Senator Richard Russell (D-Georgia). Russell was extremely influential in the Senate, and particularly revered by Southern Democrats. As chairman of the Senate Armed Services Committee and one of the few members of Congress who at that time were informed about U.S. intelligence operations (if on an irregular basis), Russell's comments were especially weighty. Although Russell had backed Johnson on Vietnam, he noted that the U.S. role in Vietnam started out with a commitment not much larger than the Congolese operation, and that it was difficult to limit such involvement once it began. No further commitment of U.S. troops or equipment was made in the Congo, and the planes were gradually withdrawn.

Fulbright later said that Russell's questioning of what constituted a national commitment "really began" what became a two-year effort to define the term, which culminated in the 1969 National Commitments Resolution.[40] The resolution, adopted by the Senate by a lopsided 70-16 vote, said a national commitment "means the use of the Armed Forces of the United States on foreign territory, or a promise to assist a foreign country, government, or people by the use of Armed Forces or financial resources of the United States, either immediately or upon the happening of certain events..." Although largely symbolic, the non-binding resolution expressed the sense of the Senate that such a commitment could result "only from affirmative action taken by the executive and legislative branches of the United States Government..."[41]

In conjunction with this effort, the Senate Foreign Relations Committee established a Subcommittee on U.S. Security Agreements and Commitments Abroad, chaired by Stuart Symington. The subcommittee's work spotlighted the growth in the U.S. involvement abroad and the number of U.S. "commitments."

The National Commitments resolution was the precursor of the 1973 War Powers Resolution, limiting the power of a President to commit U.S. forces to future hostilities without congressional authorization.[42] It was also in 1973 that renewed congressional efforts to deal with the arms transfer issue in a serious manner materialized. In the period since Congress had first begun to scrutinize arms sales, such sales had continued to grow at a rapid pace. In June 1973, the Senate Foreign Relations Committee recommended a wholesale revision of the statutory framework governing foreign military sales and grant assistance. The committee's legislation was developed with the strong personal backing Chairman Fulbright. Fulbright's efforts actually had their roots in the 1967 staff report for the Foreign Relations Committee at the time of the Country X controversy. Over the years he had grown increasingly concerned about arms transfers. Fulbright's bill would have phased out the military grant aid program and the military assistance groups (MAGs) assigned to foreign countries. The legislation also called for a new credit sales system of loan guarantees through commercial banks and would allow the Exim Bank to finance sales to developing countries--but there would be a ceiling on such sales and, unlike the Country-X program, there would be no deception involved.

Although the bill passed in the Senate, it did not become law. Still, it reflected the growing trend in Congress to alter the pattern of U.S. military grants and sales to foreign governments. The committee's report on the bill said, "For too many years, the United States has lived beyond its means abroad, maintaining vast military forces and bases, and lending and giving away our resources..."[43]

Nelson-Bingham Amendment

Finally, in 1974, Congress took more decisive action to assure a role in arms sales. The fiscal year
1975 foreign aid authorization bill (PL 93-559) contained requirements that the President must report to
Congress military sales valued at $25 million or more
and give Congress 20 calendar days to disapprove such
sales by passing a concurrent resolution of disapproval.
The Senate amendment was introduced by Senator Gaylord
Nelson (D-Wisconsin). A similar amendment had actually
been approved by the Senate in 1973, but had been
dropped in conference. In 1974, with Congress becoming
increasingly independent in the aftermath of Richard
Nixon's resignation, both Houses approved the proposal.
It was sponsored in the House by Representative Jonathan
Bingham (D-New York) and became known as the Nelson-
Bingham amendment.

The push for the amendment came from a Nelson staff
member, Paula Stern, working with Norvill Jones of the
Senate Foreign Relations staff. Concerned about the
inability of Congress to get a handle on arms sales,
Stern and Jones considered a variety of legislative
means before settling on this procedure.

Subsequently, the Nelson-Bingham amendment was refined. A major legislative initiative, the 1976 Arms
Export Control Act (PL 94-329) included a number of provisions related to arms sales. Section 36(b) of that
act, as updated, provides that Congress has 30 days,
following formal notification, during which it may act,
by concurrent resolution, to disapprove a sale. (Congress is normally given an informal notification 20 days
before the formal notice, although that is not required
by law.) The congressional review provisions initially
applied to any proposed sale of defense articles or services valued at $25 million or more, or any sale that
included more than $7 million in major defense equip-
ment. The threshhold figures were subsequently increased, with notification required for sales valued at
$14 million or more for single items or $50 million or
more for packages. The Arms Export Control Act has also
been amended to provide Congress with the authority to
veto transfers of weapons by recipient countries to
third countries (1977), and commercial arms sales
(1979). More detailed and frequent reports on arms
sales are required by Congress as well. There is still
provision, however, that the President can waive congressional review if he declared that an emergency
exists which requires that a sale be made in the national security interest.

Beginning with the efforts to exercise some control
over the Country X program, Congress has taken a series
of steps to strengthen it role in arms sales. As the

Senate Foreign Relations Committee stated in its report
on the 1976 Arms Export Control Act, "Congress in the
past has not exercised effective oversight of arms
sales matters and needs additional statutory authority
to do so."[44] With passage of the Arms Export Control
Act, Congress finally succeeded in carving out for itself a relatively active role in overseeing and influencing arms sales and arms transfer policies.

Executive Initiative

Despite these moves by Congress to insure a role for
itself in arms sales, this remains an area where the
initiative rests with the executive and where only a
concerted congressional effort can reverse an executive
decision. However, the congressional role does result,
at least in some cases, in greater leverage for Congress
and in more inter-branch consultation on proposed sales.
Congressional sentiment is usually tested by the executive, although sometimes the consultation is belated and
minimal. But some proposed sales have been delayed, and
other arms packages have been reshaped or scaled down in
order to head off congressional problems. Further, as a
result of the opportunity for congressional involvement,
there is much more pub- lic and media attention to proposed sales, which seems appropriate in light of the
growing importance of arms sales as instruments of U.S.
foreign policy.

Several proposed sales have been hotly debated by
Congress since passage of the Nelson-Bingham amendment
and the Arms Export Control Act. But in none of these
cases did Congress ultimately use the legislative veto
to stop the sales. Most of the controversial sales have
involved nations in the Middle East and Persian Gulf region. In 1975, President Ford, faced with the threat
of possible congressional disapproval, compromised on a
proposed sale of Hawk missiles to Jordan. After extensive consultation, Ford informed Congress that Jordan
had indicated that the missile systems would be perman-
ently installed in a defensive and non-mobile manner.
This pledge, which sought to insure that these weapons
could not be used in an offensive role, and thus would
pose neither a strategic threat to Israel nor affect the
power balance in the Middle East, was satisfactory to
Congress and the threat of congressional disapproval
ended.[45]

A year later, Ford had to sharply reduce the number
of Maverick air-to-ground missiles to be sold to Saudi
Arabia. The Senate Foreign Relations Committee voted
for a disapproval resolution and "repeated its concern
over the failure of the executive branch to take into
account the Congress' concern over arms sales policy or
to respond fully to the requests for information

relevant to proposed sales."[46] In order to ameliorate congressional concern and avoid possible disapproval, Ford reduced the number of missiles to be sold from 1,500 to 650.

American Arms and Iran

The next major confrontation over arms sales oc- cured in 1977, when President Jimmy Carter proposed to sell seven of the highly sophisticated Airborne Warning and Control System (AWACS) planes to Iran. Controversy over U.S. arms sales to Iran dated back to the mid- sixties. With Iran becoming an increasingly important source of oil, and with the Shah occasionally flirting with the neighboring Soviet Union, the U.S. began step- ping up arms sales to Iran. In 1967, Undersecretary of State Eugene Rostow, arguing that the U.S. should not antagonize the Shah, said in a letter to Senator Ful- bright that this nation had to decide "whether we should leave our friends without the means they feel they need to defend themselves or attempt through modest sales to help them achieve at least minimum defense capability." But Fulbright remained uncon- vinced, saying, "I have been in Iran and it is a most desolate country. There are very few rich people, but the majority could easily turn to revolution. I think you are doing a great disservice to them loading them down with these arms."[47]

Under the Nixon Administration, arms sales to Iran were stepped up further. By 1972, Nixon and Secretary of State Kissinger had agreed to sell the Shah virtual- ly any conventional weapons system he wanted, beginning with the advanced F-14 fighter plane. As one writer noted, "Within a year Iran became the bazaar for an American arms bonanza as the three military services and arms sales converged on Tehran."[48]

In the four years preceding 1973, official U.S. sales to Iran had reached a value of $1.28 billion, in itself no small figure. But in the following four-year period (1973-1976) the volume of these sales was in- creased nearly ten times, to a total of $11 billion.[49] (See Table 5.1)

However, when Carter came into office in 1977, he announced a new U.S. policy to govern the transfer of conventional arms. Carter's initiative was at least in part a response to continuing congressional pressure, and was designed to restrain U.S. sales. He said in May 1977, that the U.S. would "henceforth view arms transfers as an exceptional foreign policy imple- ment."[50] But only a short time later, Carter revealed plans to sell AWACS to Iran, a $1.2-billion deal that appeared to undercut his own policy.

Early opposition to the AWACS sale was led by two

TABLE 5.1
U.S. Arms Sales to Iran

Fiscal Year	U.S. Dollars	
1969	235,821,000	
1970	134,929,000	
1971	363,884,000	
1972	472,611,000	
1973	2,171,355,000	
1974	4,325,357,000	
1975	2,447,140,000	
1976	1,794,487,000	
1977	5,713,769,000	*
1978	2,586,890,000	*
1979	41,520,000	*
1980	0	

Source: Figures from the Department of Defense

*Some of the sales were cancelled after the Shah was deposed, and the military equipment was never delivered.

liberal Democratic senators, John Culver (Iowa) and Thomas Eagleton (Missouri). Culver and Eagleton had taken a strong interest in U.S. relations with Iran, particularly after a visit to Iran in 1976. Although congressional travel is frequently referred to as "junketing," the trip to Iran by Culver, Eagleton and others was an example of the value that can result from congressional travel when members of Congress are able to see matters for themselves and make independent judgments. The judgments made by Culver and Eagleton were contrary to the positions taken by the Ford, Nixon, and Carter Administrations, all having proclaimed great confidence in the Shah. In contrast to Carter, who was later to refer to Iran as "an island of stability," Eagleton and Culver had strong doubts about the prospects for future stability in Iran.[51]

In a rather prophetic report after their 1976 trip, the senators pointed out the lack of stable political institutions in Iran, and said U.S.-Iranian ties were too dependent on a highly personalized relationship with the Shah. They expressed concern about "Ugly American" friction caused by the huge numbers of American technicians living in Iran and raised questions about the ability of the Iranians to absorb highly advanced technology so quickly.[52] Culver later recalled that the two had raised the hackles of U.S. diplomatic and military officials in Iran with their questioning attitude.[53]

On June 16, 1977, Carter sent Congress the prenoti-
fication announcement of the proposed sales of the seven
AWACS planes. By the time the formal notification was
given on July 7, opposition, led by Culver and Eagleton,
was growing on Capitol Hill, particularly after a report
by the General Accounting Office (GAO). The GAO, the
independent investigative arm of Congress, raised questions about the sale, calling the Administration's justification "inadequate" and said the sale could pose a
threat to U.S. security if, for example, information on
the technology should leak to the Soviet Union.[54]

Despite the ardent efforts of Culver and Eagleton,
it appeared that the sale might go through unscathed.
Under the Arms Export Control Act, Congress had only 30
days to act to disapprove the sale, and opponents of the
sale found themselves in a time bind as Congress moved
toward a statutory recess period, scheduled to begin
August 5. The Senate was tied up with a Republican filibuster against a Carter-supported bill for public financing of congressional elections.

On July 22, the opponents gained a strong ally.
Senate Majority Leader Robert Byrd hand-delivered a letter to the White House asking the President to withdraw
the notification of the proposed AWACS sale. Byrd's
letter noted the scheduling problems facing the Senate
and said that under the circumstances "it will be impossible for the Senate to give the proposal the careful
and serious consideration it deserves." Byrd also expressed his own "serious reservations" about the sale
and detailed them at some length in the letter.[55] Administration officials tried to get Byrd to back down,
but Byrd insisted that Congress deserved time to consider the sale thoughtfully. When Carter did not accede to
what the Majority Leader considered to be a reasonable
and responsible request, Byrd expressed his determination to push for a congressional veto of the sale.

Carter risked alienating Byrd, a key congressional
figure, who had already proven helpful in fending off
attacks on Carter's foreign policy. But apparently convinced that withdrawing the proposal would be interpreted as a sign of presidential weakness and also damaging
to U.S.-Iranian relations, Carter refused to pull back
the proposal.

Byrd did not relent, and called on the Administration to reconsider its position. Meanwhile he began
working with the Foreign Assistance Subcommittee of the
Foreign Relations Committee, which was considering the
sale. Hubert Humphrey, who chaired the subcommittee,
was concerned by the institutional showdown he saw developing between Congress and the President. As a veteran of both branches, the former Vice President believed in the importance of consensus and comity between
the branches. Working through his former Senate colleague from Minnesota, Vice-President Walter Mondale,

Humphrey sought to convince the White House to back off from a confrontation.

With the White House showing no signs of giving in, Byrd enlisted the support of Minority Leader Howard Baker and personally appeared before the Foreign Relations Committee to urge a disapproval resolution. Byrd insisted that it was an institutional issue and that the Senate should pass the disapproval resolution if that was the only way for the Senate to get enough time to weigh the issue on its merits. Although favoring the sale, Baker agreed with Byrd on the institutional principles involved.

In view of Byrd's strong commitment, the White House recognized the probability of a Senate defeat. But since both Houses had to vote disapproval resolutions in order to kill the sale, the Administration still felt safe because it expected to win the House. Speaker Thomas P. O'Neill told the President that the House would not oppose the sale. O'Neill had not counted on the determined efforts of Culver, however. In a two-hour virtuoso performance before the House Foreign Affairs Committee, Culver pounded the table and delivered a comprehensive denunciation of the sale. When Administration officials followed with a low-key defense of the proposal, they were no match for Culver, and the committee stunned the White House by voting 19-17 to disapprove the sale.

At that point the White House recognized that it had no choice but to temporarily withdraw the sale, and Byrd commended Carter for his "statesmanlike decision" to do so.[56] Further, Carter agreed to make some modifications in the AWACS package to reduce security risks and meet other concerns expressed in Congress: for example, certain communications and coding gear would be removed from the planes. A series of other assurances were provided when Carter resubmitted the proposal after Congress resumed its session in September. Although some members remained strongly opposed and others professed continuing doubts, the sale went through without either House taking further action.

But the controversy had served to focus greater congressional and public attention on the vast amount of U.S. weaponry flowing to Iran and on the congressional review process. One of the assurances provided to Congress in connection with the AWACS sale was that the Administration would conduct a detailed study of Iran's ability to continue to absorb high technology without additional requirements for U.S. technicians. In October 1977, Byrd noted that although the AWACS sale had been approved, he remained "concerned about the immense quantity of sophisticated military equipment which we are selling to Iran" and the possible future ramifications for both the U.S. and Iran. Pointing out that the AWACS sale would bring the total sales to Iran since

1972 to $18.2 billion, Byrd called for a moratorium on such sales.[57] Byrd also suggested that Congress consider requiring explicit congressional approval--rather than a resolution of disapproval--for sales to one nation valued at more than $200 million.[58] Although Congress did not adopt this suggested change in its procedures on arms sales, similar suggestions have been repeated, particularly with arms sales having become such a significant element in American foreign policy.

The AWACS was the last major sale to Iran to be approved before the Shah's regime fell early in 1979. One of the criticisms directed at the Shah was that he expended vast amounts for sophisticated weaponry, with U.S. encouragement, while neglecting some of the critical needs within Iran. Despite all the debate on the AWACS, it was never actually delivered to Iran, because delivery was not scheduled until 1981, well after the Shah had departed. American officials shuddered at the thought that the AWACS might have fallen into the hands of an unfriendly government, such as that of Ayatollah Khomeini.

More Middle East Sales

Subsequent major controversies over arms sales have involved Israel and Arab countries. Foremost among these were the 1978 $4.8-billion package of jet aircraft sold to Egypt, Israel, and Saudi Arabia, and the 1981 agreement to sell AWACS to Saudi Arabia.

In 1978, Carter had to wage a strong battle to ward off disapproval of his proposed sale of jets to the three Mid-East countries. The principal fight was over the Saudi Arabian component of the package. This was the first proposal to transfer top-of-the-line U.S. planes to the Saudis. But Secretary of State Cyrus Vance said that Saudi Arabia was "of immense importance in promoting a course of moderation in the Middle East."[59] Groups opposing the sale, such as the American Israel Public Affairs Committee (AIPAC), argued that the weapons being sold to the Arab states were "offensive" weapons.

Once again there was an example of the executive branch moving to mollify mounting opposition in Congress by modifying the proposed sale. In this case, the Carter Administration pledged that the Saudi F-15s, which had provoked the strongest protest in Congress, would be based outside striking distance of Israel and would not be equipped with bomb racks or air-to-air missiles which would give them offensive power. However, the administration resisted efforts to separate the Saudi planes from the rest of the package. The Senate Foreign Relations Committee sent a resolution of disapproval to the Senate floor, and Chairman Frank Church

strongly objected to having to consider the three sales
as one package. He said the President was forcing Congress to accept the Saudi sale by threatening to withhold the sales of planes to Israel otherwise.[60]
This time the Administration worked closely with
Majority Leader Byrd, winning his support for the proposal. And, after the Administration agreed not to
equip the planes with "offensive" equipment and provided
other assurances, Byrd worked tirelessly to build support among his colleagues. The Senate considered the
matter in a rare closed-door session in order to discuss
classified matters relating to the sale. During the debate, Senator Abraham Ribicoff (D-Connecticut), a highly
respected Jewish Senator, spoke effectively in behalf of
the sale. Ribicoff's views were influential in the Senate's decision, after more than 10 hours of debate, to
defeat the disapproval resolution 54-44, thus allowing
the sale to go through.[61]

AWACS for Saudi Arabia

Saudi Arabia was also at the center of the next
struggle between Congress and the executive over arms
sales, this time during the Reagan Administration. After holding off several times because of congressional
pressure, Reagan formally notified Congress in October
1981 of his intention to sell five AWACS planes to Saudi
Arabia. Even before notification, there was strong opposition to the proposal. But Reagan, not unlike other
presidents, attempted to present Congress with a _fait
accompli_--arguing that a "commitment" had already been
made to the Saudis, and if Congress went back on that
commitment, it would be disastrous for U.S.-Saudi relations. The fact that any such "commitment" on arms
sales is subject to congressional review does not prevent presidents from making such arguments.
Opposition in the Democratic-controlled House of
Representatives was overwhelming, and the House passed
a resolution disapproving the sale by a 301-111 vote.
But Reagan had been enjoying great success in winning
congressional support for his domestic policies and now
his Administration turned to an all-out effort to win
the fight for the AWACS sale in the Republican-controlled Senate.
Defeating the AWACS sale was a high priority for the
American Israel Public Affairs Committee (AIPAC), which
coordinates lobbying for Jewish organizations, and has
long been a potent force in influencing Congress. (For
more on the role of ethnic lobbies, see Chapter 3.)
AIPAC stressed its concern that the AWACS planes might
be used against Israel by the Saudis, in concert with
other Arab nations, and that there was a danger that the
AWACS secrets might fall into unfriendly hands.[62]

Over the years, the Saudis had become more skillful at building support in Congress. The Saudis retained a public relations firm to work on their behalf, and a member of the Saudi royal family--a young, English-educated, American-trained pilot--met privately with many key Capitol Hill figures. Opponents of the sale charged that Saudi Arabia applied considerable pressure in behalf of the sale through business and industrial groups. Aerospace firms, including Boeing, the builder of the AWACS, plus oil and construction companies with strong Saudi ties mounted major lobbying efforts.[63]

But the major lobbying effort came from the President himself. It was a vivid demonstration of how difficult it can be to stop a well-organized campaign, led by a popular President, even in the face of strong congressional opposition. Reagan held a series of meetings for senators at the White House and met with many senators individually to convince them that the sale was vital if the U.S. was to maintain good relations with the Saudis.

Following the pattern of other executive-legislative struggles over arms sales, the Reagan Administration provided certain "assurances" to help mollify congressional concerns. Such assurances often make it easier for initially reluctant members of Congress to support a presidential action, and enables them to claim that they influenced the terms of the sale. Early in this debate, Secretary of State Alexander Haig offered "new assurances" that the Saudis would protect the AWACS secrets and would not use the planes against Israel. But, with the Senate vote nearing and the outcome still highly uncertain, Reagan had to write a letter to Senate Majority Leader Howard Baker offering further assurances that the Saudis would not misuse or compromise the AWACS. The letter was apparently an important factor in convincing several wavering senators. The Administration also argued that the death a short time before of President Anwar Sadat of Egypt--who had been considered America's best Arab friend--made it all the more imperative the relations with Saudi Arabia not be jeopardized by rejection of the sale.

Even though at one time 50 senators had announced opposition to the sale, when the vote occurred on October 28, Reagan had succeeded in getting several senators to switch their positions, and the resolution of disapproval failed by a 48-52 vote. So much attention had been focused on the issue that, in the final analysis, a number of senators were reluctant to damage an American President's prestige by opposing him. This is often a factor in congressional foreign policy decisions, and in this case the Reagan White House used it very effectively.

Despite all the lobbying by business and pressure groups, it was clearly the President who turned the tide. "The President did a whale of a persuasive job," Robert Packwood (R-Oregon), one of the opposition leaders said.[64] Packwood commented, "With 90 percent of the votes, the President was 80 percent of the deciding factor."[65] Senator David Pryor (D-Arkansas) said, "The presidential lobbying effort has been as strong as train smoke, as we say down home."[66]

Although the President was victorious, it required an all-out effort, and some questioned whether he might have used up too much political capital in fighting off disapproval of the sale, making him more reluctant to undertake a similar struggle, or at least leading to more prior consultation with Congress. Sometimes members of Congress who give the President a benefit-of-the-doubt vote on foreign policy will then feel more free to go the other way on a domestic issue. President Carter, having engaged in a number of close and difficult battles on foreign policy, gradually ran out of political capital and found it hard to convince Congress to continue supporting him on controversial foreign policy matters.

Reassessing the Congressional Role

Congress has labored, sometimes effectively, sometimes with minimal impact, to involve itself in arms sales policy and decisions. Although Congress has consistently proven to be reluctant to formally reject a sale, it has played a significant role in shaping and modifying a number of arms deals. An analysis by the Congressional Research Service noted that the threat of the legislative veto has on occasion forced administrations to consult with Congress in a manner that led to reductions or modifications in proposed sales. However, the same Congressional Research Service study, while concluding that the Arms Export Control Act compelled the executive to deal with Congress in a systematic way, argued that the executive "has almost always found ways of finessing detailed discussions and negotiations with Congress on major arms sales until it has made its basic decision to sell."[67]

While the degree of actual congressional influence can be debated, there is little question that the executive often has had to take Congress into account in considering arms sales decisions. One of those who helped shape the congressional participation, Representative Bingham, said the Saudi AWACS battle underscored the point that the Arms Export Control Act gives Congress "an important instrument for sharing in important political decisions."[68] Gaylord Nelson, who was Bingham's counterpart while serving in the Senate, said, "This kind of debate could not have occurred without this law."[69]

Senator Charles Percy, from his perspective as Chairman of the Senate Foreign Relations Committee, considers the Arms Export Control Act to be one of the "positive" steps taken by Congress in increasing its foreign policy powers. But Percy is concerned about other areas in which "Congress sought more control over foreign policy than it could handle effectively" and believes that the congressional veto could be overused.[70]

By normally receiving an informal notification prior to the actual notification, Congress is given more time to review sales than is actually required by law. But some members believe that a longer review period is needed. And the fact remains that Congress reviews a proposed sale only after it has been the subject of extensive negotiations with the prospective purchasing country. To disapprove or significantly modify a sale at that point can risk serious damage to U.S. relations with the would-be purchaser.

Senator John Tower is one who is critical of the congressional role in arms sales. He says that, as a result of the Nelson-Bingham amendments, in recent years "every major arms sales agreement has been played out amidst an acrimonious national debate, blown all out of proportion to the intrinsic importance of the transaction in question."[71] Tower notes that legislators are put in the position of posturing for domestic political considerations and often ignore the merits of a proposed sale and the long-term foreign policy consequences. Such sales become subject to inordinate influence by lobbies for various national and ethnic groups, Tower believes. The result can be impairment of "a President's ability to carry out a strategy which reflects the interests of our nation as a whole."[72]

There is also the concern that congressional debate on arms sales proposals can unnecessarily complicate relations with the purchasing nation if, for example, Congress places "trivial and humiliating restrictions" on a sale. Tower believes that has happened in some cases.[73] Representative Les Aspin (D-Wisconsin) says, "...if we do not sell, the effect is enormous. The countries involved take it as a personal affront and as a rejection. That is what gets us into trouble, that we make these deliberations in public as we do, and if the decision is negative, it can have severe consequences."[74]

Referring to the "rather elaborate procedure" for congressional consideration of sales, Aspin says that the existence of the procedure can itself be a factor in affecting executive decisions.[75] An administration may be dissuaded from proposing a sale because of the procedure and the fear that Congress might turn it down.

Andrew Pierre notes that Congress is not prepared

nor equipped in time and staff to make case-by-case or country-by-country decisions on every arms sales. But, because sales are subject to scrutiny on Capitol Hill, Pierre says, Congress has served as an inhibiting factor on some prospective sales that were likely to be seen as excessive.[76]

Senator Joseph Biden (D-Delaware), a member of the Senate Foreign Relations Committee who has been involved in considering many arms sales proposals, acknowledges that Congress may not have been particularly successful in limiting the quantity of weapons transfers. However, one of the major reasons Congress became involved in arms sales issues was because, beginning with the Country X program, arms sales were becoming an increasingly important component of American foreign policy. (See Table 5.2.) Congress acted, as Biden said, "to restrict the ability of the executive to initiate independently and to carry out, without the participation of Congress, major foreign policy changes."[77]

What Congress set out to do, Biden points out, was "to make itself part of the game,"[78] and, in that sense, it has been successful.

The Supreme Court's 1983 ruling that the legislative veto is unconstitutional left the status of the congressional procedure on arms sales in an uncertain state. (The Court, in Immigration and Naturalization Service v. Chadha, said legislative vetoes violate the constitutional requirements preserving the separation of powers.) However, even without the legislative veto, there are ample means for Congress to have an impact on arms sales if it chooses to use them. As noted earlier, Congress could, for example, require affirmative congressional action on major sales--relying on approval rather than the disapproval procedure, as has been the case under the Arms Export Control Act.

The executive will retain the initiative in arms sales. If Congress is to continue to be part of the game, it will probably have to reassert itself periodically, as it has done since its initial involvement with arms sales, and to insist on playing and active role.

TABLE 5.2
United States Arms Sales

Fiscal Year	U.S. Dollars
1950-70	12,934,000,000
1971	1,390,000,000
1972	2,950,000,000
1973	4,848,000,000
1974	10,343,000,000
1975	16,053,000,000
1976	14,673,000,000
1977	8,305,000,000
1978	11,039,000,000
1979	13,014,000,000
1980	15,277,000,000
1981	8,525,000,000
1982	21,500,000,000

Source: These figures are based on information from official government and congressional sources. However, there are contradictions and inconsistencies in the figures provided by various agencies. Therefore, the figures should be regarded as indicative of general trends rather than representative of precise arms transfers totals. There are also differences in sales agreements and actual deliveries. In recent years, the Reagan Administration has released figures showing U.S. arms sales agreements with Third World countries. According to the Administration, these were: FY 1978 - $7.5 billion; FY 1979 - $9 billion; FY 1980 - $10 billion; FY 1981 - $4.9 billion. By contrast, according to the Administration, the figures for Soviet agreements to sell arms to the Third World during the same period were: FY 1978 - $3 billion; FY 1979 - $8.9 billion; FY 1980 - $14.8 billion; FY 1981 - $6.6 billion.

NOTES

1. Andrew J. Pierre, "Arms Sales: The New Diplomacy," Foreign Affairs 60, winter 1981-82, pp.266-267.
2. Figures from Committee on Foreign Affairs, U.S. House of Representatives, cited in Congress and the Nation: Volume 2, 1967 Chronology (Washington: Congressional Quarterly Press, 1968), p.87.
3. U.S. Congress, Senate, Committe on Foreign Relations, Arms Sales and Foreign Policy, Staff Study, January 25, 1967.
4. Ibid.
5. Ibid., pp.7-8.

6. Letter, Thomas E. Morgan to Robert S. McNamara, December 20, 1963 (Agency File, Defense, National Security Files), Johnson Presidential Library, Austin.

7. Report of the Senate Foreign Relations Committee on S.1872, Foreign Assistance Act of 1967, Enrolled Legislation, P.L.90-137 (Special Files), Johnson Presidential Library, Austin.

8. Memorandum (r to M), August 26, 1964 (C.F. FG 220, White House Central Files), Johnson Presidential Library, Austin.

9. U.S. Congress, House, Hearings before the Committee on Banking and Currency on H.R.6649, July 17, 1967, p.4.

10. U.S. Congress, Senate, Hearings before the Committee on Appropriations on H.R.17788, April 20, 1966, pp.20-30.

11. Memorandum, Horace Busby, Special Assistant to the President, to Walt Rostow, National Security Advisor, September 21, 1966 (C.F. FG 220, White House Central Files), Johnson Presidential Library, Austin.

12. Senate Foreign Relations Committee, Arms Sales and Foreign Policy, 1967.

13. Interview with William B. Bader, July 9, 1982.

14. U.S. Congress, Senate, Hearings before the Committee on Banking and Currency on S.1155, July 25, 1967, p.4.

15. Senate Foreign Relations Committee, Foreign Assistance Act of 1967, pp.208-212.

16. Ibid., pp.294-295.

17. Ibid., pp.273-274.

18. Presidential Message to Congress on Foreign Aid, U.S. House of Representatives, 89th Cong., 2d sess., Doc.374, February 1, 1966.

19. U.S. Congress, House, Hearings before the House Committee on Banking and Currency on H.R.6649, September 1967, p.38.

20. Letter, John McNaugton, Department of Defense, to Walt Rostow, July 5, 1967 (Department of Defense, Agency File, National Security File), Johnson Presidential Library, Austin.

21. Memorandum, Richard Moose, National Security Council staff, to Walt Rostow, July 18, 1967 (Department of Defense, Agency File, National Security File), Johnson Presidential Library, Austin.

22. Congressional Quarterly, vol.28, 1968, pp.191-192.

23. Neil Sheehan, "Arms Sales Fight Takes New Tact," The New York Times, July 30, 1967, p.8.

24. Congressional Record, Senate, August 15, 1967, p.22639.

25. Ibid., p.22641.

26. Ibid., p.22631.

27. Ibid., p.22648.

28. Ibid., p.22643.

29. Ibid
30. Ibid., p.22655.
31. Ibid., p.22659.
32. Ibid., p.22660.
33. Felix Belair, Jr., (The New York Times), "House Unit Restrict Sale of Arms Under Aid Bill," International Herald Tribune, Paris, November 2, 1967.
34. Letter, William Gaud, Administrator, Agency for International Development, to Wilfred Rommel, Bureau of the Budget, November 13, 1967, Enrolled Legislation, P.L.90-137 (Special Files) Johnson Presidential Library, Austin.
35. Congress and the Nation, vol.II, pp.86-88.
36. Robert Siner, "President Signs Aid Bill, Bids Congress Reconsider," International Herald Tribune, Paris, November 16, 1967.
37. Congress and the Nation, vol.II, p.107.
38. Ibid., p.110.
39. U.S. Congress, Senate, War Powers Legislation, 1973, Hearings before the Committee on Foreign Relations on S.440, 93rd Cong., 1st sess., April 1973, p.148.
40. Statement by Senator J. W. Fulbright on S.3475, before the Subcommittee of Separation of Powers, Senate Committee on the Judiciary, April 24, 1972. (Fulbright Press Release #8, 1972)
41. S. Res. 85, 91st Cong., 1st sess., Congressional Record, p.S17245, 1969.
42. War Powers Resolution, P.L.93-148, approved November 7, 1973.
43. U.S. Congress, Senate, Committee on Foreign Relations, Report on S.2443, The Foreign Military Sales and Assistance Act, Report 93-189, 1973.
44. U.S. Congress, Senate, Committee on Foreign Relations, Report on S.2662, International Security Assistance and Arms Export Control Act of 1976, Report 94-605, January 30, 1976, p.6.
45. U.S. Congress, House, Committee on International Relations (Foreign Affairs), Congress and Foreign Policy--1975, Committee Print, 1976, pp.70-71.
46. U.S. Congress, Senate, Committee on Foreign Relations, Legislative Activities Report of the Committee on Foreign Relations, 94th Cong., 1975-76, February 21, 1977,
47. U.S. Congress, Senate, Committee on Foreign Relations, Hearings on Near East and South East Asia, 90th Cong., 1st sess., March 14, 1967, p.110.
48. Richard T. Sale, "The Shah's America," The Washington Post, May 12, 1977.
49. George F. Kennan, The Cloud of Danger: Current Realities of American Foreign Policy (Boston: Little, Brown, 1977), p.87.
50. Congressional Record, Senate, May 20, 1977, p.S8242.

134

51. _Public Papers of the President_, Jimmy Carter, 1977 (Washington: Government Printing Office, 1977-1978, 2 vols.), II, 2221.

52. _Congressional Record_, Senate, May 24, 1977, p.S8542.

53. Interview with John Culver, July 20, 1982.

54. Norman Kempster, "GAO Sees Peril in Sale of Radar Planes," _Los Angeles Times_, July 16, 1977; also Staff memorandum, Senate Foreign Relations Committee, July 1977, p.3.

55. Letter, Senator Robert C. Byrd to President Jimmy Carter, July 22, 1977.

56. _Congressional Record_, Senate, July 29, 1977, pp.S13085-13086.

57. _Congressional Record_, Senate, October 7, 1977, p.S16620.

58. Ibid., p.S16621.

59. Middle East Aircraft Package, Reference Papers, Department of State, March 1978; Announcement by Secretary of State Cyrus Vance, February 14, 1978, Department of State Press Release #75.

60. _Congressional Record_, Senate, May 15, 1978, p.S7435.

61. _Congressional Record_, May 15, 1978.

62. See "The U.S. in the Middle East: A Forceful or Fearful Foreign Policy?" Speech by Thomas A. Dine, Executive Director, American Israel Public Affairs Committee, AIPAC Policy Conference, Washington, D.C. May 18, 1981; Paul Taylor, "Lobbying on AWACS," _The Washington Post_, September 28, 1981.

63. Thomas B. Edsall, "Conservatives, Corporations Aided AWACS," _The Washington Post_, November 1, 1981; Steve Emerson, "The Petrodollar Connection," _New Republic_ 186, February 17, 1982, pp.18-25.

64. James McCartney, (Knight-Ridder), "President Wins Victory on AWACS," _Dallas Times Herald_, October 29, 1981.

65. Lee Lescaze, "President, Hill Make 'a Nice Save'," _The Washington Post_, October 30, 1981.

66. Howell Raines, "A One-Time Dividend on a High-Risk Investment," _The New York Times_, November 1, 1981.

67. U.S. Congress, House of Representatives, Committee on Foreign Affairs, _Executive-Legislative Consultation on U.S. Arms Sales_, Congress and Foreign Policy Series No.7, Congressional Research Service, Library of Congress (Study prepared by Richard Grimmett), December 1982, p.3.

68. _Congressional Quarterly_, October 31, 1981, p.2096.

69. Ibid.

70. Charles H. Percy, "The Partisan Gap," _Foreign Policy_ 45, winter 1981-82, pp.8-9.

71. John G. Tower, "Congress Versus the President: The Formulation and Implementation of American Foreign Policy," Foreign Affairs 60, winter 1981-82, p.234.

72. Ibid., p.237.

73. Ibid., p.235.

74. Arms Sales: A Useful Foreign Policy Tool? AEI Forum 56, American Enterprise Institute for Public Policy Research, Washington, September 1981, p.8.

75. Ibid., p.13.

76. Andrew J. Pierre, The Global Politics of Arms Sales (Princeton: Princeton University Press, 1982), p.51.

77. Arms Sales: A Useful Foreign Policy Tool? p.13.

78. Ibid.

6
Nuclear Nonproliferation

Steven J. Baker

Israel's June 1981 air attack on the Iraqi nuclear research reactor revived interest in a set of policy issues that the Reagan Administration seemed inclined to ignore, but which had enjoyed high visibility during the Carter Administration. Early in 1981, President Reagan had declared that proliferation was none of America's business, and Secretary of State Alexander Haig had sought to lower the priority of nonproliferation policy, without abandoning the objectives altogether. Newly appointed Secretary of Energy James Edwards advocated steps towards the so-called "plutonium economy," notably by proposing the licensing of the Barnwell, South Carolina nuclear fuel reprocessing plant; operation of this plant had been blocked by President Carter as part of his nonproliferation policy.

With the Israelis practicing "assertive nonproliferation," the Reagan Administration was reminded that the spread of nuclear weapons capabilities continues to be a source of instability in various parts of the world, and that this instability can directly impinge on American foreign policy objectives. In the Middle East, the United States finds itself in the uncomfortable position of seeking to be an ally of both sides in the Arab-Israeli dispute; hence the Israeli raid on Iraq had the result of worsening U.S. relations both with Israel and with major Arab allies such as Saudi Arabia. In the short run, the on-going effort by State Department negotiator Philip Habib to achieve a ceasefire between Israel and Lebanon was sidetracked, the proposed sale of AWACS to Saudi Arabia became even more controversial, the delivery of jets to Israel was suspended, and the U.S. for the first time joined with other United Nations Security Council members in a unanimous censure of Israel's action.

In the wake of the Baghdad raid, the Reagan Administration hastily issued a policy statement endorsing nonproliferation, but it was clearly responding to events rather than articulating well-planned objectives. Resolutions calling for an Administration nonproliferation policy statement had already been introduced in Congress.[1] The Administration had earlier raised questions about its nonproliferation policy by reviving the proposal to resume military and economic aid to Pakistan, even though Pakistan is persisting in its "Islamic bomb" program. And soon after the Israeli raid against Iraq, the U.S. announced that the nuclear cooperation agreement with Egypt, pending since 1974, would finally be implemented, with U.S. industries authorized to supply Egypt with nuclear power reactors. Once the shipment of jets to Israel was resumed, wags began to suggest that the Reagan Administration's nonproliferation policy was to supply Israel with the offensive capability to knock out her neighbors' nuclear capabilities, while supplying Israel's neighbors with the appropriate targets.

Policy Contradictions

Contradictions in American nonproliferation policy are nothing new. Since 1945, American policy for dealing with the spread of nuclear weapons has zigged and zagged. In the early years of the Carter Administration, a more coherent policy emerged: This involved cooperation with other industrial countries to block emergence of additional nuclear weapons capabilities through export controls and reassesment of domestic nuclear energy programs. After three years, the Carter Administration policy began to show serious contradicttions, while the Reagan Administration reached that point in six months. In fairness to the Reagan Administration, two points deserve emphasis: first, the shift toward downgrading nonproliferation as a U.S. policy objective came in the last year of the Carter Administration, not in the first year of the Reagan Administration. By proposing to resume military and economic aid to Pakistan in the wake of the December 1979 Soviet invasion of Afghanistan, the Carter Administration signaled that it was prepared to subordinate its global nonproliferation strategy to regional geopolitical objectives. In essence, this was also the Reagan Administration's nonproliferation policy.[2] The contradictions that result are less attributable to a particular administration than they are inherent in a selective nonproliferation policy, one where nonproliferation pressures are applied to some countries but not to others.

A second point that should be emphasized is that the direction nonproliferation policy takes will depend in large part on the U.S. Congress. Nonproliferation policy is no longer an exclusive executive prerogative, but is embodied in U.S. statutes. If the Reagan Administration is determined to abandon a universal approach to nonproliferation in favor of a case-by-case approach, it will have to seek the cooperation of Congress, because various legislative measures are in force that require a universal policy. Indeed, following Israeli attack against Iraq, steps were taken in Congress to initiate a review of nonproliferation legislation with an eye toward revisions that would reflect a shift in U.S. policy.[3] The need for such a revision had already been established in the last year of the Carter Administration.

President Reagan scored an initial success when Congress voted to authorize a resumption of aid to Pakistan, waiving the provisions of the Symington amendment to the Foreign Assistance Act that had been the basis for cutting off aid to Pakistan in early 1979.[4] But the Reagan Administration's attempts to get legislative approval for a major shift in nonproliferation policy were blocked. Nonproliferation policy presented the Reagan Administration with the challenge of articulating a policy that augured to be effective abroad while maintaining support in Congress.

Congress and Nonproliferation

Nonproliferation policy is a prime example of the reassertion of congressional foreign policy prerogatives in the 1970s. Congress took the lead on nonproliferation policy in the faces of indifference and occasional hostility on the part of the Nixon and Ford Administrations. Nonproliferation policy achieved some coherence during the first three years of the Carter Administration because a convergence of views between Congress and the Administration made cooperation possible. These views diverged in the last year of the Carter Administration, particularly as a result of the controversy over shipping nuclear fuel to India.

The Indian case was an important turning point. Its significance predated the Carter Administration and its effects will last long into the future. Although India refused to comply with the provisions of the Nuclear Nonproliferation Act of 1978 (NNPA), President Carter approved the shipment to India of 38 tons of nuclear fuel for U.S.-supplied power reactors. The President's action was overwhelmingly disapproved by the House of Representatives, but narrowly upheld by the Senate. Thus, even before the advent of the Reagan Administration in 1981, there was an apparent shift in U.S. nonproliferation policy that raised fundamental questions about both the role of Congress in foreign policy and about the future of nonproliferation policy: Had Congress lost the initiative, so recently acquired, in foreign policy? Had U.S. nonproliferation policy lost its coherence?

Joint Committee on Atomic Energy

Congressional involvement in nonproliferation policy can be traced back to the immediate postwar years. The 1946 Atomic Energy Act created the Atomic Energy Commission (AEC), and entrusted supervision of the Atomic Energy Commission to two political authorities-- the congressional Joint Committee on Atomic Energy (JCAE) and the President. While there was initial uncertainty as to who was favored in this distribution of authority, over time the Joint Committe on Atomic Energy came to play a role in nuclear policy that went far beyond legislative oversight, often prevailing over the President.[4]

The Joint Committee on Atomic Energy was designed to reconcile the demands of nuclear technology and democracy. The Joint Committee's nine representatives and nine senators were given broad jurisdiction over the nations' nuclear activities, but were also enjoined to maintain a high level of secrecy to protect national security. This secrecy, combined with the highly technical nature of nuclear policy questions, reinforced the Joint Committee's statutory monopoly on nuclear policy in Congress.

The President also had advantages in his role in the nuclear policy field. The President's predominance in foreign policy, his power to appoint Atomic Energy Commission members, and to propose the Atomic Energy Commission budget made him a key source of nuclear policy initiatives. But often the Joint Committee on Atomic Energy proved to be the more assertive of the two political masters of the Atomic Energy Commission.[5] The predominance of the Joint Committee over the President in nuclear policy was further strengthened as civil nuclear policy became a policy priority along with nuclear weapons, reducing the national security implications of nuclear policy.

Powerful and ambitious Joint Committee members pursued a few, well-defined nuclear policy goals. Through long tenure on the Committee, men such as Senators Brian McMahon, Burke Hickenlooper, Clinton Anderson, John Pastore, and Representatives Craig Hosmer, Chet Holifield, and Melvin Price were able to acquire a high degree of specialized knowledge which gave greater authority to the Joint Committee and reinforced their personal influence in Congress. This influence was used to foster a "vigorous, imaginative, and aggressive atomic energy program, demanding boldness and risk-taking rather than caution and economy."[6] Successive presidents lagged behind the committee in enthusiasm for bold nuclear programs, often preferring small-scale projects.

While the Joint Committee divided internally, some-times along partisan lines, on issues such as public versus private electric power, the committee generally supported the twin goals of developing commerical nu-clear energy and modernizing nuclear weapons. The Joint Committee could claim major responsibility for such significant steps as development of the H-bomb, expansion and diversification of American nuclear ar-senal, development of nuclear-propelled submarines, and development of a commercial nuclear power plant for generating electricity.

Given its central role in nuclear policy, the Joint Committee necessarily influenced U.S. foreign policy as well as domestic policy. Generally, the committee tended to resist the relaxation of nuclear secrecy against pressures from the executive and private indus-try for greater access. For example, the Joint Commit-tee completely rewrote the Eisenhower Administration's Atoms for Peace proposals. The resulting revision of the Atomic Energy Act permitted the sharing of peaceful nuclear technology with friendly countries and nuclear weapons technology with selected allies subject to the committee's authority to oversee this sharing.[7]

The Joint Committee was more reluctant than the Ad-ministration to share nuclear weapons technology with allies. For example, the Joint Committee helped to block nuclear aid to France when Secretary of State John Foster Dulles seemed to favor such a possibility.[8] The committee was also concerned lest the Administra-tion "give away" peaceful nuclear technology developed at the American public's expense. For example, the 1958 U.S.-Euratom Joint Program subsidized the export of several power reactors to Western Europe, along with fuels and technical assistance for European research and power programs. The Joint Committee supported this program as a means of opening the European market to the eventual sale of American nuclear power plants.[9]

New Congressional Role

Given this history of involvement in all aspects of nuclear policy, it is not surprising that Congress should have taken the initiative on nonproliferation policy in the mid-1970s. What was new about nonprolif-eration policy as it emerged from Congress in the mid-1970s was that it reflected a different set of concerns and involved a different set of actors than before. The Joint Committee had been concerned with reconciling national security interests in maintaining the secrecy on nuclear technology with economic interest in promot-ing the development of a nuclear energy industry. As dependence on nuclear energy grew in the late 1960s, doubts began to be expressed about the safety and economic viability of nuclear plants. As the salience of the nuclear energy question grew, a larger number of people sought to influence nuclear policy, challenging the monopoly of the Joint Committee within Congress.[10] The first casualty of this shift in the policy context was the Atomic Energy Commission. It was broken up in 1974 because its goals of promoting and regulating nuclear energy were seen as increasingly incompatible. The Energy Research and Development Agency (ERDA) and the Nuclear Regulatory Commission were set up to take the place of the Atomic Energy Commission, and in 1977, the Department of Energy replaced the Energy Research and Development Agency.

The Indian nuclear test explosion in May 1974, served as a catalyst for linking growing doubts about the wisdom of U.S. domestic nuclear energy policy with growing concern about the worldwide proliferation of nuclear weapons. There was a feeling that the Joint Committee had been co-opted by the nuclear energy promoters, and, ironically, the Joint Committee was seen as having been insufficiently cognizant of the dangers of nuclear proliferation inherent in the export of U.S. nuclear fuels and facilities. In sum, nuclear policy had become too important to be left to a small number of "initiates."

In the wake of the Indian nuclear test, there were several congressional attempts to make American nuclear export policy more restrictive, initiatives that were generally opposed by the executive branch. Under President Ford, preventing the spread of nuclear weapons capabilities began to receive more emphasis. The Ford Administration began to seek cooperation among nuclear suppliers, but did not welcome efforts in Congress, usually led by Democrats, to legislate nonproliferation policy changes. In the House, Representatives Richard Ottinger (D-New York), Clarence Long (D-Maryland), and Jonathan Bingham (D-New York) were active in moves to wrest control of nonproliferation policy from the Administration and the Joint Committee. In the Senate, the Government Operations Committee, under the leadership of Abraham Ribicoff (D-Connecticut), attempted to draft a comprehensive nonproliferation policy. Democratic Senators Stuart Symington and John Glenn sponsored legislation to cut off U.S. aid to countries importing uranium enrichment facilities and plutonium reprocessing facilities because these would provide direct access to weapons material.[11] Finally, in 1977 the Joint Committee on Atomic Energy was disbanded. From that time forward, a number of Senate and House committees would compete for control over various aspects of nuclear policy.

Nonproliferation Legislation

The advent of the Carter Administration in 1977 provided a favorable climate for cooperation with Congress, with the Democrats controlling both Houses as well as the White House. Carter had seized on the nonproliferation issue early in his presidential campaign, and in April 1977 he submitted to Congress his Nuclear Nonproliferation Policy Act. Over the next year, the Administration bill was considered by several committees in both Houses, along with two other major pieces of nonproliferation legislation--one emanating from the House Foreign Affairs Committee and one reflecting the views of Senator Glenn, Charles Percy, and others. What resulted from these deliberations was the Nuclear Nonproliferation Act of 1978 (NNPA), a tangled compromise among the major actors that fully satisfied no one but was acceptable to most. Passed in the House by a vote of 411 to 0 and in the Senate by a vote of 88 to 3, the Nonproliferation Act of 1978 was signed into law on March 10, 1978.

The Nonproliferation Act is a dense, often redundant piece of legislation that establishes statutory guidelines for a universally applicable nonproliferation policy based on restricting American nuclear energy exports. First, it establishes "fullscope safeguards" as a criterion for receiving any nuclear material or nuclear facilities from the U.S. In other words, if nations are to receive nuclear materials or facilities from the U.S., they must allow international inspection of all of their nuclear facilities, not just those supplied by the U.S. This provision has been referred to as a kind of "poor man's Nonproliferation Treaty," having direct impact on a handful of nations that have nuclear agreements for cooperation with the U.S., that have not ratified the Nonproliferation Treaty (NPT), and that have some nuclear facilities not presently being inspected by the International Atomic Energy Agency (IAEA)--nations such as India, Argentina, Spain, and South Africa.

A second, corollary provision of the Nonproliferation Act called for the renegotiation of all existing agreements for cooperation with othe countries to reflect the changes in American law embodied in the Nonproliferation Act. If the renegotiation efforts failed in the 18 months alloted, then the Nonproliferation Act requires an end to nuclear cooperation with the country in question.

A third provision of the Nonproliferation Act gives the Nuclear Regulatory Commission (NRC) a role in nuclear export license approval. For example, the NRC is to judge whether full-scope safeguards are in effect, and whether physical security measures are adequate in countries seeking to import nuclear fuels or facilities

from the U.S. Giving this responsibility to an independent regulatory agency diminished the control of the
President over nuclear exports and enlarged the formal
responsibilities of the NRC, extending its responsibilities abroad.

A fourth provision of the Nonproliferation Act
asserts American control over other nations' reprocessing of spent nuclear fuel of American origin. Most
existing agreements for cooperation establish that no
American-supplied fuel can be reprocessed without
mutual agreement between the U.S. and the country in
question; however, the agreements are not uniform and
this provision of the Nonproliferation Act was intended
to close any possible loopholes.

Finally, the Nonproliferation Act allows the
President to waive the provisions of the act and
authorize a nuclear energy export if he judges that
"withholding the proposed export would be seriously
prejidicial to the achievement of United States nonproliferation objective, or would otherwise jeopardize
the common defense and security." A presidential
waiver would, however, be subject to review by Congress through a "legislative veto"*--the President's
waiver could be blocked by a concurrent resolution of
disapproval, requiring a majority vote of both
Houses.12

With the Nonproliferation Act, Congress had enacted
a stringent nonproliferation policy, based on the perceived link between civil nuclear energy programs and
nuclear weapons capabilities. This policy was nondis-
criminatory, applicable to all countries that cooperate
with the U.S. in nuclear energy. The Carter Administration enthusiastically endorsed nonproliferation,
only objecting to a few of the most restrictive provisions of the Nonproliferation Act such as the legislative veto of a presidential waiver.

On the other hand, Congress balked at one part of
the Carter Administration's nonproliferation policy:
Carter sought to bring U.S. domestic policy into line
with his international nonproliferation objectives by
discouraging U.S. moves toward the reprocessing of
spent nuclear fuels by the recycling of plutonium in
light water and breeder reactors. Carter also sought
to discourage other nations from reprocessing spent
fuel, avoiding the development of a so-called "plutonium economy" worldwide. But while Congress acquiesced
in postponing indefinitely commercial reprocessing in
the U.S., it frustrated Administration efforts to
eliminate the Clinch River fast breeder reactor proto-
type under construction in Tennessee. As a result of

---

*See Chapters 1, 5, and 8 for discussion of the 1983
Supreme Court decision concerning legislative vetoes.

porkbarrel politics, Congress kept alive the plutonium-fueled fast-breeder program at Clinch River. The result was a $15-million-a-month boondoggle that was no longer a logical part of the nation's nuclear energy program. Congress' action on Clinch River suggested to some foreigners that America might not be completely sincere in its efforts against the plutonium economy.

The Indian Nuclear Fuel Case

The controversy over the export of 38 tons of nuclear fuel to India came to a head in the summer of 1980. This controversy was important for two reason: it was the first major test of the provisions of the Nonproliferation Act of 1978, and it came in the wake of the Soviet invasion of Afghanistan. Therefore, this issue was widely perceived as pitting nonproliferation policy against geopolitical preoccupations in South Asia. Since the Carter Administration had vigorously supported nonproliferation policy during its first three years, its advocacy of the Indian nuclear fuel exports was seen by many as a significant reversal, the kind of policy zig-zag for which the Administration was widely criticized. The question was whether Congress would follow the President's lead in this policy shift, and if it were to do so, what the implications would be for nonproliferation policy in the future.

As provided in the legislation, during the 18 months after the March 1978 enactment of the Nonproliferation Act, the U.S. had sought to persuade the Indian government to accept the "comprehensive safeguards" on all of its nuclear facilities, as a condition for continuing to receive American nuclear fuels. The Desai government in India seemed genuinely opposed to further nuclear tests or a nuclear weapons development program, but it refused to accept comprehensive safeguards as a matter of principle. The negotiations on revising the nuclear cooperation agreement foundered. The return to power of Indira Gandhi in January 1980, changed both the tone of Indian policy and the substance. Mrs. Gandhi refused to rule out future nuclear tests, and her government openly threatened that the U.S. failure to supply India with nuclear fuel would be considered a unilateral U.S. abrogation of the 1963 agreement for cooperation.

The Gandhi government argued that abrogation would remove existing safeguards from U.S.-supplied facilities and spent fuel stockpiles in India, and permit India to seek nuclear fuel supplies for American power reactors elsewhere--i.e., from the Soviet Union. India would also feel free to reprocess the 200 tons of U.S.-supplied spent fuel stockpiled in India, and to recycle the plutonium obtained from the spent fuel in the

Tarapur reactors, or use reprocessed fuel in its breeder reactor program. India might even use U.S.-derived plutonium as part of a weapons program at some time in the future.[13] The State Department denied that the Indian threats constituted a case of "nuclear blackmail," but the U.S. government fears about the consequences of stopping the supply of nuclear fuel to India proved an ironic twist to the "leverage" argument that is so often used to justify American nuclear exports: far from inhibiting India's pursuit of its own nuclear policy objectives, U.S. nuclearaid had given India considerable influence over U.S. nonproliferation policy.

Two legal questions dominate the controversy. First, did the Nonproliferation Act of 1978 supercede the 1963 U.S.-India agreement for cooperation? The Indian government argued that the U.S. could not unilaterally alter the terms of an existing international agreement, and the State Department agreed that the U.S. had a legal commitment to continue to supply fuel to India.[14] The second legal question was more complicated: could shipments of nuclear fuel be made after 24 months from the Nonproliferation Act's passage if, as in the Indian case, these licenses were properly filed during the law's 18 month renegotiation period? The Administration argued that these licenses should be approved, even though India did not conform to the standards of the Nonproliferation Act, because the licenses were filed within the 18-month period.[15] But the Nuclear Regulatory Commission ruled that because 24 months had elapsed from the date of passage of the Nonproliferation Act, the 18-month renegotiation period and a 6-month grace period, no licenses could be approved to countries not meeting Nonproliferation Act standards.[16] Unfortunately, the legislative history was not clear on Congress' intent regarding the relevant provisions of the Nonproliferation Act.

These legal arguments raised important policy questions. Supporters of nuclear exports argued that the U.S. had a legal commitment under the 1963 agreement to supply the Tarapur reactors with nuclear fuel. However, opponents of the exports pointed out that the Indian government had flaunted the 1963 "peaceful uses" agreement when it used American-supplied heavy water to produce the plutonium for its 1974 nuclear explosion. Export opponents also argued that the 1963 agreement and agreements pursuant to it had to be consistent with American law, and that there were ample precedents for changes in American law governing foreign ownership and use of nuclear materials.[17]

Although the Administration insisted that support for these two fuel shipments would not constitute a precedent, Deputy Secretary of State Warren Christopher refused to rule out additional shipments to India beyond the disputed licenses.[18] But opponents argued that if the U.S. were to refuse fuel shipments in the future, the Indians would once again cry "abrogation." Opponents also argued that the approval of the two pending licenses would only add to the stockpile of spent fuel that the Indians would eventually feel free to use, or abuse, as they saw fit--better to end cooperation now than in the future.

Beyond a possible precedent for future Indian fuel shipments, approving these licenses might have implications for nuclear fuel shipments to nations such as South Africa, Spain, and Argentina. Each of these nations has fuel-supply agreements with the U.S. that predate the Nonproliferation Act; none has been willing to accept comprehensive safeguards, and each had fuel license applications pending in 1979. South Africa is suspected of having a nuclear weapons development program, and Argentina is a "nuclear threshhold" country.

It is significant that legal arguments should play so prominent a part in the resolution of a question that is fundamentally political. For legislators, many of whom are lawyers, legal arguments have deep appeal, especially where the level of interest in or information about the political substance of the issue is relatively low. It may well be, as Senator Glenn concluded, that the Administration's legal case tipped the scales in the President's favor in the Senate, and thereby determined an outcome favorable to the Administration.[19]

Compared to these rather arcane legal points, the geopolitical calculations behind the Carter Administration's endorsement of the fuel export licenses were obvious. The Russian invasion of Afghanistan in December 1979 reinforced frantic attempts to bolster the U.S. position in an area which had already been seen as volatile as a result of the Iranian hostage crisis. The initiative for these attempts, like much of the foreign policy of the last year of the Carter Administration, came from the National Security Council.

It was National Security Advisor Zbigniew Brzezinski who publicly offered to extend military aid to Pakistan without first consulting either Pakistan or the Congress. The failure to consult Pakistan contributed to the ultimate rejection by General Mohammed Zia-ul-Haq, the Pakistani leader, of the $450 million aid package as "peanuts."[20] Brzezinski made a highly publicized trip to Pakistan, and was photographed pointing a rifle in the direction of Soviet troops on the other side of the Khyber Pass. Thus, Brzezinski managed to further increase tensions with the Soviet Union while failing to win the support of Pakistan. Advance consultation with Congress was important, since assistance to Pakistan had been cut off earlier in 1979 as a result of the 1975 Symington amendment to the Foreign Assistance Act. Pakistan is known to be proceeding with a clandestine uranium-enrichment program as part of the effort to construct an "Islamic bomb."[21] The U.S. aid cutoff was required by the Symington amendment, and only a presidential ruling that supreme U.S. interests were involved could clear the way for the necessary congressional approval of aid to Pakistan. Given the situation in Southwest Asia after the invasion of Afghanistan, there was support in the Senate for allowing the resumption of military aid to Pakistan. However, there was little support in Congress for what General Zia really wanted and what Brzezinski proposed informally: a long-term militray commitment guaranteeing Pakistan's security. The Senate was prepared to go no further than responding to the present emergency, without assuming long-term obligations. Sentiment toward Pakistan was not altogether favorable on Capitol Hill: only a few months earlier, a mob had sacked and burned the U.S. Embassy in Islamabad, and the Zia government had done little to protect the American personnel and their dependents.

Administration support for the Indian nuclear fuel licenses emerged as part of a regional balancing act. If the U.S. proposed to help Pakistan, and had to bend U.S. nonproliferation policy in order to do so, then the U.S. had to do something for India at the same time. The pending nuclear fuel licenses provided a neat solution. However, the Administration persisted in trying to provide the fuel to India even after the collapse of the effort to renew aid to Pakistan. President Carter promised to deliver the fuel to India in a private letter to Mrs. Gandhi, and the Administration thereafter argued that the U.S. was "committed" to this course of action.

The $1.6-billion arms deal between the U.S.S.R. and India, announced in May 1980, paradoxically strengthened the determination of the Carter Administration to deliver the nuclear fuel to India. Opponents of the fuel export pointed to Mrs. Gandhi's growing dependence on the U.S.S.R. and her initially uncritical reaction to Soviet intervention in Afghanistan, and asked, "Why should we do her any favors?" But the Administration argued that because Soviet influence in India was growing, the U.S. had to compete.[22] The nuclear fuel export licenses were a pending issue that could be implemented quickly, without major resource allocation problems.

The bureaucratic line-up on the nuclear fuel license case was more complex than usual. Brzezinski and the National Security Council initiated the policy to bolster the U.S. position in South Asia, but the execution of the fuel license policy was largely left to the State Department. The State Department was divided internally along fairly predictable lines. The country office people--those who followed U.S.-India

relations on a day-to-day basis--supported the fuel
exports as a means of bettering relations with India.
Many State Department area specialists had never given
more than luke-warm support to a comprehensive
nonproliferation policy. By training and institutional
interest, they tended toward a "case-by-case" approach
to nonproliferation, which usually meant trying to prevent nonproliferation policy from damaging U.S. relations with their particular countries. This approach
had prevailed in the Nixon-Ford Administration decision
to not protest the 1974 Indian test explosion, and in
moves to improve ties with Brazil in the wake of the
1975 German-Brazilian nuclear energy agreement. Within
the State Department, support for the Carter Administration's comprehensive nonproliferation policy was to
be found mostly in those offices with functional responsibilities that cut across specific regional bound-
aries--International Security Assistance, Political-
Military Affairs, and Policy Planning. The influence
of nonproliferation advocates in the State Department
waned with the departure of key Carter appointees such
as Joseph Nye and Leslie Gelb, and many believed that
Carter's appointee as especial ambassador for nonproliferation, veteran diplomat Gerard Smith, had stepped
back from the earlier, aggressive nonproliferation policy. Coincidentially, Smith had negotiated the 1963
nuclear cooperation agreement with India and he strongly supported the President's decision to ship nuclear
fuel to India.

However, it came as a surprise to many that the new
Secretary of State Edmund Muskie, chose to side with
the supporters of the Indian fuel exports. Muskie had
resigned from the Senate in April 1980, to succeed
Cyrus Vance at the Department of State. Muskie's record in the Senate and the views of some of his staff
created speculation that Muskie might reverse the
decision to go ahead with the Indian fuel licenses as a
last-minute "midnight judges" attempt to present the
new Secretary of State with a fait accompli. If this
was indeed the intent, it apparently worked; within a
few days of becoming the Secretary of State, Muskie
became the Administration's most effective advocate on
behalf of the nuclear fuels exports to India.

The other important institutional actor was the
Nuclear Regulatory Commission. Of the five commissioners, only Victor Gilinsky had a strong record in
favor of a vigorous nonproliferation policy. Gilinsky
lobbied actively against shipping nuclear fuel to
India. The positions of most of the other Nuclear
Regulatory Commissioners against the Indian nuclear
licenses indicated that their unanimous rejection of
the licenses was based on their limited statutory authority. In other words, even though they felt prohibited by the terms of the Nonproliferation Act from

approving the licenses themselves, they did not necessarily oppose the President acting by executive order.[23] The legally circumscribed position of the Nuclear Regulatory Commission did, however, serve to put
the burden of proof on the President--and, given the
situation in the summer of 1980, President Carter was
forced, in turn, to convince the U.S. Senate.

Focusing on the Senate

The ultimate responsibility for deciding the Indian
fuel licenses export question fell to the Senate because the Nonproliferation Act requires a concurrent
resolution of disapproval to block a presidential executive order--i.e., a majority vote of both Houses
against the President. Under the Nonproliferation Act,
the Congress provided a check on the executive by giving the authority to license nuclear exports to the independent Nuclear Regulatory Commission. By giving the
President the option to proceed counter to a Nuclear
Regulatory Commission ruling, Congress provided the
President with discretion and flexibility to be used in
exceptional circumstances. And, by retaining the option to review a presidential exception, Congress provided a mechanism for assuring that the intent of the
Nonproliferation Act would not be ignored unless Congress agreed with the President that it should be.
This is an example of the kind of legislation device
that Congress sees as essential to its "oversight"
functions but which the executive branch often feels
encroaches on its prerogatives to "execute" the law.
From the beginning, the House seemed certain to
reject the presidential order. On June 11, Clement
Zablocki, Chairman of the House Foreign Affairs Committee, warned the President privately that a majority of
his committee would oppose the fuel shipments, with the
implication that a majority of the House would probably
follow suit. Zablocki and Representative Bingham were
the main nonproliferation spokesmen in the House and
two of the legislators most responsible for the passage
of the Nonproliferation Act. They were neither "anti-
India" nor "anti-Carter;" indeed, Zablocki, Bingham,
and others were interested in the possibility of some
sort of compromise that might avoid a direct confrontation with the President on this issue. Proposals such
as approval of the shipment of reactor spare parts and
components without nuclear fuel were discussed with the
Administration. Former State Department spokesman on
nonproliferation, Joseph Nye, proposed the approval of
one of the two fuel licenses as a way of avoiding an
embarassing defeat for the Administration that would
also compromise U.S. foreign policy objectives.[24]
It soon became clear that there was little hope for

winning House approval, even of a compromise. The Indian government's expressed willingness to sell food and other supplies to Iran to break the U.S. blockade did little to improve the climate of opinion in the House.[25] Since a negative vote in the House alone would not block the President, the Administration wrote off the House and concentrated its lobbying on the Senate. The September 10 voice vote of the House Foreign Affairs Committee in favor of the resolution of disapproval and the September 18 House vote of 298-98 in favor of disapproval had been long anticipated by the Administration. However, the nearly 3 to 1 margin of the House vote did raise fears that the anti-nuclear export momentum would spread to the Senate.

The House has a reputation in the eyes of the foreign policy community, fairly or not, as being erratic in its behavior on foreign policy questions--too easily influenced by domestic constituency pressures and other considerations that foreign policy professionals often consider "extraneous." Images to the contrary notwithstanding, the House vote to overrule the President and deny the nuclear fuel shipments to India would appear to be more consistent with established nonproliferation policy that the subsequent Senate vote; in effect, the House was acting responsibly to maintain the continuity of American foreign policy in the face of the Carter Administration's policy shift. The Senate has the image of being more "responsible," i.e., more inclined than the House to follow the President. This has not always been true, but, in this case, the Senate did follow the Administration lead.

For most senators, the Indian nuclear fuel license question was not a major issue; certainly, as a foreign policy concern it was subordinate to the ongoing hostage crisis in Iran and the Soviet intervention in Afghanistan. And the issue came to the Senate just as the 1980 campaign season was heading into its most intense period. Some senators who had been interested in the issue of nonproliferation in the past--such as Stuart Symington--were no longer in the Senate; others --such as Ribicoff--showed limited interest in the question. The key Senate spokesman on behalf of nonproliferation policy in 1980 was John Glenn. His membership on the Foreign Relations Committee and his chairmanship of the subcommittee of the Government Operations Committee that handles nonproliferation questions put him in an influential position and provided him with an able and experienced staff to help handle this issue. But Glenn was also in the middle of a re-election campaign, as were Foreign Relations Committee Chairman Frank Church and ranking Republican Jacob Javits, and all were frequently out of Washington in the summer of 1980. However, the delay in Senate consideration of the President's executive order until well into the 60-day period provided by law was largely

due to Administration requests for time to lobby uncommitted senators.

The Administration sought the support of Senate
Majority Leader Robert C. Byrd. His help had been crucial in the Panama Canal Treaties debate, and he had
done a great deal to keep alive the possibility of approving the SALT II Treaty through early 1980. But, by
the summer of 1980, relations between the Carter White
House and the Senate leadership were at an all-time
low. Byrd made it clear early on that the Senate would
study the Indian nuclear fuel question carefully,[26] but
he was not personally very interested in the issue.
When preoccupied with other matters, Byrd was inclined
to follow the lead of his committee chairmen. Without
a major push from the Democratic leadership, the Administration had to carry the burden of convincing a majority of the Senate to support its position on the
Indian nuclear fuel licenses. A resolution of disapproval was filed in the Senate by Harry F. Byrd, Jr. of
Virginia on June 20, two days after the President
signed his executive order; a substitute resolution was
considered by the Foreign Relations Committee, where
Senator Glenn was its sponsor and principal advocate.

The State Department began to lobby the Senate in-
tensively at all levels. U.S. Ambassador to India
Robert F. Goheen was brought home to Washington to personally plead India's case with senators; however the
Indian Ambassador in Washington kept a low profile
throughout. Secretary Muskie spent an extraordinary
amount of time lobbying his former colleagues in the
Senate on this issue; he became the first Democrat ever
to address the Republican Policy Committee.[27] And in
the days immediately preceeding the final vote on the
Senate floor, the President took time away from a mid-
west campaign swing to lobby senators; he phoned several senators from Air Force One in what was conceded by
Senator Glenn to be a very effective lobbying effort.[28]

Committee Action

The first test of the Administration's strength
came in the Senate Foreign Relations Committee. From
the first, key committee staffers, some of whom were
former foreign service officers, strongly favored nuclear fuel exports to India. Both majority and minority staffers sought to bolster the Administration's
case for the exports, in part to "carry water" for the
State Department, and in part out of a preference for
the "case-by-case" approach to nonproliferation. Bipartisan support for the Administration was equally
evident in the committee membership. Ranking Republicans Javits and Percy were the strongest proponents of
shipping nuclear fuel to India, both in the committee
and during the floor debate. Javits, often called the

"Senate's lawyer" by his colleagues, based his advocacy
on his interpretation of the legal obligations flowing
from the 1963 agreement for cooperation,[29] while Percy
stressed the importance of improved relations with the
Indian government to overall U.S. foreign policy.[30]
Percy's position was particularly interesting because
he had been one of the promoters of the Nonproliferation Act in 1978, and because he subsequently became
Chairman of the Foreign Relations Committee when the
1980 elections returned a Republican majority to the
Senate. (Javits would have become chairman had he not
been defeated in 1980.) Foreign Relations Chairman
Frank Church admitted that there were good arguments on
both sides of the issue, but concluded that because it
was a close call, he was inclined to support the Administration.[31] This position probably accurately sums up
the feelings of many senators who had no particular
interest in the question. Church also revealed an Administration promise that only one of the two fuel
shipments would be made immediately.[32]

Senator Glenn led the fight against the President's
action, arguing that it was a betrayal of the Administration's own nonproliferation policy that would sow
doubt about America's steadfastness and raise problems
in our relations with other nuclear threshhold countries.[33] Glenn scored a signal victory when the Foreign Relations Committee voted to disapprove the President's executive order by a vote of 8-7.

The Administration was surprised by the loss and
the unpredictability of the line-up: Glenn was joined
by liberal Democrats George McGovern, Paul Tsongas,
Joseph Biden, and Claiborne Pell, and the Republican
conservatives Jesse Helms, S. I. Hayakawa, and Richard
Lugar. Republican Minority Leader Baker joined Percy
and Javits, and Democratic Senators Church, Paul
Sarbanes, Richard Stone, and Edward Zorinsky in support
of the President.

The Senate Vote

When the debate moved to the Senate floor on September 23, there was a replay of the arguments within
the Foreign Relations Committee but with a different
outcome. The major figures in the debate were Percy
and Glenn. Senator Daniel Patrick Moynihan (D-New
York), an ex-Ambassador to India, predictably supported
the full shipments. Senator Alan Cranston (D-Cali-
fornia) took a strong stand against shipping the fuel
and in favor of adhering to the letter and spirit of
the Nonproliferation Act, a position he had earlier
enunciated as a witness before the Foreign Relations
Committee.[34] The arguments which seemed to carry the
most weight were the legal points, especially the

Administration's contention that the U.S. had an ob-
ligation to supply nuclear fuel when licenses were
filed before September 10, 1980. And, while there was
no great outpouring of affection or support for India,
there was obviously a belief among many senators that
the geopolitical situation in South Asia required some
attempt to improve the U.S. position there.

On September 24, the resolution of disapproval
failed by a 46-48 vote; therefore the Senate upheld the
President's decision to authorize the shipment of 38
tons of nuclear fuel to India. As in the Foreign Relations Committee, the vote on the Senate floor cut
across party and ideological lines--Majority Leader
Byrd voted with the President while Majority Whip
Cranston voted against. Minority Leader Baker and Minority Whip Ted Stevens both voted to support the Administration. Conservatives such as Helms, Gordon
Humphrey, and Harry Byrd voted against the Administration, while conservatives such as James McClure and
Jake Garn voted with the Administration. Liberals from
both parties were on each side of the issue--Republican
Charles McC. Mathias and Democrat Thomas Eagleton voted
with the Administration, Democrat Edward Kennedy and
Republican Mark Hatfield voted against. Nor did being
up for re-election seem to incline senators one way or
another--George McGovern and Gary Hart voted against
the Administration, while Church and Javits voted with
the Administration. The result was a narrow victory
and a source of satisfaction for an embattled Administration, whose foreign policy woes were a major lia-
bility in its fight for re-election.

Influences on Congressional Action

There are several factors that seem to account for
Congress' behavior in the Indian nuclear fuel case. To
the extent that the same or similar factors are found
to be important in other cases, these factors may have
explanatory as well as descriptive significance.

Nonproliferation is one of those issue areas that
bridge the gap between foreign and domestic politics,
and between security concerns and economic interests.
America's stake in limiting the spread of nuclear weapons in an uncertain world has to be reconciled with
America's economic interest in civil nuclear energy
exports. The overlap of "high politics" and "low politics" guarantees the active interest and involvement of
Congress in this kind of issue. However, in the case
of the Indian nuclear fuel licenses in 1980, national
security calculations of a traditional, geopolitical
sort clearly predominated in the actions of the Carter
Administration. American economic interests were very
limited in this particular case: At stake were future

fuel supplies, but no major reactor or other nuclear
equipment orders. Mired in other problems, the U.S.
nuclear industry did not mount a major lobbying effort
in support of continuing fuel shipments to India. Furthermore, there was no domestic ethnic group lobbying
on this issue--either on behalf of or in opposition to
India. In the absence of the two most potent domestic
interest factors that have an impact on most "intermestic" issues (issues on which the international-domestic
distinction is blurred), the Carter Administration succeeded in posing the question in a national security
vein. On national security questions, the Congress is
still inclined to defer to the President, even if it
does so less automatically than in the past.

The Indian nuclear fuel case provides a good example of the use of the "legislative veto" provisions
Congress wrote into a number of laws.[35] It is important to note that in spite of all the controversy surrounding the legislative veto, there is no example of
Congress successfully blocking an important foreign
policy initiative by the President by this device; however, the threat of a legislative veto has compelled
the President to consult with Congress. If, as in the
case of the Indian nuclear fuel licenses, the President
is prepared to fight for what he wants, he often gets
his way.

How an issue is perceived is closely related to the
salience of the issue to the President and to members
of Congress. The more a question is seen as a traditional national security issue, the more the President
might be expected to prevail over his congressional
competitors. This is reflected in the attitude of some
senators that if it was a close call, then the President should have his way. But obviously, this feeling
did not prevail in the House, which sought to uphold
the letter and spirit of the Nonproliferation Act in
the Indian nuclear fuel case and to block the President's waiver. If the issue had been of higher salience, if more senators had been convinced that the
question was fundamentally important, then more might
have been willing to challenge the President on the
nuclear fuel question. Many senators did not see this
as an important issue, and this worked to the advantage
of the Administration. Because the stakes were higher
for the President--both in terms of his foreign policy
objectives in South Asia and in terms of his image at
home in the presidential campaign--he was willing to
expand extraordinary effort on the Indian nuclear fuel
question, and many senators were inclined to allow him
to have his way.

The structure of the Senate was an important factor
influencing the outcome in this case. The leadership
was not crucial in marshalling support for the President either in the Foreign Relations Committee or on
the Senate floor, but leadership also posed no major

obstacles to the President. In the absence of strong
push from leadership, Senator Glenn was able to use his
position as chairman of a subcommittee of the Government Operations Committee to lead the campaign against
the Administration on a foreign policy question. Given
the low salience of the issue and the state of relations between the White House and the Senate leadership, Glenn was never in danger of being sanctioned because of his efforts.

Personalities played a very important role in determining the outcome in this instance. The major
actors, Glenn and Percy, were both popular among their
colleagues; there is no evidence of personal scores
being settled in this case. The fact that ex-Senator
Muskie had recently become Secretary of State was undoubtedly the major asset the Administration had at its
disposal. Muskie's active lobbying of his former colleagues on this question, his first major foreign policy initiative, was effective. Muskie was widely liked
and respected in the Senate, more than the President he
served. Some of those who did not feel strongly about
the question of the Indian nuclear fuel licenses were
doubtless swayed to back Secretary of State Muskie on
this issue, even though on questions they might perceive as more important, they would have been prepared
to oppose him.

It would be excessively rational to conclude that
the outcome of the deliberations of a legislative body
necessarily constitute a judgment on the merits of the
issue. Obviously, secondary questions and sometimes
wholly extraneous matters can influence, if not determine, the outcome. Rationally, one might assert that
the Senate vote in this case was a judgment on the
merits of U.S. nonproliferation policy generally and
its specific application to India. However, a close
examination of the record suggests that secondary considerations may have been more persuasive than the primary arguments.

The legal dimensions of the problem helped to muddy
the waters. Even those senators who might have been
inclined to uphold nonproliferation policy and fidelity
to the letter of the law could differ on what the law
demanded: unilateral abrogation of a contract is a
difficult thing for senators to approve, especially
those with legal training; it was easier to argue that
these two particular licenses should be exempt from the
requirements of the Nonproliferation Act, without passing judgment on the merits of the law itself. Thus,
the decision to side with the Administration was not a
clear-cut vote to endorse local geopolitical objectives
at the expense of universal nonproliferation objectives. In sum, the Senate acted to support the President by a very close vote, in circumstances that make
it difficult to conclude that there was a meaningful
consensus on a shift in U.S. nonproliferation policy.

Whither Nonproliferation?

There are two general questions about the future of U.S. nonproliferation policy that the Indian fuel case raises: whether the universal approach to nonproliferation established by the Nonproliferation Act should be abandoned in favor of a selective application of nonproliferation measures, and whether this kind of foreign policy issue is better left to wide executive discretion or narrow statutory limits.

The consensus on a universal approach to nonproliferation seems to have been lost--abandoned first as a matter of expediency by the Carter Administration, then as a matter of principle by the Reagan Administration. The former is more comprehensible than the latter: there will always be a tension between following a "policy" and responding ad hoc to events, and in the third year of the Carter Administration the latter won out. And yet, the record of the first three years of nonproliferation policy was substantial and positive.36 Certainly, making an exception for India in 1980 was a policy failure, bringing none of the supposed benefits in terms of U.S.-Indian relations. In the first few months of 1981 nuclear cooperation between the two nations broke down and termination of the 1963 agreement was again a possibility. And, as predicted, India insisted that the U.S. was guilty of abrogating the contract, and therefore would have no control over the accumulated stockpile of nuclear fuel of U.S. origin. During Mrs. Gandhi's visit to Washington in August 1982, it was announced that the U.S. would allow France to assume the responsibility of supplying fuel to the Tarapur reactors. However, this "solution" may have been no more than a diplomatic way to paper over persisting problems. After Mrs. Gandhi's return home, it was unclear whether France would be much more accomodating than the U.S. had been with regard to plutonium separation and Indian rights to re-use plutonium as they see fit.37 And the Reagan Administration appeared ready to resume some forms of nuclear cooperation with India, such as the supply of spare parts for Tarapur.

The major objection to a universal approach to the nonproliferation problem is that such a policy must be, by definition, insensitive to specific circumstances, especially to the differences between friendly nations and others. Such a rigid policy can only be defended when compared to the defects of the alternative case-by-case approach. First, and most important, a case-by-case approach easily amounts to having no "policy" at all. In international politics, there are only special cases, as every diplomat knows. The choice is between being blind to the rich diversity of international politics or being arbitrary, choosing to oppose the aspirations of one nation while favoring the aspirations of others. A universal nonproliferation policy offends those few countries who are friends and whose nuclear programs will be negatively affected; a selective nonproliferation policy offends the many who are inclined to support nonproliferation objectives but who resent exceptions being made for a chosen few.

The second defect of a selective, case-by-case approach to nonproliferation is that it is almost impossible for the U.S. government, as presently constituted, to implement such a policy successfully. The formulation and implementation of American foreign policy is a complex process involving multiple institutional actors. To be successfully implemented, foreign policy positions must be clearly stated and communicated to all parts of the foreign policy apparatus. That is why a universally applicable set of nonproliferation standards is a more effective basis for American policy than a selective, case-by-case approach, varying from country to country. To be successful, selectivity requires a degree of flexibility and secrecy that are imcompatible with American political practices. The choice is between tailoring institutions to fit policy objectives, or tailoring policies to what political institutions will permit.

While there was an apparent shift in U.S. nonproliferation policy in 1980, there were no immediate changes in nonproliferation legislation, and this was a source of ambiguity. The Nonproliferation Act was one of several recent attempts by Congress to legislate foreign policy in substantial detail. Policies grounded in law have the advantage of providing coherence and continuity because laws do not change as often as events. Policies embodied in statutes reflect not the transitory judgment of the executive foreign policy establishment but also the judgment of Congress. These policies are more likely to be effective, less subject to being undermined in their implementation. Such policies also have a better claim to public support as representing the national interest. And finally, legislating foreign policy is an attempt to master international events rather than allowing events to dictate policy.

As long as the executive and Congress generally agree on the problem in question, legislating policy may work well--President Carter's position on nonproliferation policy was strengthened by the fact that this policy had a statutory base. However, when the executive and Congress diverge on an issue--as occurred in the Indian case, with the House voting overwhelmingly against the President--then institutional confrontation and legal confusion threaten. Paradoxically, legislating policy seems to work best when it is least needed, when the executive and Congress generally agree on what should be done; legislating policy seems to work worst when it is most needed, when substantial differences exist about what the policy is or should be. The latter was the case under the Reagan Administration, which sought to remove some of the nuclear export restrictions in the face of resistance from Congress.

There are two ways to avoid an impasse on nonproliferation policy: either the policy can be adjusted to conform to legislation or the legislation altered to conform to the prevailing policy. Failing to do one of these two things breeds policy confusion and disrespect for law. Neither confusion nor disrespect serve the interests of American foreign policy. The Indian nuclear fuel controversy posed this problem without answering it.

NOTES

1. _Congressional Quarterly_, July 25, 1981, pp.1348-49; and July 12, 1981, pp.1223-28.

2. James L. Malone, "Nuclear Cooperation and Nonproliferation Strategy," U.S. Department of State, Current Policy N.354, December 1, 1981; see also Lewis Dunn, _Controlling the Bomb_ (New Haven: Yale University Press, 1982).

3. _Congressional Quarterly_, December 10, 1981, pp.2497989; General Accounting Office, _Report to the Congress: The Nuclear Nonproliferation Act of 1978 Should Be Selectively Modified_ (Washington: Government Printing Office, May 21, 1981).

4. Thomas Morgan, _Atomic Energy and Congress_ (Ann Arbor: University of Michigan Press, 1963).

5. Harold P. Green and Alan Rosenthal, _Government of the Atom_ (New York: Atherton Press, 1963).

6. Ibid., p.105.

7. Harold Nieburg, _Nuclear Secrecy and Foreign Policy_ (Washington: Public Affairs Press, 1964), p.4.

8. William Bader, _The United States and the Spread of Nuclear Weapons_ (New York: Pegasus, 1968), pp.26-35.

9. "Review of the International Policies and Programs of the U.S." "Report to the Joint Committee on Atomic Energy," October 1960 (Washington, GPO, 1960); and Irvin C. Bupp and Jean-Claude Derian, _Light Water_ (New York: Basic Books, 1978), esp. Chapter 1.

10. Clarence Long, "Nonproliferation: Can Congress Act in Time?" _International Security_, spring 1977, vol.1, no.4.

11. Ibid.; and Warren Donnelly, "Congress and Nonproliferation, 1945-1977," in Alan Platt and Lawrence D. Weiler, eds., _Congress and Arms Control_ (Boulder: Westview, 1978).

12. Public Law 95-242, March 10, 1978.
13. See The Times of India, March 20, 1980; and Robert F. Goheen in The Washington Post, June 27, 1980.
14. Testimony by Warren Christopher before the U.S. Senate Committee on Foreign Relations and Committee on Governmental Affairs, June 19, 1980.
15. "Application of Section 128 of the Atomic Energy Act of 1954 with Respect to Fuel Exports to India," Memorandum of Law, Department of State, June 18, 1980.
16. Leonard Bickwitt, "Application of Section 127 and 128 of the Atomic Energy Act to Proposed Exports to India," Nuclear Regulatory Commission, May 12, 1980; and Memorandum and order, CLI-80-, Nuclear Regulatory Commission, May 16, 1980.
17. See "Separate Views of Commissioners Gilinsky and Bradford," in The Matter of NSC Export License Application XSNM-1222, March 23, 1979, p.5, fn.15.
18. Christopher statement.
19. Congressional Quarterly, September 27, 1980, p.2872.
20. The New York Times, January 18, 1980, p.1.
21. The Christian Science Monitor, November 30, 1981.
22. Christopher statement.
23. NRC Memorandum and Order CLI-80.
24. The New York Times, August 30, 1980, p.15.
25. The Washington Post, June 14, 1980.
26. Congressional Record, Wednesday, May 21, 1980, p.S5669.
27. Congressional Record, September 23, 1980, p.S13216.
28. Congressional Record, September 23, 1980, p.S13211.
29. Congressional Record, September 24, 1980, pp.S13249-52.
30. Congressional Record, September 23, 1980, pp.S13215-19.
31. Congressional Record, September 24, 1980, pp.S13255-57
32. Ibid., p.S13255.
33. Congressional Record, September 23, 1980, pp.S13209-27; and September 1980, pp.S13249-83 ad interim.
34. Congressional Record, September 24, 1980, pp.S13265-66.
35. See, for example, Thomas E. Cronin, "A Resurgent Congress and the Imperial Presidency," Political Science Quarterly; vol.95, no.2, summer 1980, pp.222-25; and Congressional Quarterly, July 13, 1982, p.1567.
36. See, for example, Joseph S. Nye, "Maintaining a Nonproliferation Regime," International Organization, winter, 1981.
37. Link (New Delhi) September 5, 1982, pp.33-34.

7

The Senate and Arms Control: The SALT Experience

J. Philip Rogers

If Congress is to play a significant role in the formulation of United States foreign policy, it could scarcely address a more critical issue than nuclear arms control. However, while all agree that avoiding nuclear war is an essential goal, there is considerable disagreement over the best means to achieve this goal. Given the gravity and controversial nature of the issue, the involvement of Congress might be seen as desirable since Congress is ostensibly the most "representative" branch of government. This normative concern for democratic decision-making has been coupled with the pragmatic belief that the Senate might be more likely to approve an arms control treaty which it had a hand in developing. Finally, congressional involvement in the area of arms control has been advanced as a means for keeping this issue at the forefront of executive branch attention. When executive interest in arms controls seems to lapse, as many believed was the case early in the Reagan Administration, congressional debate can reinvigorate the issue.

Taken together, these arguments seem to make a strong prima facie case for congressional involvement throughout the arms control process. How well do these arguments fare in the light of empirical evidence?

The first major episode of congressional involvement in the nuclear arms control process occurred in the late 1950s and early 1960s. At that time, the primary concern of the public was the effects of radioactive fallout from the atmosphere nuclear tests. Eventually, the Senate would approve the 1963 Limited Test Ban Treaty. In that case, the Senate was able to work well with the Kennedy Administration to accomplish the arms control objectives it sought. Significantly, Congress did so without sacrificing an open and vigorous debate on the issue.

While this early experience tended to support the argument for congressional involvement, later experience raised some serious questions. The most important

160

period for arms control is the era of SALT--the Strategic Arms Limitation Talks. The SALT process stretched
from 1969-1979. During this time, two formal agreements, SALT I in 1972 and SALT II in 1979, were produced. SALT I was overwhelmingly approved by the Senate after relatively little debate and little prior
consultation, while SALT II was shelved after lengthy
Senate hearings and the intense involvement of various
senators throughout the negotiating process.

With the failure of the Senate to approve the SALT
II Treaty, it might be argued that perhaps the Senate
is inherently ill-suited for major participation in
arms control negotiations. Nuclear arms agreements may
be an exception to a generally valid principle--an area
of foreign policy in which normally desirable institutional characteristics such as public debate are imcompatible with the overriding goal of securing nuclear
arms agreements. The Senate's failure to complete
action on SALT II after it was signed in 1979 could be
at least partially attributed to factors not directly a
part of the treaty. Nonetheless, the failure of the
Senate to approve an agreement negotiated over a period
of seven years by three presidents points up the need
to weigh normative considerations favoring congressional participation against an equally valid need for consistency in foreign policy, and for what many see as
the critical need to secure arms control agreements.

There are five arguments that have been made in
questioning a major role for Congress in arms control
negotiations:[1]

(1) Members of Congress do not have the
    requisite expertise to understand the
    arcane facts of arms control.
(2) Open congressional debate on U.S. arms
    control policy weakens U.S. bargaining
    leverage in dealing with the Soviets.
(3) The decentralized nature of Congress and
    its "adverserial" relationship with the
    President makes presidential consultation
    difficult. This further inhibits the
    development of coherent policy.
(4) Congressional approval frequently comes
    at too high a price; e.g., with promises
    of increased defense spending in areas
    not covered by the agreement.
(5) Congressional involvement throughout the
    process "politicizes" the issue. Arms
    control agreements are particularly sus-
    ceptible to "grandstanding." The open
    and political nature of debate in Con-
    gress forestalls the achievement of ser-
    ious progress and makes final approval
    problematic.

For those who favor arms control, these arguments do merit serious examination. To explore the validity of the arguments both favoring and opposing Senate involvement in arms control it is necessary to look at the historical record of the SALT process, examine the impact of the Senate's involvement in this process, and cull from this experience lessons for the future role of the Senate in this vital area.

SALT I

Senate participation in SALT I was sporadic.[2] Initially, there was a flurry of Senate involvement, which centered on three issues: the possibility of a ban on multiple independently targetable re-entry vehicles (MIRVs); the threat imposed by the Soviet "heavy" missiles; and the desirability of the anti-ballistic missile (ABM) system. However, once negotiations began, the Nixon Administration effectively shut Congress out of the decision-making process. The resultant lack of information, coupled with a declining congressional interest meant that there would be relatively few committee hearings on the subject.[3] However, there were periods intense Senate interest, particularly the ABM debate and attempt to restrict MIRVs.

The ABM debate typifies the complex interaction between Congress and the executive in the field of arms control. Rather than being a contest of Congress versus the executive, in almost all cases both institutions splinter into different factions that seek allies in the other institutional branch. In this case, the Joint Chiefs of Staff (JCS), the President, and the Senate Armed Services Committee were pitted against the Senate Foreign Relations Committee, the State Department, and the Arms Control and Disarmament Agency (ACDA).

The ABM debate was an annual event from 1967 until 1975, but the most intense debate occurred in 1969 and 1970, right before and after the onset of SALT. In the 1969 debate, the pro-ABM forces won by a one-vote margin, partly because President Nixon provided Senator Henry Jackson (D-Washington) with classified information to use against the ABM opponents. These opponents were handicapped in attempting to respond the Senator Jackson without equal access to these classified studies. The 1970 debate was also heated, but, thereafter, the Administration's "bargaining chip" argument began to prevail.[4] Congressional interest declined precipitously after that; so much so that by the time of the 1972 debate on the ABM treaty, Senate Majority Leader Mike Mansfield chided his fellow senators for their disinterest:

We are considering one of the most important

treaties to come before this body in a good
many years. Yet, there seems to be little interest on the part of the membership to discuss the pending business. We will have to
twiddle our thumbs and wait for the expiration
of the time limit unless...(someone) under-
takes their constitutional responsibility.

Despite Mansfield's plea, the debate was short and
the treaty was overwhelmingly approved by an 88-2
margin.[5]

The SALT I agreement actually consisted of two
parts: the treaty restricting the deployment of ABM
systems and an agreement imposing certain limits on offensive weapons. If public and congressional information was sparse with regard to the evolution of the ABM
Treaty, it was virtually non-existent concerning the
offensive weapons negotiations. Throughout the entire
negotiation period, with only rare exceptions, Congress
and the public were kept totally in the dark on the developments. A few senators did make an attempt to
gather more information. Senator John Sherman Cooper
(R-Kentucky) attempted to attend the negotiations in
Vienna, but his visits were without official sanction.
(Chief SALT negotiator Gerard Smith is said to have
favored his participation, but Henry Kissinger vetoed
it.) Cooper never was allowed to participate in or
even observe any substantive negotiations.[6]

Brooke Resolution

The primary congressional concern in the area of
offensive weapons was the widespread belief that a restriction or ban on MIRVs should be sought. Throughout
1969 a plethora of congressional resolutions were submitted calling for a limit or a ban on MIRVs. Probably
the most widely supported of these was proposed by Senator Edward Brooke (R-Massachusetts) in June 1969.[7]
Despite its widespread support, however, Brooke's resolution languished in the Foreign Relations Committee
for almost a year without action. According to Alton
Frye, the reason for Senate inaction was that various
senators were given the impression by the Nixon Administration that actual deployment of U.S. MIRVs would be
held in abeyance during the upcoming SALT negotiations
in hopes that a ban could be obtained. In addition,
some senators believed that even further MIRV testing
would not be conducted since the Soviets still had not
achieved their first successful test. Apparently the
feeling on Capitol Hill was that since the basic "legislative intent" of the Brooke Resolution was satisfied, actual formal passage would be superfluous.
Since Brooke's proposal was merely a "sense of the

Senate" resolution, which is not legally binding, it made little sense to recommend to the Administration to do what it already intended to do.[8]

This attitude received a sharp jolt in March 1970 when in testimony before the Armed Services Committee, Secretary of the Air Force Robert Seamans inadvertently let slip that deployment of MIRVs would begin that June. The reaction of the Senate was immediate and negative. The Foreign Relations Committee activated testimony on the somnolent Brooke's resolution, and shortly thereafter passed a revised version by a unanimous vote. President Nixon's response to the Foreign Relations Committee's initiative is perhaps indicative of his Administration's attitude toward congressional participation. Nixon stated that the resolution was "irrelevant to what we are going to do."[9] Perhaps in response to such a politically insensitive pronouncement, the resolution picked up additional momentum, including the endorsement of Republican Minority Leader Hugh Scott, and eventually passed 72-6.

SALT I produced no MIRV ban of any form however. Kissinger has claimed that the Administration tried and failed to get the Soviets to agree on some sort of MIRV restrictions.[10] He repeatedly assured members of Congress that the Administration was as interested as they in securing MIRV restrictions, and was in fact making proposals to the Soviets along those lines. Since the senators were kept in the dark, with no basis on which to challenge the Kissinger assertions, little objection was made at the time. Recently, however, in two separate accounts, Gerard Smith[11], chief SALT negotiator, and Lawrence Weiler[12], a key assistant, have argued that the Administration's MIRV proposal was intentionally constructed as a non-starter, something that the Soviets would reject out of hand. The base their case on three points:

First, it called for extensive on-site inspections, something that until recently the Soviets have been adamant in rejecting. Perhaps most incredibly of all, the Kissinger proposal lumped on-site inspection of the MIRVed missile sites with inspection of Soviet surface-to-air missiles (SAMs) as well. Smith says that the Soviets told him this was an obvious attempt to engage in surveillance of the Soviet air defense system.

Second, the Administration's proposal was dropped a mere two months after is was proposed, with no subsequent attempt at a counter-proposal to the Soviet MIRV proposal. This failure to follow up occurred despite the repeated calls of Smith and others for more exploration of the topic.

Finally, Smith cites the fact that before the proposal was submitted to the Soviets the SALT verification panel never was instructed to do a study on how on-site inspections might actually be carried out.

According to Smith, this was not the normal procedure for more "serious" proposals.

Unaware of all this at the time, the Senate apparently believed that with the passage of the Brooke resolution it had discharged its responsibility on the issue.

The MIRV issue ceased to capture significant congressional interest after that. Only a minority would later support the more binding MIRV proposals advanced by Senators George McGovern (D-South Dakota) and Hubert Humphrey (D-Minnesota). Humphrey's proposal would have put MIRV deployment funds in "escrow" until "the President and Congress jointly determined that Soviet testing and MIRV development necessitated U.S. resumption of its program as a guarantee of retaliatory capability." Humphrey's legally-binding proposal failed to engender the widespread support given to the Brooke "sense of the Senate resolution." Apparently, many senators believed that to enact such binding legislation during negotiations would be to step beyond the bounds of institutional propriety. Perhaps even more importantly, Senator Humphrey failed to convince the Senate leadership of the necessity of undertaking such "drastic" measures, so the amendment was brought up by the leadership on a day when many of Humphrey's supporters were absent. It was easily defeated.[13]

The ABM debate and the Brooke resolution were rare flickers of congressional assertiveness. More typical of the congressional pattern in this period was the indifference and/or acquiescence to Administration proposals. This attitude was reinforced by an Administration that had no intention of including Congress in the development of policy. Congressional hearings, when they occurred at all, often consisted of a perfunctory questioning of Administration officials.[14]

Jackson Amendent

There was one significant exception to this pattern. Congress did take one action that would have a major long-term impact on arms control negotiations. This was the approval of the Jackson amendment to the resolution approving the 1972 Interim Agreement on Strategic Offensive Arms. On June 13, 1972, when Senator Jackson was finally made aware of the terms of the Interim Agreement, he angrily denounced the "inequities" in the agreement. His major objection was to the fact that the Soviets were allowed to keep a larger number of missile launchers, which, with their advantage in missile launch weight, made for a tremendous potential advantage in throw-weight. Since the agreement was temporary, Jackson agreed to support it if the resolution of approval was amended by one important qualification, to the effect that:

> future treaties on offensive weapons not limit
> the United States to levels of intercontinent-
> al strategic forces inferior to those of the
> Soviet Union.

Jackson argued that these agreements should be based on
"equality." There was considerable debate on the floor
of the Senate about what equality should mean (i.e.,
whether it applied to just aggregate launcher numbers
or to other aspects as well, such as throw weight). A
number of amendments were offered in an attempt to
loosen the language, but these were all defeated. In
the end, the Jackson amendment was passed, and subsequently, the Interim Agreement also received Senate approval. The legislative history of the Jackson amendment suggests that Jackson intended it to apply to
dimensions such as throw weight as well as numbers of
launchers. This would be as issue of considerable importance later.[15]

SALT II-A (1972-1976)

The SALT II negotiations began not long after SALT
I was ratified. The pattern of congressional involvement in this period was similar to that of the earlier
period, with the exception that Senator Jackson increasingly used his Subcommittee on Arms Control to
conduct critical investigations. Immediately after
SALT I, Jackson is reported to have met with Nixon to
discuss the number of "soft-headed" negotiators in the
Arms Control and Disarmament Agency. It appears to
have been at Jackson's instigation that a "mini-purge"
of ACDA officials was conducted, in a deliberate effort
to begin SALT II with a new set of "tougher"
negotiators.[16]

The most significant congressional involvement during this period occurred at an executive session of
Jackson's Armed Services Subcommittee on Arms Control
on June 24, 1974. Paul Nitze, who had recently resigned his post as a SALT negotiator (Nitze was one negotiator of whom Jackson approved), told the subcommittee that the Administration had left a number of 'loopholes' in SALT I. According to Nitze, these loopholes
were only closed after Kissinger made some secret
agreements with Soviet Ambassador Anatoly Dobrynin.
Nitze also asserted that President Nixon had given secret assurances to the Soviet leaders that the U.S.
would not increase the numbers of submarine-launched
ballistic missiles (SLBM) to the maximum permissible
level. Jackson made the most of this information in

putting the heat on the Administration to disclose the contents of their "secret" negotiations. It was later suggested that Jackson's real intention in holding the hearings was to sabotage the next round of SALT II talks until he could get adequate information on the positions being put forth.[17] In any case, this episode proved to be a watershed in congressional attitude toward the executive. After this incident, senators were increasingly suspicious of the executive branch and less willing to stand on the sidelines.[18] The nascent congressional assertiveness would not fully emerge until the Carter Administration, but the tide had turned.

During this period, Senator Jackson's influence began to be felt, not just in his public hearings, but on the actual substance of U.S. negotiating position. President Ford had wanted to conclude SALT II during his Administration, but the 1976 Republican primaries and the criticism from Ronald Reagan made this difficult. What was accomplished during his tenure was the signing in 1974 of the Vladivostok accords, which were supposed to serve as the basis for the formal SALT II agreement.

As noted, the Jackson amendment actually had no impact whatsoever on the 1972 Interim Agreement. What it did effect, in an important way, was subsequent offensive arms agreements (the Vladivostok accords and, eventually, SALT II). The Vladivostok accords were the first agreement with "parity" in terms of equivalent numbers of strategic nuclear delivery vehicles (SNDV). However, this parity did not extend to the numbers of heavy missiles nor to the overall throw-weight comparisons. Therefore, one could argue that, although it was a step toward the provisions of the Jackson amendment, it did not fulfill the requirment of that amendment in all respects. Probably the actual manner in which the Jackson amendment affected the accords was indirect; i.e., by reinforcing the position of those in the executive bureacracy who had similar goals.

During the 1972-1976 period a few other senators pursued the issue of arms control. Many of these individuals adopted the opposite position from Jackson. Rather than believe, as Jackson did, that the Administration had gone too far in SALT I, these senators thought that it had not gone far enough. Senators Charles McC. Mathias (R-Maryland), McGovern, Humphrey, and Thomas McIntyre (D-New Hampshire) tried to encourage the Administration to pursue deeper cuts, but without notable success. These "arms controllers" stirred little interest among their colleagues. The overall characterization of congressional participation during the 1972-1976 period is largely on of disinterest.[19]

SALT II-B (1977-1979)

Jimmy Carter came into office promising an open
administration, which implied greater congressional
participation in foreign policy. Compared to his pred-
ecessors, this policy was largely realized. From
February 1977 until the signing of SALT II, Administration officials briefed congressional committees almost
50 times. Counting informal briefings of individual
senators, the number of briefings exceeded 140.[20]
While the quality of these briefings might be questioned, the quantity certainly could not. Congress responded to this new openness with a new assertiveness
of its own.

One significant example of this assertiveness occurred during the 1977 confirmation hearings of Paul
Warnke as Director of the Arms Control and Disarmament
Agency (ACDA) and chief SALT negotiator. Confirmation
hearings for these positions were normally pro forma,
with little effort to probe or influence policy position. Not so with the Warnke hearings. Warnke was
questioned closely by the Foreign Relations Committee.
He also consented to go before the Armed Services Committee, although this was not a requirement. It was
here that he received his most severe grilling. There
were also opposition witnesses, including Paul Nitze.
Although the Senate could have opted to conduct the
confirmation vote for the two positions as one vote, it
chose instead to split the vote. The importance of
this change was that it allowed those Democratic senators who were concerned about Warnke's "toughness" as a
negotiator to register their concern without embarras-
sing a new Democratic president. Consequently, there
was a major difference in the vote margins on the two
votes. Warnke was easily confirmed for the less-con-
troversial position as head of ACDA by a vote of 70-
29. However, the vote on Warnke as chief SALT negotiator was much closer--the final tally was 58-40. (See
Chapter 1.) Warnke has suggested that Majority Leader
Robert Byrd's floor leadership was critical for this
successful (albeit close) outcome.[21]

It is significant that this margin of victory was
less than the two-thirds margin which would be necessary for Senate approval of any SALT treaty. Even Senator Alan Cranston, a strong SALT supporter, admitted
that this vote accurately reflected the Senate's intent to "send a message" to President Carter to the
effect that any SALT agreement would be carefully
scrutinized.[22]

One of the most dramatic differences between SALT I
and SALT II was the fact that during the summer of 1977
25 senators, (and a number of Representatives as well)
were invited by Warnke to participate in the ongoing
negotiations. They were even allowed to converse

directly with the Soviet delegation. In addition, over the next two years, six members of the Foreign Relations Committee traveled to Geneva on several occasions to keep track of the progress of the negotiations. Another Senate delegation went to Moscow and spoke with Soviet officials there. Finally, after the completion of the SALT II agreement in June 1979, Majority Leader Byrd went to the Soviet Union to explain the Senate's role to Soviet President Leonid Brezhnev and other Soviet leaders. One important objective of Senator Byrd's mission was to clarify for the Soviet Premier the differing legal implications of the various forms of understandings, reservations, or amendments the Senate might attach to the treaty.[23]

While executive-congressional relations had been fairly good throughout the spring and summer of 1977, by the early fall some significant congressional opposition had begun to emerge. It coalesced around Senator Jackson. President Carter had made a concerted attempt early in his administration to enlist Jackson's support. He had allowed Jackson to make a number of proposals to the government on what the U.S. position should be--a few of which were incorporated in the March 1977 proposals. The provision of the March 1977 proposals that Jackson liked most was a proposal that, in effect, would amount to sharp reduction in the number of Soviet "heavy" missiles (the SS-18 in particular). However, the Soviets rejected the proposals, citing the reduction of the "heavies" as one of the more objectionable provisions. In September, Carter decided to stop pursuing a cutback in heavies, to focus instead on attempting to reduce the total number of MIRVed intercontinental ballistic missiles (ICBM). This may or may not have been a wise decision. But the significant fact was that the Carter Administration made this change without consulting key senators. Jackson was particularly incensed not only by the change in policy, but because he learned about it in The New York Times. It is doubtful that prior consultation with Jackson would have convinced him to forego his long-time fixation on the "heavies," but perhaps prior notification might have mitigated his outrage.[24] Other congressional participants echoed this refrain about an inconsistency of consultation. One Armed Services aide, for example, called the Carter consultations "a triumph of quantity over quality."[25] Senator Charles Percy was later to remark, "The Administration failed to consult frequently with key senators about substantive changes at crucial points in the negotiations. Consulations would have lessened the subsequent opposition within the Senate..."[26]

These charges against Carter may be overdrawn. He did, after all, consult to a greater extent then ever before--in both qualitative and quantitative ways.

What can be said with some degree of certainty is that
Carter was inconsistent in his consultation and that in
the case of SALT II, congressional demands for participation grew faster than the willingness of the Administration to comply.

It was in the midst of this growing tension between
the President and Congress that the Administration
realized that the 1972 Interim Agreement on Offensive
Weapons was about to expire (Octoger 4, 1977)--with no
immediate prospect for a replacement. Something had to
be done, or hopes for SALT II could disintegrate in the
midst of a renewed arms race. Given the climate in
Congress at the time, the Administration was hesitant
to submit any decision to extend the Interim Agreement
for fear the congressional hardliners would embroil the
negotiations in controversy. Instead, the State Department and the U.S.S.R. issued simultaneous "parallel
unilateral declarations," that the Administration maintained were not subject to congressional review. Few
in Congress bought that argument. There was a widespread belief in the Senate--among both SALT supporters
and detractors--that the Administration had violated a
provision of the 1961 Arms Control and Disarmament
Agency Act which states:[27]

> no action can be taken under this law or any
> other law that will obligate the U.S. to dis-
> arm or reduce or limit the armed forces or
> armaments of the U.S., except pursuant to the
> treaty-making power of the President under the
> Constitution or unless authorized by further
> affirmative legislative action by the Congress.

Senators Cranston, Jackson, and other key senators co-
sponsored a resolution declaring approval for the extension of the Interim Agreement. Their intent was to
reassert the congressional prerogative in this area.[28]

Linkage Issue

The debate on SALT II (which centered primarily in
committee hearings) did not stick strictly to the
merits of the treaty. In fact, one of the most important areas of concern was whether or not to "link"
favorable treatment of SALT II with Soviet behavior.
Because of the extreme preoccupation of a number of
senators with the "linkage" issue, it is not unreasonable to argue that SALT II was not approved because it
was seen in the context of deteriorating relations with
the Soviets while SALT I passed because it was considered during the heyday of detente. SALT II failed to
gain approval because its fate became linked to international events, especially the international

activities of the Soviets.

As hard as President Carter tried to decouple the debate over the merits of the treaty from world events, this proved increasingly difficult to do. In the spring of 1979, for example, a poll of senators found roughly 40 who considered themselves generally favorably disposed to arms control agreements, but who were undecided on SALT II because of the Soviet military build-up and activities in the world.[29]

Eventually "linkage" would become the dogma of the Republican Party. There were various calls for a break in negotiations in response to Soviet activities. Linkage is a rather broad concept that can be used to apply to both the internal and external "behavior" of the Soviet Union. A good example of an application of "internal" linkage, was in regard to the trial of Anatoly Shcharansky, a Soviet dissident. Unfortunately the Soviets chose to try Shcharansky just prior to a critical meeting between Secretary of State Vance and Soviet Foreign Minister Andrei Gromyko. Senator Robert Dole (R-Kansas) called on Vance to cancel the meeting. Senator Jackson said to go ahead would be to "send the wrong signal, at the wrong time."[30]

More typically, however, the SALT II treaty was linked to Soviet international behavior, especially to activities in the Third World. The argument for linkage was that the U.S. can use agreements such as SALT II as leverage to induce the Soviets to change their international or internal behavior. Many senators had the notion that by signing SALT I, the Soviets had tacitly agreed to "behave." The activities of the Soviets in the Third World (e.g., the Horn of Africa) were seen as clear evidence that SALT I had not achieved these objectives.

Later, in the minority report filed by Republican Senators Howard Baker, Richard Lugar, S. I. Hayakawa, and Jesse Helms explaining why they voted against SALT II in the Foreign Relations Committee, "linkage" accounted for three of the four reasons cited. At one point the Senators stated:[31]

> We disagree with the Administration's contention that SALT and our consideration of this treaty should not be linked to the overall geopolitical relationship between the Soviet Union and the United States.

The debate in the Senate (which centered in committee hearings) was not by any means totally focused on the "linkage" issue. There was, in fact, a good deal of debate on the merits of the treaty in three key respects:[32] (1) SALT II's impact on the strategic balance, (2) verification concerns, and (3) implications of SALT for NATO.

Strategic Balance

To the arms control hardliners, SALT II simply did
not deal with the critical issue: the "window of vulnerability." The window of vulnerability refers to the
hypothetical vulnerability of American ICBMs to a
Soviet ICBM first strike. One of the most important
differences between 1972, when SALT I was signed, and
1979, when SALT II was signed, was the evolution of
Soviet strategic forces. The Soviets had always had a
numerical advantage in terms of large ICBMs. This was
not considered a problem by many senators in 1972 because Soviet missiles were not very accurate and none
of them were MIRVed. However, once the Soviets began
MIRVing their large missiles and making drastic improvements in their accuracy, the situation changed.
The fear of Paul Nitze and others was that unless the
number of Soviet heavy missiles was drastically reduced, the Soviets would be able to capitalize on this
strategic advantage for political gain. Nitze and his
congressional allies charged that because SALT II did
not reduce the number of Soviet "heavies," the "window"
was left wide open.[33]
On the other side, proponents of the treaty argued
that the fear of a Soviet preemptive strike was unrealistic, and could never be translated into strategic advantage for the Soviets for a number of reasons, including the relative invulnerability of the other legs
of the U.S. strategic triad.[34] (The triad consists of
the three elements of U.S. strategic capability--land,
air, and sea-based.) Moreover, the proponents argued
that the fractionation limits imposed by SALT II; i.e.,
the limitation of the number of warheads which could be
placed on the Soviet "heavies" would greatly reduce the
utility of these behemoths.
There was also a third group of senators, typified
by Senators McGovern and Mark Hatfield (R-Oregon), who
questioned SALT II on the grounds that it did not go
far enough, that it made no progress toward real reduction.[35] SALT supporters responded by saying that although SALT II would not result in any dramatic reductions, it was an important and necessary first step in
checking the arms race before seeking some significant
reductions in SALT III. The proponents of the treaty
contended that SALT critics tended to focus on the
matters not covered by the treaty and to ignore what
was dealt with, such as the fractionation limits.
One reason that the final SALT II product disap-
pointed both the Hatfield and Jackson viewpoints was
that it did not measure up to earlier expectations. In
March 1977 Carter had called for deep cuts, including
cuts in the Soviet heavy missiles. But when Carter
pulled away from these "deep" cuts after the Soviet

rejection, disillusionment set in. Another benchmark
against which SALT II was unfavorably compared was the
Jackson amendment. Since Jackson could make a convincing case that the amendment mandated parity for throw-
weight as well, the SALT II treaty did not fulfill this
aspect of that amendment.

Verification Concerns

A major concern of some senators who generally were
inclined to support SALT II (e.g., John Glenn) was
whether the treaty could be adequately verified. Since
SALT I, there had been growing doubts about whether the
Soviets could be trusted to honor their agreements.
This perception was fed by the fact that the Soviets
had taken advantage of certain loose definitions in
SALT I. This particularly related to the rather vague
definition in SALT I of exactly what a "heavy missile"
was. Staying bearly within the letter, if not the
spirit of the agreement, the Soviets were able to in-
troduce a new generation of missiles (the SS-19) that
was substantially larger than what the U.S. had intended to allow.[36]

Secondly, there was the assertion by some of the
anti-SALT forces that the Soviets had actually violated
the literal terms of the agreement. The primary charge
was that they had used various radar set-ups "in an ABM
mode."[37] The Carter Administration argued that when
questions concerning such activities had been raised
that, in every case, the Soviets had either changed
their behavior or presented an explanation that satisfied the terms of SALT I.[38] Some treaty opponents were
not convinced, however, and persisted in their belief
that the Soviets had cheated on SALT I.

The consequences of all this led to a fixation with
verification issues that was unrealistic and counter-
productive. A good example of this came in an exchange
between Senator Glenn and Secretary of Defense Harold
Brown. Glenn contended that with the existing state of
technology, the U.S. could not monitor all the qualitative restrictions imposed by SALT II. In particular,
he maintained that while the agreement prohibited improvements of missiles by more than 5 percent on certain dimensions, in actuality, the intelligence capacity was no where near that sophisticated. Brown
countered that Glenn's logic might lead him to seek an
agreement that was verifiable, but totally undesirable
(e.g., setting improvement levels at 50 percent).[39]

Implications for NATO

The final major area of concern in the debate on

the merits of SALT II was over the implications of the agreement for U.S. allies. The major question was whether the U.S. was giving too much away in allowing restrictions on the ground-and-sea-launched cruise missile scheduled to be placed in Europe at a later date. The fear was that even though these restrictions were scheduled to expire in three years (before the cruise missiles could even be deployed) certain aspects of SALT suggested that these restrictions might be extended. Various senators, Sam Nunn (D-Georgia) in particular, worked assiduously to prevent any problems for the NATO allies from SALT II.[40]

Committee Action

If the quantity and quality of congressional participation from 1977 until the signing of SALT II greatly exceeded that of previous years, the involvement of the Senate after the signing of the agreement was also dramatic. One important change was that committees other than the Senate Foreign Relations Committee were involved to a greater degree than before.

One new committee that played a role in SALT II was the Senate Select Committee on Intelligence on the verification implications of the SALT II treaty. The Intelligence Committee received briefings on Soviet compliance with SALT I and on the technical ability of the United States to monitor the new requirements of SALT II (especially the qualitative requirements). The committee recommended that Congress appropriate money to increase U.S. capabilities. With this improvement, it was generally argued that any "strategically significant" violation could be detected in time for a U.S. response.[41] Although the overall conclusion tended to support SALT II, there was enough controversial material in the report to keep the verification issue a major point of contention. There was no Intelligence Committee in the Senate in 1972, so this investigation was a major change from SALT I.

In addition to the Intelligence Committee's hearings, the Senate Armed Services Committee also conducted hearings on the "Military Implications" of SALT II.[42] At the conclusion of the hearings, Senator Jackson and nine other members attempted to report out a negative evaluation of SALT II, over the protests of Chairman John Stennis and six other members. A report from this committee could not become the basis for legislative action, but it did serve as a vehicle for the anti-treaty forces. Of course, the fulcrum of the SALT debate continued to be the Foreign Relations Committee.

On SALT I, the Foreign Relations Committee had held seven days of hearings on the treaty, and the Senate

Armed Services Committee held nine days of hearings. The increase in number of hearings held by both committees on SALT II was dramatic. For example, on SALT II the Foreign Relations Committee held 11 sessions on procedure alone. In addition, there were 30 public hearings and 13 executive sessions prior to "mark-up." During this mark-up period--when the committee discussed and voted on the provisions of the treaty and proposed changes--there were a total of 22 sessions. The Foreign Relations Committee eventually reported favorably on the treaty by a narrow 9-6 margin. A number of important conditions were attached to the treaty when the committee approved it. In all, the committee voted for 20 conditions which would have been sent to the Senate floor along with the treaty itself. What is most significant about the mark-up process is that the committee did not recommend any amendments.[43] This action was largely the result of Majority Leader Byrd and Chairman Church of the Foreign Relations Committee. Both men were well aware that had any amendments passed, and been approved by the full Senate, this would have necessitated eventual renegotition of the treaty. Some of these potential "killer amendments" came within one vote of being passed by the Foreign Relations Committee.

Committee Changes

Perhaps the most significant change the Foreign Relations Committee proposed related to an item in the Joint Statement of Principles and Basic Guidelines for Subsequent Negotiations (an annex to the SALT II agreement). A provision in this document stated that: The parties shall, in the course of future negotiations, pursue certain objectives, one of which is "resolution of the issues included in the protocol" to the SALT II Treaty.[44]

The problem with this provision was that the items covered in the protocol were exactly the items many in Congress did not want to see become the basis for future negotiations. One of these items was the basing of ICBMs in a mobile mode. The Foreign Relations Committee included a statement in its report on the SALT II treaty saying that the United States should issue a declaration of its intent to deploy a mobile-based "missile experimental" (MX) once the protocol expired. In its report, the Foreign Relations Committee also recommended that the Senate accept language stating that nothing in the treaty or protocol:

Establishes a precedent for any limitations which may be proposed in future negotiations relating to systems limited in the protocol.[45]

More important than even the MX basing mode was the restriction on sea-and-ground-launched cruise missiles, also in the protocol. Given the passage from the Joint Statement for Future Negotiations, which suggested that the protocol did form the basis for future agreements, this was a significant action by the committee. This interpretation in the committee report was complicated, however, by the fact that Senator McGovern introduced a resolution (endorsed by the committee) which seemed to support the idea of using the protocol for future negotiations.[46] This apparent contradiction was left unresolved by the committee.

The committee also recommended that the Senate adopt a sense-of-the-Senate resolution to the effect that the protocol could not be extended unilaterally by the President without Senate approval. Obviously, this was an attempt to avoid the type of controversy that arose from Carter's extension of the Interim Agreement.

Another important change which resulted in a loosening of the provision of the SALT II agreement was the committee's interpretation of the circumvention clauses. The circumvention clauses were vaguely worded provisos that papered over a basic difference between the United States and the Soviet Union. The difference concerns whether or not the U.S. would be permitted at some future point to transfer cruise weapons and/or cruise technology to its NATO allies. Senator Nunn had been instrumental in ensuring that these provisos were vague in the first place. The Foreign Relations Committee recommended loosening the restriction even more, by an explicit statement that "nothing in the treaty or the protocol...precludes cooperation in modernization" (i.e., by transfer of cruise weapons).[47]

SALT and International Circumstances

The Foreign Relations Committee's review of the SALT II Treaty was protracted well beyond the original timetable. The delay was largely caused by a series of international events that clouded the atmosphere for treaty considerations and raised questions about Soviet intentions. When the Senate began its August recess, it was thought that the Foreign Relations Committee was nearing completion of its consideration of the treaty. Although there had been some strong criticism of the treaty during the committee's hearings, much of the criticism related to the overall U.S. defense posture rather than to the specific provisions of the treaty. And Administration witnesses, particularly the Joint Chiefs of Staff, and other supporters had made a strong case for SALT II. Thus, the pro-treaty forces appeared to be gaining momentum, which supporters hoped would carry through to the time when the full Senate took up the treaty.

However, when the Senate returned to session in early September, prospects for SALT II had been badly damaged by the "discovery" of a Soviet military brigade in Cuba. Foreign Relations Chairman Frank Church and several Administration officials quickly made sweeping, categorical statements about the Soviet troops before the full facts of the situation had been established. (See Chapter 1.) SALT critics quickly seized upon the issue and pointed to three "lessons" from this incident that proved that SALT II should not be approved. They argued that: (1) The Soviets went to great lengths to hide the presence of the troops, proving once again that they could not be trusted. (2) The troops had apparently been in Cuba for some years. This cast doubt on the ability of U.S. intelligence to detect Soviet activities. (3) The presence of Soviet troops in the Western Hemisphere was proof of the Soviet aggressive tendencies.[48]

The controversy over the Soviet troops in Cuba diverted attention from the merits of the treaty it- self, and necessitated a further delay in Senate floor debate. In the course of this delay, much of the pro- SALT momentum dissipated.

At the height of the flap over the Soviet troops, Senator Russell Long (D-Louisiana) announced his oppo- sition to the treaty, citing the incident as a factor in his decision. Senator Long was one more key Senate figure whose support the Administration had needed.

The strong statements made by Senator Church upon first learning about the Soviet brigade were a major factor in the controversy. Church was facing a stiff challenge from the right wing in his bid for re-elec- tion in Idaho, and was under attack for his support of the Panama Canal Treaties. Almost reflexively, he latched onto the Cuban issue as an opportunity to demonstrate his resolve and a tough-minded attitude. Immediately after being informed about the Soviet troops, Church made several remarks he would later regret, including the statement that, "There is no likelihood whatsoever the Senate will ratify the treaty while there are Soviet troops in Cuba."[49] Coming from a leading SALT supporter and the man who, with Majority Leader Byrd, had been expected to lead the SALT floor debate, this was a damning statement. Byrd labeled the incident as a "pseudo-crisis" and noted indications that the troops had been in Cuba for some time. Church later tried to back away from his statements, while saving a little face. He introduced a condition to the treaty whereby the President would have to certify before the treaty could be approved that these troops were not engaged in a combat role and would not become a threat to any country in the Hemisphere.[50] But by that time the damage to SALT II had been done. The damage was not so much in terms of a loss of specific votes but in the loss of crucial momentum.

Another international development that complicated the environment for SALT II consideration was the turmoil in Iran. The fall of the Shah in early 1979 had led to fears that the Soviets might rush in to fill this "power vacuum." A more direct consequence for SALT II was the loss of certain U.S. "listening posts" in Iran after the Shah's fall. These had been used by the U.S. to monitor Soviet missile testing. The loss of these stations was one of the reasons Senator Glenn had questioned the ability of the U.S. to effectively monitor compliance with SALT II.[51]

There was another and broader sense in which the developments in Iran had a debilitating effect on SALT II. Paul Warnke has stated that arms-control agreements are an "index of a nation's self-confidence."[52] In late October 1979, SALT II proponents were beginning to show signs of regaining momentum, as the controversy over the Soviet troops in Cuba died down. But, in early November, the United States Embassy in Tehran was seized by Iranian militants, and embassy personnel were taken as hostages. The Iranian situation dealt a serious blow to U.S. self-confidence and to the chances for SALT II approval.

The coup de grace to SALT II prospects came with the Soviet invasion of Afghanistan at Christmas-time 1979. In early January 1980, President Carter and Majority Leader Byrd agreed that the consideration of SALT II should be suspended. In light of these international events, consideration of the treaty on its merits seemed highly unlikely.

The Case For and Against Senate Involvement

The Senate's record on SALT I and II provides an historical framework for consideration of the validity of the arguments for and against major Senate involvement in the arms control process. The discussion will be structured around the arguments made against Senate involvement, but, in the process, the arguments for Senate involvement will also be covered.

Lack of Expertise

The first argument against major Senate involvement in the arms control process is in many respects the weakest argument. Briefly stated, this argument asserts that senators are typically not arms control experts and hence lack the requisite expertise to grapple with such a highly technical, arcane subject. This argument is actually a vestige of a more general argument against congressional involvement in foreign policy that had much more validity in a previous era. Now, the argument makes little sense. Present-day senators have much greater access to technical information and expertise. One factor increasing this access is the quantitative and qualitative improvements in Senate staffing. In preparation for SALT II consideration, all the Senate leadership and many of the interested senators contracted their own staff experts on arms control. Those who did not had access to the staff experts assigned to the relevant committees. Secondly, senators can utilize research services such as those of the Office of Technology Assessment or the General Accounting Office to do specialized studies.

Finally, some individual senators became arms control experts in their own right. A few, such as Senator Glenn, already had a technical background from which to draw. Glenn, for example, with the help of key aides, made some improvements to the treaty during the Foreign Relations Committee hearings. These conditions, attached to the resolution for ratification passed by the Foreign Relations Committee, dealt with such technical subjects as a tighter definition of cruise missile range and the composition of elements of the "bus" or MIRVed missile carrier.[53]

Glenn's focus on definitions suggests another broader aptitude at which members of Congress generally are well-practiced: the refining of procedure. Representative Les Aspin (D-Wisconsin) has argued that one of Congress' major strengths is the refinement of governmental or legal process.[54] The aptitude comes both from the fact that many senators are lawyers and perhaps more importantly, because such is the warp and woof of their legislative endeavors. This aptitude can and should be harnessed--at the negotiation stage, as well as final approval stage. It is not inconceivable to argue that the examination of the proposed SALT I Interim Agreement by a critical Senate might have detected the loose definitions before the process was too far along.

Reduction of Bargaining Leverage

The second argument against Senate involvement during the negotiations asserts that the public nature of Senate debate, with its concomitant criticism of the prevailing U.S. position, weakens U.S. bargaining leverage in dealing with the Soviets. The implicit assumption here is that a lack of unity necessarily results in a weaker bargaining position--at least when this disagreement is apparent to the adversary. This does not appear to be universally valid, however.

In some cases the argument does seem to be intuitively correct: for example, in those cases in which many senators are advocating positions closer to the adversary than the administration. Henry Kissinger has argued that the mood of Congress during the Paris negotiations on Vietnam led to a greater recalcitrance on the part of the North Vietnamese.[55] Applying this logic to SALT, had the Senate been more informed during the negotiations on SALT I, that particular Congress might have "weakened" the U.S. position. But that is speculation; it might also have worked in the opposite direction.

In any event, this whole line of reasoning does not fit SALT II. In this case there appears to be clear empirical evidence that the involvement of the Senate strengthened U.S. bargaining leverage. Paul Warnke has remarked that he intentionally exposed the Soviet negotiators to some "hard-line" U.S. senators so that the Soviets might better understand why certain positions would be unacceptable to the Senate. Warnke indicated that this seems to have strengthened his bargaining position with his Soviet counterpart.[56]

A less confrontational variant of this tactic was used on at least one occasion to extract a specific and significant concession from the Soviets. When Senator Mathias met with the Soviet negotiator, Vladimir Semyonov, they apparently developed a personal rapport. Based on this rapport, and on Mathias' reputation as an arms control advocate, Mathias was able to credibly argue that the Senate simply would not approve a treaty that was not accompanied by an "agreed data base" (on the number of Soviet weapon systems of different sorts). This had been a frustrating sticking point for the American SALT delegation ever since SALT I. Consequently, when Semyonov responded positively to Mathias' suggestion, it greatly surprised some of the professional negotiators.[57]

Difficulty of Presidential Consultation

The third argument against Senate involvement represents an attack on some of the more widely recognized institutional flaws in the legislative branch: specifically, its decentralized nature and its alleged confrontational relationship with the executive. Although these two factors are analytically distinct, they are said to produce similar effects. Both factors are said to make it more difficult for effective presidential consultation, which has the ultimate result of making the articulation of a coherent arms control policy extremely difficult.

This third argument has a basis in truth, but its

significance is all too often exaggerated. The Senate
is indeed decentralized to the point where the clear
articulation of policy is often difficult. This decentralization or lack of unity has occurred for a
whole litany of reasons that should be familiar to any
student of political science: the decline of party
loyalty, the diminishing power of the Senate leadership, and the fragmentation of responsibility being
primary factors. One direct result of the fragmentation of responsibility is that there is no one focal
point for presidential consultation. The President
cannot simply send his representatives to one committee, but instead must stay in touch with several committees and subcommittees in both Houses, as well as
the leadership of both parties, plus some interested
individual senators. Consequently, some of the inconsistency which some members of Congress attributed to
President Carter, may have been due in some part to
this institutional flaw.

Another well known systematic "flaw" is the fact
that the executive and legislative branches exist in an
inherently adversarial relationship. This has its
strengths, but it also makes articulation of a coherent
policy more difficult. Evidence of the tension between
the two branches during SALT can be seen in the dispute
over the "parallel unilateral declarations" which represented a presidential attempt to circumvent a congressional prerogative.

While all this is true, care must be taken not to
exaggerate either the extent or the significance of
congressional decentralization and legislative-executive tension. The SALT II experience provides a number
of illustrations indicating that the situation is a
good deal more complex than is sometimes suggested by
simplistic models of Congress. For example, the Warnke
confirmation hearings exhibit both evidence of the tension between branches and proof that the systems works
rather well despite that tension. The tension is ex-
emplified by the fact that in the vote on Warnke's
nomination as chief SALT negotiator, he failed to get
two-thirds of the votes cast. As mentioned, this was a
deliberate signal to the President that the Senate
would not passively accept any arms control initiative
that the executive sent, but would examine any such
proposal diligently.

What may have escaped notice about this episode
however is the deft political maneuver employed by the
Democratic leadership to separate the votes on Warnke's
two positions. This adroit move enabled Democratic
senators to express their concern to the President in a
manner that minimized political embarrassment to him
and mitigated the tension between the two branches.
Not incidentally, Warnke was confirmed for both
positions.

Perhaps even more significant in this regard than the Warnke nomination was the careful coordination between President Carter, Majority Leader Byrd, and Foreign Relations Chairman Church to ensure that in the formal committee consideration of SALT II no "killer amendments" were added. Such amendments would have required renegotiation with the Soviets. Since in the resultant process of renegotiating the entire agreement was likely to unravel, the amendments were said to have the potential to "kill" the treaty.

Despite the addition of some 20 conditions by the Foreign Relations Committee, none were of such a nature as to require sending the treaty back for renegotiation. Given the great opposition to SALT II, this was no mean achievement. Both this example and that of the Warnke confirmation demonstrate that at certain crucial points, despite the problems, the system works remarkably well.

SALT and Defense Spending

The fourth argument made against Senate involvement in the arms control process is a cogent one, which is difficult to refute from the SALT experience. This argument asserts that Senate involvement in SALT II led to an increase in military spending through two mutually reinforcing dynamics:

A.   The need to "win over" some of the more defense-minded senators to a pro-SALT position induced President Carter to raise the proposed levels of military spending.

B.   Because so much of the discussion in the SALT II debate focused on the expanding military prowess of the Soviet Union, many senators, (both for and against SALT) became 'sensitized' to the need (or perceived need) for an increase in military spending to bolster U.S. military forces.

Jimmy Carter was elected on a platform of reducing military spending. However, after the SALT II Treaty encountered opposition in the Senate, he appeared to reverse his position. Although one might attribute this change of heart to a reassessment of the Soviet military threat, it is equally plausible that he was motivated by "political" considerations. During the discussions on the fiscal year 1981 military budget, Carter agreed to a real increase of 3 percent in military spending. At that point Carter desperately needed the support of a "defense-minded" senator to pull in

undecided votes. With the loss of Senators Jackson and
Baker, Senator Nunn became a pivotal figure. Senator
Nunn's position on the Armed Services Committee and his
credentials as an advocate of a strong defense policy
enhanced his attractiveness. Best of all, Nunn appeared truly open on SALT. However, Nunn was adamant
(as were Senators Tower of Texas and Ernest Hollings of
South Carolina) that a 3 percent defense increase would
not be sufficient. Senator Nunn kept pushing for a 5
percent increase, and eventually Carter relented.[58]
Although Nunn never made a firm commitment on SALT II,
after the increase in the proposed defense budget, he
was reported to be leaning toward support of the
treaty.[59]

In the second type of linkage between congressional
involvement in SALT and increased defense spending the
dynamics are different. Here the argument is that high
congressional involvement led to increased military
spending because the extensive discussions of Soviet
military power "sensitized" many senators to the issue. Many of these senators had not been well informed
about the Soviet military build-up before this point.
The SALT II debate changed that. It is ironic that a
congressional debate on an arms control treaty should
lead the participants to favor a military build-up (in
areas not covered by the treaty); but that seems to
have been the case. One very important point that
should be stressed here is that this dynamic worked on
both proponents and opponents of SALT. It was not just
the traditional hawks who were fueling this debate.
One reflection of this dualistic attitude (pro-arms
control; pro-military spending) can be seen in one of
the conditions added to the Foreign Relations Committee
report on the treaty. The same committee that voted
approval of the SALT II treaty supported a "sense-of-
the-Senate" declaration calling for funds for an MX,
"advanced penetrating bomber," Trident II submarine and
missile, and other weapons systems.[60]

The interaction of domestic political and systemic
factors can be seen in the debate on how to deploy the
MX missile. The argument for a mobile MX was that a
mobile ICBM would provide a means of redressing the
perceived vulnerability of American ICBMs to a Soviet
preemptive strike. The validity or likelihood of a
preemptive strike may be questionable, but Paul Nitze
and senators such as Henry Jackson were convinced that
the threat was real enough. From the Carter Administration perspective, the beauty of deploying the MX in
a mobile mode was that while it could theoretically
reduce the threat to the ICBMs, this only made sense
within the context of a SALT agreement that limited the
number of Soviet warheads by various means. In other
words, if Carter accepted the logic of the mobile
basing, he would have at least a plausible response

to the Nitze-Jackson charge that he was doing nothing
about the much-discussed "window of vulnerability."
Nitze and Jackson never accepted that argument; they
said that even with SALT II the Soviets could still
threaten the missiles.[61] However the Carter Administration hoped that the argument would be plausible to
other uncommitted senators. Moreover, Carter's decision to support the idea of a mobile MX (an idea that
had a passionate support of the Joint Chiefs) helped
get the military leaders "on board."[62]

"Politicization" of Negotiations

The final argument made against Senate participation in arms control negotiations is probably the
most important. The gist of this argument is that
Senate involvement "politicizes" the negotiations to
such an extent that the chance for "serious progress"
in the negotiations and/or eventual approval of the
agreement are greatly diminished. Obviously, there are
two different, and somewhat contradictory, applications
of the politicization argument. The first application
pertains to the substance of the treaty while the
second application pertains to the chances for ratification. The assumption of the first is that serious
progress can occur only under conditions of secret
diplomacy where neither party will be tempted to engage
in propagandistic blasts instead of concentrating on
formulating a substantive agreement.[63]

The second application of the politicization argument is based primarily on the SALT experience. Before
SALT the prevailing wisdom was that the Senate would be
more likely to support policies it had a hand in developing. This assumption was called into question, however, because SALT I was approved after only minimal
debate and little prior consultation while SALT II was
not approved despite extensive Senate involvement. So
this "new" wisdom suggests to some that the involvement
of the Senate early in the process politicized the debate to such an extent that approval became extremely
difficult, if not impossible. The logic of this argument is based on two mutually-reinforcing dynamics.
First, the involvement of a greater diversity of viewpoints made negotiating the agreement more difficult
and protracted the entire process. Second, because of
the protraction of the negotiations and the open nature
of the debate, opposition groups could more effectively
mobilize.

Before discussing the different applications of the
politicization argument, it is useful to deal with the
general point that the involvement of the Senate in the
arms control process "politicizes" the issue. In the

extreme variant of the argument, which is easily re-
futed, the implicit assumption is that it is the specific involvement of senators that introduces the political element into the equation. This assertion is
patently false. It ignores the highly politicized nature of the executive branch as a whole, not to mention
any ulterior motives the President may have. The President is directly involved in the electoral process
himself, and so large an issue as arms control cannot
help but have major political ramifications. There is
good evidence to suggest that in response to criticism
from the right wing of the Republican Party (especially
his opponent for the 1976 Republican nomination, Ronald
Reagan), President Ford initiated a slow-down in SALT
activity.[64]

Moreover, bureaucratic politics is just as applicable to arms control as it is to other issues. The
various "actors" all have certain perspectives on the
issue, which are at least partly grounded in an organizational bias. Each actor has certain vested interests
to protect.[65] The involvement of the Senate did not
create the splits or disagreements among executive
policy makers. The Senate might be more accurately
described as mirroring policy differences that already
existed both in the executive branch and the public at
large. Although Senate involvement reinforces this
trend, given the differing bureaucratic and ideological
perspectives within the executive branch, merely elim-
inating legislative involvement will not somehow mirac-
ulously produce unaminity and coherence. Of course, if
the involvement of most of the actors in the executive
branch is curtailed as well--something Henry Kissinger
largely succeeded in doing in SALT I--this might result
in a closer approximation of a "unified" position.
Such a tactic has its own costs however, and these
costs may be too high of a price to pay. Gerard Smith,
the SALT I chief negotiator, has suggested that when
Kissinger took most of the negotiations into his own
hands, the agreement that Kissinger finally negotiated
was less favorable to the U.S. on several key points
than what was "in the works" through more formal
channels.[66] However, even if the "extreme" version of
this argument is fallacious, there is still a great
deal of truth to the assertion that the involvement of
the Senate exacerbates the difficulty in securing an
arms control agreement. This is true if for no other
reason than that the number of political actors is
greatly increased when the Senate is involved.

Senate Involvement and "Substantive Progress"

Granted that Senate involvement does increase the

"political" nature of the issue, does the inherently
public nature of congressional debate prevent the
achievement of "substantive progress?" The results are
mixed. One partial refutation of this objection can be
found in the number of improvements to SALT II that can
partly be attributed to Senate pressure.

For example, Senator Thomas McIntyre insisted that
the negotiators establish a time for the dismantling of
the strategic nuclear delivery vehicles (SNDVs) that
did not overlap with the end of the protocol. McIntyre
reasoned that if the Soviets delayed the dismantling of
their systems, they might be able to use this as leverage to force continuation of the protocol limits. He
wanted to allow the U.S. the option to extend or dis-
continue the protocol. McIntyre's proposals were written into the language of the agreement.[67]

Senator Gary Hart (D-Colorado) was a major force in
pushing for significant qualitative limits on "new
types" of missiles. At Hart's urging, the restrictions
on modernization were pushed down to the 5 percent
range. This was an important change, because previous
arms control agreements concentrated on quantitative
dimensions. So Hart's insistence was an important step
forward.[68]

Another example of a qualitative restriction that
was encouraged by congressional interest was the
fractionation limit (the limit on the maximum permissible number of warheads per missile). It is not that
the members of Congress originated this idea or any of
the others. This was rarely the case. However, it can
be argued that the long-term interest of the Senate in
attempting to get some sort of MIRV ban finally came to
fruition with this Carter Administration proposal.
Perhaps the most accurate description is that congressional interest in a fractionation limit reinforced the
positions of those in the executive branch who desired
this option as well.

However, the general objection to _extensive_ public
discussion of specific proposals may have some validity. Many analysts believe that it was a mistake for
President Carter to publicly disclose some of the
specifics of his March 1977 proposals before submitting
them to the Soviets. The desire to secure Senate
support may have been part of his motivation. Consequently, the best alternative may be some sort of
compromise between secret, executive-dominated diplomacy (as in SALT I) and a wide-open public debate on
specific proposals during the negotiations. Putting
this compromise into operation would be difficult, but
one possibility would entail limiting congressional
debate in the early stages to committee "executive
session" discussion.

Impact of Early Senate Involvement

The second aspect of the politicization argument focuses on the question of the impact of early Senate involvement on chances for final favorable treatment of the agreement. This whole question is closely tied to the relationship between electoral politics and arms control. The American political process seems to demonstrate its more deleterious effects on the arms control process as election times near. Jimmy Carter was intensely aware of this. Consequently, he began negotiations on SALT II very early in his Administration. The hope, and indeed the belief, was that the treaty would be signed and presented to the Senate well before the approach of the 1980 election. This would have meant that domestic political factors would have had less of an impact on the decision.

Unfortunately, for a number of reasons, including the early involvement of the Senate, the negotiations dragged on much longer than had been anticipated. By the time the treaty was finally presented to Congress in the summer of 1979, the support for the President had dwindled, and powerful SALT opposition groups had emerged to challenge the treaty.

One such group was the American Conservative Union, which took out ads on 350 television stations arguing against SALT II before it was even signed.[70] This could only be possible in an atmosphere in which at least some of the general terms of the prospective agreement were known in Congress. Secretary Vance remarked at one point:[71]

> One of my real frustrations has been that the protracted negotiations have prevented us from laying out the strengths of the agreement and from answering some of the misleading statements.

Still, all of this might not have mattered, had it not been for the fact that the 1980 elections were rapidly approaching. The calculation of the pro-SALT strategists was that since moderate Republican support for the treaty was absolutely essential (to get the necessary two-thirds), the Senate debate had to take place as soon as possible and before spring of 1980. Spring would signal the start of presidential primary season, and an increasingly partisan atmosphere in Congress. There would be a powerful incentive for Republicans to criticize the President, and a disincentive for them to adopt bipartisan positions. On SALT II, the moderate Republicans would also come under intense pressure from the conservative wing of their party to vote against the treaty. Against this backdrop, the equivocation of many moderate Republican senators is politically understandable. Therefore, as international events forced the continued postponement of the SALT II debate, and with the 1980 elections looming increasingly closer, the prospects for SALT II approval dimmed.

An interesting case in point is that of Howard Baker, who was Senate Minority Leader at the time. Baker planned to run for the Republican presidential nomination in 1980. He was faced, however, with considerable opposition from the conservative wing of his party for his support of the Panama Canal Treaties. Baker's support had been absolutely critical to the success of those treaties. (See Chapter 4.) His backing of the treaties made it easier for other Republicans to support them. The support of the Republican moderates was crucial because of the constitutional requirement that a two-thirds majority is necessary for treaty approval. Carter was hoping for this same support in the SALT II debate. Therefore, Baker's denunciation of SALT II as "fatally flawed" dealt a serious blow to the chances for eventual treaty approval. When this situation is contrasted with that at the time of SALT I (a Democratic majority in the Senate and a Republican President) it can be concluded that the divided leadership of the Senate in SALT II proved to be more important than divided party affiliation between President Nixon and Congress in SALT I. In other words, intra-institutional tension may be more important than inter-institutional division.

Although many of these arguments would appear to militate against congressional involvement, particularly in the early stages, a return to the era of congressional acquiescence is not likely.

Influence of Politics and Experience

Any attempt to circumvent the Senate's prerogative is apt to be met with stiff resistance. The growing assertiveness of the Senate in the field of arms control was apparent in 1979. There were a number of reasons for this increased assertiveness. One major reason might be labeled the "legacy of SALT I." A pervasive belief in Congress was that past administrations had not been as forthright as they might have been. This suspicion was reflected in a statement by Senator Church to Secretary Vance:

When the committee held hearings on SALT I, the Secretary of State, William Rogers, declared categorically that there are no secret agreements. Within six weeks after the Secretary made that statement, we were later to

> discover that Mr. Kissinger had entered into a
> secret agreement with Anatoly Dobrynin about
> the Soviet G-1 subs...Then later it was dis-
> covered that Nixon informed Brezhnev the U.S.
> would not deploy the maximum number of sub-
> marine missiles...I don't want any surprises
> of this kind in the course of our consider-
> ation of this SALT II agreement.[72]

In addition to this fear of executive secrecy, there
was also a widespread belief that the U.S. had been too
lax with the Soviets in SALT I. Many senators saw it
as their duty to prevent this from happening again.

Coupled with this "rational" explanation of increased assertiveness, there are several factors that
reinforced this trend. The first factor was a shift in
the public attitude toward detente and the Soviet
Union. Politically, this meant that those politicians
who advocated arms control during the SALT II period
were vulnerable to political attack. The public opinion polls at the time presented an interesting contrast: Although a healthy majority of the American
public continued to support arms control in general, a
large majority were also suspicious of the Soviet
Union. Perhaps most significantly, some of the later
polls indicated that many of those citizens who were
most informed about SALT (and hence were likely to take
it into account when they voted) were opposed to the
agreement.[73]

Finally, there were what might be called the "lessons of Panama." Many of those serving in the Senate
in 1979 at the time of SALT II had not been there in
1972. Consequently, much of their attitude toward the
treaty process derived from the Panama Canal debate.
In the course of the Panama debate, many senators
learned the ropes, so to speak, with regard to treaty
consideration. This infused them with self-confidence
in regard to the SALT II agreement. Many of them
generalized the experience of the Panama debate and applied that to SALT II. As a consequence of the experience in the Panama debate, many in the Senate believed
they could make substantial improvements in the SALT II
Treaty itself and not destroy the arms control process.

Given this congressional assertiveness, it can be
argued that Senate involvement in the SALT process did
increase the odds for favorable treatment of the treaty
relative to what the odds would have been without that
participation. If the only effective voice the Senate
has is in the approval phase, an assertive Senate might
be much less careful to avoid "killer amendments."

Also it must be stated that the political process
does not necessarily hinder arms control--it could
conceivably facilitate it. If there is a situation in
which the executive is not seriously committed to arms

control, while the public is, then the involvement of
the Senate should enhance the pressure for arms control
initiatives. Signs of this could be seen in the early
1980s, with Congress as a "link" between a public with
a strong interest in arms control and the Reagan Administration, which many believed was not seriously
committed to arms control.

Summary

The historical record indicates that Congress had a
neglible impact on SALT I. This study suggests that
the reasons for this are two-fold: (1) The Nixon Administration effectively kept the process of policy
development in the White House by drastically restricting the amount of information Congress had concerning
the substance of U.S. proposals or the status of the
talks. (2) There was a broad willingness in Congress
to allow the executive to have control. Congress did
not press the Administration to any great degree. A
major reason for this aquiescence was the indifference
of the part of many members toward arms control issues. There were a few strong supporters of arms control centered in the Foreign Relations Committee during
the chairmanship of J.W. Fulbright, but except for this
group, plus Senator Jackson and a few others, there was
relatively little interest in arms control issues.
This attitude persisted through the mid-seventies
before a more assertive attitude gradually emerged,
which finally expressed itself during the more "open"
Carter Administration. It appears that the efforts of
congressional involvement in the arms control process
are mixed. From an arms control perspective, some of
these efforts militate for congressional involvement,
and some militate against it.

One the one hand, congressional involvement resulted in these effects which could be seen as negative
from an arms control perspective:

1. In the case of SALT II, it led to an increase in military spending because:
   a. The desire to secure the support of
      defense-minded senators induced
      President Carter to increase the
      proposed levels of military spend-
      ing. The need to secure the support
      of these senators was brought about
      at least in part, by the constitu-
      tional requirement for a two-thirds
      majority.
   b. So much of the SALT II debate fo-
      cused on the expanding military
      prowess of the Soviet Union, this

"sensitized" many senators to the need to increase U.S. military spending.

2. The decentralized nature of Congress and the lack of party loyalty made it difficult for the President to consult with Congress and for Congress to articulate a clear, consistent policy direction.

3. The involvement of the Senate early in the process did increase (though it did not create) the "politicization" of the issue. The effects of this were mixed, though the major negative impact was to contribute to the protraction of the negotiations. The length of the negotiations and the openess of the debate allowed opposition groups to mobilize early. Finally, the proximity of the 1980 elections to the formal consideration of the treaty made favorable treatment more difficult.

4. The failure of the Senate to approve the SALT II Treaty led to an inconsistent U.S. foreign policy and raised questions abroad about the ability of the executive branch to commit the U.S. on major foreign policy issues.

On the other hand, there were some positive results from congressional involvement as well:

1. It increased U.S. bargaining leverage in dealing with the Soviets.

2. Congressional involvement improved the substance of the treaty. There were several examples, but the most important ones related to the push in Congress for a greater qualitative emphasis in SALT II.

3. Congressional involvement, imperfect though it may be, is still the best means for encouraging representative government (or as close an approximation of it as may be possible in a pluralistic society).

4. Congressional involvement in the early stages of SALT II increased the chances for final approval compared to the odds if there had not been that involvement. If the Senate had been denied initial participation, the Senate would have been much more likely to amend the treaty. This would probably have killed it. As it was, the Senate leaders might have been able to steer it through to approval without the addition of "killer

amendments" had international events not
kept the full Senate from debating the
treaty in 1979-1980.

On balance, the SALT experience suggests that a
stronger case can be made for congressional participation in strategic arms negotiations than can be made
against it. This is particularly true because of such
actions as the attempt of the Senate in SALT I to
encourage the pursuit of a MIRV ban. This suggests
that the impetus from arms control initiatives can come
from Congress as well as the President.

However, there are changes that could be made in
Congress that might mitigate some of the negative
tendencies. One possible improvement would be the
establishment of some type of ad hoc national security
committee. Such a suggestion has frequently been made
to facilitate better congressional participation in
foreign policy in general. It has special relevance
for arms control negotiations, however, because of the
necessity for a central Senate focal point for executive consultation. Establishing a small, clearly identified group of senators would serve the dual purpose
of encouraging more consistent presidential consultation while making it easier for Congress to articulate
policies and proposals. Such a consultative committee
could be made up of the majority and minority leaders,
the ranking members from the Intelligence, Foreign
Relations, and Armed Services Committees (as well as
the ranking members from the Arms Control Subcommittees), plus a small number of interested senators to be
selected by party caucus. Obviously such a consultative committee would not resolve all the problems, and
might even create a few of its own, but it would probably be an improvement over the present diffuse system.

There have also been suggestions that the constitutional requirement for a two-thirds majority for treaties should be changed. Such a change is seen as highly
desirable by many arms control advocates. The two-
thirds requirement not only makes it more difficult to
secure approval for arms control agreements, but is
viewed by some as undemocratic (in that it is anti-
majoritarian). Approval of arms control agreements by
a simple majority vote--perhaps of both Houses--would
still allow Congress to block agreements that did not
have widespread support, but it would prevent a minority from exercising veto power over U.S. arms control
policy. Nonetheless, the constitutional two-thirds
requirement is likely to continue in effect and to
remain an important consideration when it comes to arms
control treaties, particularly as long as the Senate
insists on retaining an active role in this area.

NOTES

1. These arguments are a composite of typical arguments taken from several sources, especially John Spanier and Eric Uslaner, Foreign Policy and the Democratic Dilemmas (3rd ed.) and Lawrence Weiler "Secrecy in Arms Control Negotiations," in Congress and Arms Control, Lawrence Weiler and Alan Platt, eds., (Boulder: Westview, 1978), pp.157-184.

2. SALT I actually consisted of two parts: the ABM Treaty and the Interim Agreement on Offensive Weapons. While Senate approval was necessary on both parts, the House was allowed to consider only the Interim Agreement. The House was brought into the approval process as a result of a 1961 act which mandated approval (a regular majority was sufficient for approval) from both Houses for arms control agreements couched in the form os an executive agreement rather than a treaty.

3. Alan Platt, The Senate and Strategic Arms Policy, 1969-1977 (Boulder: Westview, 1978), pp.29-30.

4. John Newhouse, Cold Dawn: The Inside Story of SALT (New York: Holt, Rinehart, and Winston, 1973), pp.66-101.

5. Recounted in Platt, p.25. See Congressional Record, August 3, 1972 for full account.

6. Platt, p.20.

7. Senate Resolution 211, Passed April 1970.

8. Alton Frye, A Responsibile Congress, (New York: McGraw Hill, 1975), pp.55-71.

9. Nixon remark reported in Washington Post, March 22, 1970, p.A-1. See Platt, p.14 for discussion of episode.

10. Henry Kissinger, Years of Upheaval (Boston: Little, Brown, 1982), pp.256-274.

11. Gerard Smith, Doubletalk (New York: Doubleday, 1980), pp.154-178.

12. Weiler, pp.162-170.

13. Platt, p.18. See also Congressional Record, June 14, 1971, p.24992.

14. Platt, pp.30-31.

15. U.S. Congress, Senate, Hearings before the Committee on Armed Services, 92nd Cong., 2d sess., 1972, pp.511-567.

16. Joseph Kruzel, cited in Congressional Quarterly, June 15, 1974, p.1546.

17. Leslie Gelb, "The Story of a Flap," Foreign Policy 16, fall 1974. Gelb makes a compelling argument that Jackson's charges are overblown.

18. Platt, p.57.

19. Ibid., p.65-68.

20. Stephen J. Flanagan, "The Domestic Politics of SALT II," in Congress, the Presidency, and American Foreign Policy, John Spanier and Joseph Nogee, eds., (New York: Pergamon, 1981), p.74.

21. Statement by Paul Warnke at seminar On Nuclear Negotiations: Reassessing Arms Control Goals in U.S.-Soviet Relations. Lyndon B. Johnson School of Public Affairs, Austin, Texas, February 26, 1982.

22. U.S. Congress, Senate, Warnke Nomination, Hearings before the Committee on Foreign Relations, 95th Cong., 1st sess., February 8-9, 1977. See also Congressional Record, March 9, 1977.

23. U.S. Congress, Senate, The SALT II Treaty, Report of the Committee on Foreign Relations, 96th Cong., 1st sess., (Exec. Report 96-14), pp.10-12. (Hereinafter referred to as SFRC Report.)

24. Strobe Talbott, Endgame: The Inside Story of SALT II (New York: Harper Colophon, 1980), p.290.

25. Thomas M. Franck and Edward Weisband, Foreign Policy by Congress (New York: Oxford University Press, 1979), p.290.

26. Charles Percy, "The Partisan Gap," Foreign Policy 45, winter 1981-82, p.13.

27. Public Law 87-297.

28. Congressional Record, October 15, 1977.

29. Congressional Quarterly, April 15, 1979.

30. Talbott, p.154.

31. SFRC Report, Minority Views, p.491.

32. These categories are taken from Flanagan, pp.61-69.

33. U.S. Congress, Senate, The SALT II Treaty, Hearings before the Committee on Foreign Relations, 96th Cong., 1st sess., (Hereinafter referred to as SFRC Hearings), Part 1, pp.435-440. See also SFRC Minority Report, pp.464-494.

34. SFRC Hearings, Part 1, pp.481-482 and Part 4, pp.405,434.

35. Flanagan, p.50.

36. SFRC Hearings, Part 2, pp.265-280.

37. This pertained to the Soviet SA-5 radar. See SFRC Hearings, Part 5, pp.15-25. See also Congressional Record, June 16, 1977.

38. U.S. Department of State, Special Report, "Compliance with the SALT I Agreements and Verification of the Proposed SALT II Treaty," Department of State Bulletin, April 1978.

39. SFRC Hearings, Part 2, pp.273-275.

40. SFRC Hearings, pp.228-252.

41. U.S. Congress, Senate, Principal Findings on the Capabilities of the United States to Monitor the SALT II Treaty. Report of the Select Committee on Intelligence, 96th Cong., 1st sess. (Hereinafter referred to as SASC Hearings) Parts 1-4.

43. SFRC Report, pp.27-28.

44. SFRC Report, p.7. See also SASC Hearings, Part 1, pp.23-50.

45. SFRC Report, p.73. Resolution of Ratification I-E.

46. Ibid., p.75. Resolution of Ratification I-L.

47. Ibid., p.72. Resolution of Ratification I-B.

48. SFRC Hearings, Part 5, pp.40-88.

49. Ibid., Part 5, p.77.

50. SFRC Report, pp.73-74. Resolution of Ratification I-F.

51. SFRC Hearings, Part 2, pp.273-275.

52. Paul Warnke, panel discussion remarks at seminar on Nuclear Negotiations, Austin, Texas, February 1982.

53. SFRC Hearings, Part 1, p.119.

54. Les Aspin, "Congressional Procedure and Arms Control," in Platt and Weiler, eds., Congress and Arms Control, pp.43-58.

55. Henry Kissinger, The White House Years (Boston: Little, Brown and Co., 1979), pp.1375-1400.

56. Paul Warnke, remarks at seminar on Nuclear Negotiations, Austin, Texas, February 26, 1982.

57. Talbott, pp.95-98.

58. The 5 percent increase would go into effect in later years.

59. Congressional Quarterly, December 15, 1979.

60. SFRC Report, pp.55,76.

61. SFRC Hearings, Part 1, pp.481-482 and Part 4, pp.405,434. See also SASC Hearings, Part 1, pp.210,257.

62. Talbott, pp.179-180.

63. See Weiler, "Secrecy in Arms Control Negotiations," for an excellent rebuttal of this argument.

64. Flanagan, p.59.

65. Gerard Smith's discussions of the bureaucratic battles in SALT I are very interesting in this regard. See Doubletalk, especially Chapters 7-8.

66. Ibid., pp.223-229.

67. Franck and Weisband, p.290.

68. Ibid.

69. Talbott, pp.38-67.

70. The New York Times, April 13, 1979.

71. Talbott, p.204.

72. SFRC Hearings, Part 1, p.119.

73. Janice Olsen, SALT II: A Review of Public Opinion Polls, Congressional Research Service, Issue Draft #1B79065.

8
Conclusion: Sharing Responsibility

Steven J. Baker

The five policy studies--arms sales, the Panama Canal Treaties, strategic arms limitations, relations with Turkey, and nonproliferation--cover a wide range of problems. However, there are common features that make these studies interesting as a group as well as individually.

First, each of these is a policy area in which traditional national interest/national security dimensions of the problem predominated. Characteristics that play an increasingly important role in making foreign policy in an interdependent world--economic interests, transnational actors, concerns about human rights--played subordinate roles in these policy studies. Second, each represents a policy area in which Congress has had a major impact, and where Congress' activity intensified as a result of the resurgence in the early 1970s. Third, each had at least one critical episode in the 1978-1982 period; each affords at least one example of how the Congress exercises the foreign policy prerogatives that it reasserted in the early 1970s. Finally, the issues range in salience from high visibility (Panama and SALT) to relatively low visibility (the Indian nuclear fuel shipments) to varying salience (the highly controversial 1981 AWACS deal as opposed to the more routine arms transfers). Considered as a group, these studies tell a great deal about how well Congress performs its foreign policy chores.

In Chapter 2, five standards were outlined for judging Congress' foreign policy performance: legitimacy, interest articulation and public information, expeditious consideration, coherence, and effectiveness. By applying these standards to the policy studies, it should be possible to evaluate Congress foreign policy performance, and to determine those areas where Congress' performance might be improved.

(1) Legitimacy

In each of these five policy areas, Congress has a
legitimate role to play, stemming from its basic oversight functions (aid to Turkey, nonproliferation, and
arms sales) or from the Senate's treaty functions (SALT
and Panama Canal). However, the policy studies also
deal with extensions of congressional authority that
may be questionable, e.g., the participation of senators in direct discussions and negotiations with a foreign government during consideration of the Panama
Canal Treaties, and the legislative veto provisions in
arms sales and nonproliferation legislation.

The SALT and Panama experiences show the Senate exercising its responsibility to advise and consent to
treaties. However, the Panama treaties were approved
by a narrow margin and only after a long and involved
process; SALT II was never called up for debate on the
Senate floor. The need to obtain two-thirds majority
approval of a treaty proved to be very difficult in
both of these cases, and combined with the often-cited
Versailles Treaty experience, has led to suggestions
for amendments to the Constitution, e.g., reducing the
required two-thirds majority to a simple majority.
Certainly, both the SALT II and Panama treaties could
probably have been approved relatively quickly by a
simple majority with fewer of the political problems
that encumbered these controversial treaties.

The principle behind the qualified majority--that
solemn international obligations should only be under-
taken with broad support--has not lost its force. But
the practice of foreign policy has greatly eroded this
principle. Most treaties are routine, often dealing
with economic, technical, or consular affairs, and are
routinely approved by the Senate. In the last several
years, the Senate has received from 12 to 30 treaties
per annum, and has approved up to 80 percent without
amendment. Controversial treaties such as Panama and
SALT II are the exception to the rule. Amending the
Constitution to deal with a few exceptions might not be
warranted.

On the other hand, the Senate often disposes of
substantial policy matters on the basis of a simple
majority. For example, most defense budget votes probably have a greater impact on U.S. national security
than most treaty votes. Why should treaties continue
to be subjected to the very demanding two-thirds "super
majority" requirement, when equally important questions
are decided by a simple majority?

Moreover, presidents have increasingly resorted to
the use of executive agreements, avoiding the need for
congressional approval. In the year 1979, for example,

30 treaties were presented to the Senate, but 360 executive agreements were concluded. Since the passage of
the Case-Zablocki Act in 1972, all executive agreements
are supposed to be transmitted to the Congress so that
Congress will at least be informed of the agreements
and the President is less free to make secret commitments. In fact, the substance of the executive agreements is often as routine as the substance of the
treaties that the Senate routinely approves.

Treaty approval by a simple majority would perhaps
reduce the incentive for resort to executive agreements
because one justification given for the increasing use
of executive agreements is the obstacle posed by the
two-thirds Senate approval requirement for treaties.
However, while there are undoubtedly instances where
potential Senate recalcitrance is a factor, it seems
questionable that this is the major reason for presidential preference for executive agreements. Executive
agreements reinforced a presidential mode of conducting
foreign policy, enhancing the executive's role and au-
tonomy vis-a-vis Congress. Thus, presidents might well
prefer executive agreements to treaties, whatever the
terms of congressional involvement in treaty approval.

The fact remains that treaties of substantial importance, even if few in number, have been blocked by
the Senate: in other words, the Senate's exercise of
its treaty approval function has an important qualitative impact even if its quantitative impact is slight.
An alternative proposal for constitutional change would
replace the requirement for two-thirds Senate approval
with approval by a simple majority of both Houses.
This is what the Constitution requires for a declaration of war: why should treaty approval requirements
be made more stringent? If such a change was aimed at
making the approval of treaties easier, submitting controversial treaties to both Houses would seem highly
problematic. For example, a majority in the House
might well have voted against the Panama treaties in
1978. Involving both Houses would almost certainly
lengthen the time necessary to consider treaties. Persuading the Senate to share its constitutional prerogatives in the treaty approval would mean overcoming formidable institutional barriers. Of the several proposed constitutional amendments under discussion in the
early 1980s, changes in the treaty approval provisions
are among the most sensible and least likely. Alternatives to the two-thirds rule have little evident political support, certainly nothing comparable to the political forces mobilized in support of efforts on behalf of the Equal Rights Amendment, or the proposed
amendments that would allow prayers in public schools,
prohibit abortion, or balance the federal budget.
Whatever their substantive merits, constitutional
amendments to streamline treaty consideration seem

dubious in practical and political terms.

The direct participation of senators in international negotiations during consideration of the Panama Canal Treaties was the most questionable exercise of treaty authority by the Senate in these studies. Although the discussions had no formal status, in effect they constituted a second stage of negotitations, coming after the treaty had already been signed by President Carter.

During the SALT negotiations, senators went to Geneva, but as observers, not as negotiators. Majority Leader Byrd traveled to the Soviet Union to meet President Brezhnev in July 1979, after SALT II had been signed, but he went to explain the Senate's role in considering the treaty, not to negotiate changes. Byrd explained to Soviet leadership that the Senate has an independent role in the treaty process and discussed areas of possible Senate action to clarify terms of the treaty.

The involvement of senators in actual negotiations with foreign nations is not unprecedented. In the Nineteenth Century, senators receiving diplomatic charges from a President usually resigned from the Senate. But around the turn of the century, the practice of making sitting senators members of diplomatic missions was used in order to help overcome an institutional impasse: from 1871-1898, the Senate failed to pass a single important treaty.

Today, a senator's responsibilities limit the role that he could play in protracted international negotiations. At best, members of Congress can observed the proceedings and advise and consult with U.S. negotiators. As noted in Chapter 3, Democrat Tom Connally and Republican Arthur Vandenberg, the senior members of the Senate Foreign Relations Committee, played active roles when appointed by President Truman as delegates to the San Francisco meeting to draw up the United Nations Charter, and also served on U.S. delegations on the European peace conferences at the end of World War II. But in the case of the Panama treaties, the senators in question were not appointed by the President to negotiate, nor did they confine themselves to observation. Because of the statesmanship and wisdom of the principal senators involved, especially Byrd and Baker, the "second-stage" negotiations on Panama were concluded on terms acceptable to all parties, making it possible for the treaties to win approval. But this type of senatorial involvement in diplomatic negotiations could constitute a dangerous precedent. It is easy to imagine that the consequences of direct involvement in other diplomatic negotiations might not end so well.

Questions about the constitutional propriety of the congressional role also arise in regard to the nuclear proliferation and arms sales statutes. These laws

provide for a so-called "legislative veto," an opportunity for Congress to review formally the executive
branch's execution of the law. In 1983 the Supreme
Court ruled unconstitutional the scores of legislative
vetoes that are written into laws dating back to the
1930s. In the Nuclear Nonproliferation Act (NNPA) of
1978, having given the President the authority to make
an exception to the law's nonproliferation standards,
Congress reserved the right to review that exception.
The 1976 Arms Export Control Act gave Congress 30 days
to disapprove a major arms sale. Recent Presidents
have seen legislative veto provisions as an unwarranted
intrusion into the executive's prerogative to "execute
the law," and a violation of the separation of powers.
For example, the Carter Administration formally pro-
tested the congressional veto provision of the Nuclear
Nonproliferation Act, even though the President proceeded to sign the law.

The Supreme Court's 1983 ruling ostensibly sides
with the executive branch in prohibiting the legislative veto as a means of congressional oversight. However, the majority opinion calls into question the
whole pattern of congressional delegation of power to
the executive, and therefore may lay the basis for restricting the scope of power the President has come to
wield. If this interpretation is sustained, Congress'
error may not be in seeking to limit the President's
authority through a legislative veto, but in delegating
authority to the executive in matters that more properly should be legislated. Ironically, the 1983 decision
could lead to more "legislating foreign policy" rather
than less. For example, in the future Congress may
press for legislation that requires all nuclear exports
and all arms exports to have legislative sanction,
greatly increasing congressional involvement in implementing foreign policy. In foreign policy, Congress
exercised its legislative veto rights very sparingly,
chosing to selectively challenge the executive only when
there were irreconciliable differences between the two
branches. Without the pragmatic tool of the legislative veto, Congress may be compelled to become involved
indiscriminately in even routine foreign policy matters.
While the legislative veto provisions of major foreign
policy legislation such as the Nuclear Nonproliferation
Act, the Arms Export Control Act, and the War Powers
Resolution may have been nullified, the rest of the
legislation remains in force. And, therefore, even after the Supreme Court decision in 1983, Congress insisted that the Reagan Administration comply with the
extant provisions of the War Powers Resolution regarding the stationing Marines in Beirut as a peace-keeping
force.

In conclusion, the legitimacy of Congress' actions
in general is confirmed in the five policy areas, but

in three cases there is reason to question the manner
in which Congress exercised its legitimate functions.
This conclusion affirms the propriety of congressional
involvement in foreign policy, but leaves open important questions about the manner of that involvement.

(2)   Interest Articulation and Public Information

Congress serves as a transmission belt between public opinion and national policy: it both reflects public preferences and contributes to shaping them. Of
course, Congress is not unique in this respect: the
President and even the court system also interact with
public opinion. The major distinction between Congress
and the President is that different constituencies and
staggered elections mean that public opinion is often
reflected differently by the two branches. The President has a structural advantage in seeking to shape
public opinion: he can speak authoritatively for the
entire executive branch, and in foreign affairs for the
whole U.S. government. No single leader of either
House can speak for Congress, much less the nation.
The five policy areas provide examples of Congress
leading public opinion, following public opinion, and
operating in a public opinion vacuum. In the case of
the Panama Canal Treaties, there was much discussion in
the Senate of whether senators should lead or reflect
public opinion. At the beginning, public opinion was
clearly against approval of the treaties. The exhaustive Senate action was in part an attempt to persuade
the public that the treaties were in the national interest. However, there is little direct evidence that
the debate in the Senate had a positive impact. The
shift in public opinion toward a more favorable view
was largely the result of extraordinary Administration
public relations efforts. Had the Senate simply represented and reflected public opinion, the treaties might
well have been rejected. The Senate approved the
treaties, albeit narrowly and after long and involved
consideration, and not without a strong dose of arm-
twisting and logrolling by the administration.
The justification for taking a position contrary to
popular opinion in a case such as Panama would seem to
lie in the exhaustive Senate deliberations. The Panama
Canal Treaty votes were taken after a long debate and
careful consideration on the part of most senators.
Many of those who voted in favor of the agreements believed that statesmanship rather than political expediency was necessary. And some senators paid a price for
this statesmanship: the Panama treaty votes were an
issue in the campaigns of several Senate liberals in
1978 and 1980, an issue that conservative political action groups emphasized in successful campaigns against

such Democratic Senators as McIntyre (New Hampshire), Culver (Iowa), Church (Idaho), and McGovern (South Dakota).

In the case of the SALT II Treaty, the Senate was certainly concerned about public opinion and reflected changes in public opinion in the course of the SALT deliberations. The Panama precedent was much on the minds of senators, although the impact of the Panama vote on re-election prospects was not clearly established until after the November 1980 elections, long after SALT II had been shelved. The greatest impact of the Panama fight was to make some senators reluctant to publicly commit themselves on SALT II prematurely, in part because of the anticipated reaction in public opinion, and in part because those who had taken early positions on Panama believed that they were ignored in the Administration's effort to garner support among doubters. Holding back from committing themselves could leave senators in a better bargaining position. For example, Senators Nunn, Glenn, and Zorinsky each held back from public support for the SALT II Treaty in order to acquire some quid pro quo from the Administration--defense spending increases, greater intelligence monitoring capabilities, strategic force modernization, etc. Had the SALT II Treaty reached the Senate floor, there would have been an all-out White House effort to persuade doubting senators that support for the treaty was also good for their constituencies. Robert Beckel and the White House staff members who had helped to deliver votes on the Panama treaties were ready to make a maximum effort to win approval of SALT II.

Consideration of SALT II was suspended before a floor debate occurred in the Senate, although it had held up very well through the long weeks of hearings by three separate Senate committees. The technical level of the debate in public and in the media was certainly raised by the Senate hearings, which were broadcast live over public radio. On the other hand, linkage with other issues--e.g., the "Soviet troops in Cuba" issue--also resulted from the actions of a few senators, and served to detract from discussion of the merits of the SALT II agreement. Public opinion showed little change as a result of Senate hearings.

In failing to debate the SALT II Treaty, the Senate reflected the changing climate of public opinion. It was Majority Leader Byrd's opinion, widely shared, that, considering the public mood in late 1979 and early 1980, the SALT II Treaty could not be debated on its merits. In the wake of the flap over Soviet troops in Cuba and the seizure of the U.S. hostages in Iran, the Soviet Embassy in Washington apparently concluded that by December 1979, SALT II was a dead letter, and that an invasion of Afghanistan would do no more than seal its fate. The Soviets seemed to credit the claims of

Senator Jackson and other treaty opponents more than the view of pro-treaty senators such as Byrd and Cranston, who believed that SALT II still had a chance for approval before the election campaigns began. The Afghanistan invasion aroused American public opinion against the Soviet Union, led to a major shift in Carter Administration policy, and sealed SALT II's fate in the Senate.

In the three other policy areas, aid to Turkey, the Indian nuclear fuel case, and arms sales, there was less direct impact of the opinion of the general public on Congress. However, when the Turkish embargo was imposed, there was a very direct impact on the Senate by a small segment of the public, the Greek-American lobby. And, on specific arms sales to the Middle East, the American Jewish community can have a major effect on Congress.

When issues are of low salience to the general public, it is easier for small numbers of concerned individuals and groups to have a major impact on how Congress behaves. The Turkish invasion of Cyprus was not an issue that created widespread public concern, nor was the question of whether or not to lift the embargo on aid to Turkey a high visibility issue. But to Greek-Americans, these were crucial questions, and Greek-American groups were very active in trying to influence Congress. Middle East arms sales may not always be major concerns for the general public, but for the well-organized supporters of Israel, these are of the highest importance. They have also been a matter of increasing concern to American firms with business interests in the Middle East.

That a policy outcome should be heavily influenced by well-organized groups representing very few people--either ethnic groups or economic interests such as weapons manufacturers and oil companies--poses a problem: should special interests be allowed to determine U.S. national interests? "Special interests" can, of course, be a loaded term, but there is a perceived difference between "special interests" and the kind of issue-oriented organizations that are active in many high-visibility public policy debates. Issue-oriented groups that are not tied to specific material or ethnic interests project an image of disinterested public involvement, as a means for citizens to express their views in an organized, collective way. In the Panama Canal case, the Conservative Caucus was one such example; in the SALT II case, the Committee on the Present Danger and Americans for SALT were examples of issue-oriented groups. Ethnic lobbies and economic groups are by definition "interested" and are perceived as benefiting from the policies that they advocate. This direct link to policy benefits places the activities of a special interest group in a somewhat different light from the activities of issue-oriented groups which are motivated only by a concern for public policy.

Interest groups in the foreign policy field do not perceive themselves as working in opposition to the national interest of the United States. Rather, they see themselves as participating in the process by which the national interest is defined, an inherently political process. According to its peculiar strengths, each of the foreign policy lobbies seeks to influence Congress through standard techniques of political influence--campaign contributions, public information or disinformation, and the mobilization of voting blocs.

The imposition of an embargo on aid to Turkey was seen as a triumph for one ethnic lobby, Greek-Americans. But it would be a mistake to attach too much influence to the Greek-American lobby. There were a varity of factors contributing to the congressional decision, which came at a time of particularly troubled relations between the executive and legislative branches. The fact that the Greek-Americans could argue that the existing law was on their side clearly made their case more persuasive in the eyes of Congress. The decision to lift the embargo four years later was taken in spite of the Greek-American lobby, and required that members of Congress waive domestic political considerations and look beyond the earlier "violation" of U.S. law in favor of geopolitical calculations. As this case demonstrates, no special interest always prevails in Congress.

The Senate's decision to support the sale of AWACS aircraft to Saudi Arabia represented a defeat for the pro-Israel lobby in general, and the heretofore spectacularly successful American Israel Public Affairs Committee (AIPAC) in particular. The intensive lobbying of economic groups--weapons manufacturers and companies doing business in Saudi Arabia, such as the engineering and construction giant, Bechtel Group Inc.-- showed how competitive foreign policy lobbying has become. Groups such as AIPAC have advantages, especially their ability to mobilize voters; but they may find it difficult to match the financial resources of economic interests such as the petroleum and arms industries. If defining the national interest is a political process, some special interests seem more likely to prevail than others.

In the case of the Indian nuclear fuel question and nonproliferation policy, there was little public interest and no ethnic group nor economic interest group pressures. Perhaps this helps to explain the different decisions reached by the Senate and the House. There were no outside organizations or groups exerting pressures that would have given more coherence to the actions of the two Houses, leaving the decision to support or oppose the President to the internal dynamics of each House.

There were bureaucratic pressures in the Indian nuclear fuel case. While the executive branch was officially united behind the President's action, dissidents in the State Department and elsewhere were in constant contact with like-minded staffers on Capitol Hill and those at the Nuclear Regulatory Commission who were working to block the Indian nuclear fuel shipment. These actors had some impact on Congress, but not much on public opinion. Informed opinion, as reflected in editorials around the nation, was against supplying nuclear fuel to India. The House actions reflected this view, but the Senate narrowly decided to support the President.

No overall pattern emerges from these policy studies with respect to the role of public opinion. In part this is because the standard itself allows for potentially contradictory conclusions: Congress' action can be consistent with public opinion, in which case it may be said to reflect it; or Congress's action can be contrary to public opinion, in which case it can be argued that Congress is attempting to inform and educate the public. There is little in these policy studies to suggest that Congress had a major impact on shaping the public's views on foreign policy. However, through media coverage of congressional debate and action, on issues ranging from arms control to U.S. policies in Central America, public interest has been heightened. The televised hearings of the Senate Foreign Relations Committee on U.S. involvement in Vietnam began a gradual awakening of the American public to U.S. policies in Southeast Asia. When a treaty or proposed arms sales is before Congress, members of Congress may become the focal point of interest groups and of public attention. Nonetheless, instances when the public looks to Congress for leadership on foreign policy issues--such as evenutally occurred with the Vietnam War--seem to be exceptional.

(3) Expeditious Consideration

There is a sense of urgency that attaches to foreign policy issues. A genuine international crisis often requires an immediate response, but even non-crisis situations require a timely response if that response is to relevant in quickly changing international environment. On routine foreign policy issues, lengthy or delayed consideration may not cause problems, but in most cases an expeditious disposition of a foreign policy problem is beneficial to the national interest.

No collective body is able to act as quickly as a unitary entity, at least in principle. In practice, however, the differences in response time between legislative and executive institutions can be

exaggerated. Bureaucratic processes can slow executive
responses, just as Congress is sometimes capable of
moving with considerable dispatch. International
events can either precipitate or slow action in both
institutions. A sense of proportion has to be maintained: when it took more than a decade for the executive to negotiate the Panama Canal Treaties, it is not
unreasonable that Senate consideration of these treaties consumed eight months.

Judgment is essential in weighing whether Congress
acted too slowly and, as a result, some substantial
foreign policy objective was jeopardized, or whether
Congress acted with appropriate speed. If it is judged
that Congress did not act quickly enough, the explanation for the delay is important. If cumbersome procedures account for the lack of timely action, then there
are organizational remedies that should be considered.
If political differences account for the delay, then
organizational remedies may be of little value. The
question of expeditious consideration is important because one of the principal arguments against a strong
congressional role in foreign policy is that Congress
is incapable of acting quickly and, therefore, Congress' role in foreign policy must be circumscribed.

Of the policy areas surveyed, the time span of Congress' involvement ranges from a few weeks to a period
of years. Some cases involve recurring issues, as in
relations with Turkey--particularly the arms embargo,
which was imposed in 1974-1975 and lifted in 1978--or
the reviews of successive arms exports. Some issues
occupy the attention of particular committees of Congress or a few members for long periods of time, while
consuming relatively little attention of the body as a
whole: the SALT II Treaty was the subject of careful
study by dozens of senators and lengthy hearings by
three Senate committees, but it never reached the Senate floor. On Panama, the Indian nuclear fuel question, and on most arms sales, there seemed to be a good
correspondence between the amount of time and attention
devoted to the issue by Congress and overall importance
of the issue as a foreign policy objective. However,
during the first four months of 1978, while being debated on the Senate floor, the Panama treaties occupied
the attention of the Senate to the exclusion of almost
all other issues, foreign or domestic.

The imposition of the arms embargo on Turkey provides examples of Congress acting both expeditiously
and in a drawn-out way. Congress responded to the
Cyprus situation rather quickly in 1974 and voted to
impose the embargo on Turkey. However, Congress resisted executive pressures to lift the embargo for
several years. In the end, the crucial factor was
support from key members of the congressional leadership for ending the embargo. Even in these days of

relative decentralization in Congress, there is much
that a determined leadership can do to affect the pace
and substance of legislation.

The Arms Export Control Act gave Congress 30 days
to consider proposed sales and to take action to disapprove them if Congress so chose. No major arms sales
have yet been blocked by congressional action, but
clearly both the content and timing of major sales such
as the 1978 Middle East arms package have been affected
by Congress' participation in the approval process.
The arms export legislation gave Congress a reasonable
period of time to act and it has proven capable of doing so. More important, anticipation of congressional
review has led to a pattern of executive branch consultation with Congress prior to making major arms sales
commitments. If Congress' role in arms sales jeopard-
izes American foreign policy objectives, it is due less
to the length of time that a debate over a proposed
sale may take than to the substance of the debate, the
public airing of the issue--during which an arms recipient may be offended even though the arms sale is approved. This is a wholly different problem from expeditious consideration.

The Indian nuclear fuel case is another example in
which the relevant legislation, the Nuclear Nonproliferation Act, mandated a particular period of time for
congressional consideration. Both the House and Senate
consumed much of the 60 days allowed before acting.
The Senate delays were less the result of Senate procedures than they were of Administration preferences:
the Administration sought to postpone action until it
could muster as much support as possible for the President's position. On the timing question, the Administration had the support of Majority Leader Byrd and of
Foreign Relations Committee Chairman Church, each of
whom had his own reasons for accepting delay. Using
the full time allowed by law did not jeopardized foreign policy objectives. The Indian licenses had been
pending for nearly two years, blocked at the discretion
of the Administration. While the Administration insisted on the urgency of the matter in June 1980, it
could be argued that U.S.-Indian relations had already
been damaged. Had the vote on the nuclear fuel shipment been negative, the negative impact on U.S. relations with India would probably not have been much
greater.

Treaties such as SALT II and Panama are subject to
special rules and procedures in the Senate. Unless
waived by unanimous consent, these special treaty rules
can require more time on the floor than most legislation. The SALT II Treaty was reported out by the
Foreign Relations Committee and placed on the Senate's
Executive Calendar, but it was never called up during
1979 or 1980. At the end of the 96th Congress, SALT II

was taken off the Executive Calendar and returned to the Foreign Relations Committee. That committee had held 30 public hearings and 12 closed hearings on the SALT II Treaty; floor debate was expected to consume as much as six weeks. In the eyes of treaty supporters, the fact that the treaty was never debated or approved did jeopardize U.S. foreign policy objectives. And there were some attempts by the Carter Administration to revive consideration of the treaty in the spring and summer of 1980, which were resisted by the Senate leadership. In the climate prevailing in 1980, it seems difficult to believe that the treaty would have been approved without some substantive changes or without a debate that would have greatly exacerbated relations with the Soviet Union. Practically, failing to debate the treaty may have jeopardized national interests less than rejection would have. Had the treaty been debated and defeated, the Reagan Administration would not have had the option of adhering to the unratified treaty's terms.

The Senate consideration of the Panama Canal Treaties was the most thorough since the Versailles Treaty debate. If the implementation legislation and oversight procedures are included, it could be said that congressional involvement in the Panama issues has not ended. But the length of the Senate's consideration of the Panama treaties was less likely to jeopardize national interests than the type and substance of that involvement. The Senate leadership of both parties was successful in moving the treaties along in the face of numerous attempts at obstruction. The almost unprecedented degree of Senate involvement in negotiations with a foreign government, which did consume some time, could easily have resulted in an outcome that would have thwarted Administration objectives; fortunately, it did not.

Frequently, the executive and legislative branches are at odds over scheduling. Executive branch officials are often frustrated when Congress does not respond quickly to foreign policy initiatives. In some instances the executive will overstate the "crisis" aspect of an issue in order to spur congressional action. As noted earlier, Congress can move quickly, particularly if its leaders are committed to doing so. But normally Congress prefers to move at its own pace, and that can be very deliberate, especially when its procedures are given full play.

There are numerous examples in the policy studies of the timetable for legislative action becoming an issue between the two branches. In the case of President Truman's proposal for aid to Turkey and Greece, the Senate quickly made it clear that the administration's timetable was seen as unrealistic. In 1977, President Carter eventually had to defer to the Senate

leadership in a showdown over scheduling of the proposed AWACS sale to Iran. Perhaps drawing on that experience, Carter looked to Majority Leader Byrd to set
the schedule for consideration of the Panama Canal
Treaties. Finally, in the case of SALT II, scheduling
problems obviously affected the prospects for favorable
Senate consideration, although in this case there were
a variety of factors that delayed action. To begin
with, the Carter Administration encountered repeated
delays in concluding treaty negotiations, thus submitting it to the Senate much later than anticipated.
Once it was sent to the Senate, the treaty was victim-
ized by a series of unexpected developments and a
changing political environment.

On the whole, these policy studies indicate that
Congress is capable of acting expeditiously in perform-
ing its foreign policy responsibilities. In two cases,
SALT II and efforts to resume aid to Turkey, there was
either imcomplete action or action later than would
have perhaps been preferable from the point of view of
U.S. foreign policy interests. But, in neither case
did procedural problems prove to be a significant hin-
drance to moving more rapidly, except for the two-
thirds treaty approval requirement impact on SALT II.
In both cases, substantial political considerations
dictated the lack of timely congressional action: Congress was able to act but chose not to. There does not
seem to be any obvious remedy to this kind of politically determined check on presidential action in foreign policy.

(4) Coherence

Without coherence it is arguable whether a nation
has a foreign policy, if policy is understood as a set
of means to implement a relatively well articulated
goal. Coherence in foreign policy is important for external and internal reasons. It provides a basis for
predicting what the U.S. will do, and this should reduce other nations' mistakes and miscalculations in
their relations with the U.S. But coherence in American foreign policy serves domestic political functions
as well: policy coherence is necessary if public support is to maintained, essential to conducting foreign
policy in a democracy. And coherence is necessary if
foreign policy is to be successfully executed by a complex, farflung bureaucracy.

There are two principal dimensions to foreign
policy coherence with respect to Congress: agreement
between the executive and legislative branches, and
agreement between the two Houses. Disagreement in
either of these dimensions contributes to incoherence,
but the most important source of confusion in U.S.

foreign policy results from disagreement between the two branches. The importance of foreign policy coherence gives the President an advantage over the Congress in making foreign policy: as the initiator and executor in most foreign policy situations, the President is able to argue that failure to agree with him will weaken his ability to pursue American interests in dealing with other nations. But this fact is also the source of Congress' leverage over the President in foreign policy: the President must tailor his foreign policy initiatives to congressional preference unless he wishes to risk a defeat that would diminish his effectiveness. Congress too must weigh the consequences of disagreeing with the President on foreign policy questions. Congressional action alone often has little impact on the behavior of other countries; to be effective, Congress usually requires the positive support of the executive branch. Thus, coherence is a concern for both branches of government. Coherence does not simply mean that Congress must always go along with the President; rather, it means that the President must also go along with Congress, reinforcing the norm of compromise that is so important in American politics.

These foreign policy issue areas provide examples across the spectrum from coherence to confusion. On the Panama Canal Treaties, the two branches reached an agreement, contributing to coherence. In imposing the arms embargo on Turkey in 1974, the two branches disagreed but the two Houses of Congress agreed with one another. In one of the most recent major arms sales controversies, the Saudi AWACS case, and on the most significant test to date of the nonproliferation legislation, the decision to ship nuclear fuel to India, the President and the Senate were able to reach an agreement, while the House dissented. The judgment with respect to the SALT II Treaty is unclear because the process was stillborn; the Senate Foreign Relations Committee reported out the treaty favorably, indicating agreement with the Administration, but the subsequent failure of the Senate to approve the treaty contributed to incoherence in U.S. foreign policy.

The Senate's approval of the Panama treaties brought to fruition years of negotiations by several presidents. That the Senate amended the treaties does not necessarily mean that its actions detracted from policy coherence. To the extent that the amendments and other conditions attached to the treaties by the Senate were in line with the negotiations conducted by the two governments, the Senate's action was coherent in effect. Obviously, however, the results could easily have been different.

The Turkish example provides a mixed picture. In imposing an embargo in 1974, the Congress was applying existing law. But this was opposed by the President

who believed that the law should be ignored because
Turkey is a valued NATO ally. The willingness to impose sanctions on Turkey demonstrated that Congress was
prepared to stand behind the restrictive provisions
that are part of U.S. laws on the transfer of military
equipment to other countries. However, it soon became
apparent, if it was not from the first, that the circumstances surrounding the Turkish embargo were very
particular and would not be a precedent for other
situations. For example, Israel repeatedly used arms
provided for defensive purposes for attacks on Pal-
estinian positions in Lebanon, and in the bombing of
the Iraqi nuclear research reactor in 1981, but was
never seriously threatened with even a diminution in
U.S. aid until 1982. Because Congress would not follow
its own precedent, its action on Turkey created confusion in U.S. policy not only because Congress dif-
fered with the President, but also because Congress
behaved inconsistently.

On issues such as arms sales and nuclear exports,
where legislative vetoes threatened, there is an incentive for the President to accomodate some congressional
demands in return for the support of at least one of
the two Houses. In both the AWACS and Indian nuclear
fuel examples, the President was allowed to proceed
having convinced barely enough senators that the initiative in question would serve the national interest
more than rejection. The early opposition of the House
in both cases probably inclined the President to be
more accomodating to demands for concessions to senatorial concerns. There is one major difference between these two examples, and that has less to do with
coherence of foreign policy than with consistency.
Major arms sales to Middle East countries are an established part of the U.S. policy in the region, however
controversial a particular arms deal might be. Consistency reinforced the coherence on selling AWACS to
the Saudis. The nuclear fuel case was different in
that the President's initiative itself was a departure
from U.S. nonproliferation policy, one that required
waiving provisions of the Nonproliferation Act. The
President's action and Senate support for it were both
contrary to the spirit (but not the letter) of U.S.
nonproliferation legislation, signaling a dramatic
shift in policy that was not then followed by a change
in the law. The Senate and the House split over the
question. As a result, U.S. nonproliferation policy
was going off in two different directions and so were
the two Houses of Congress. Inconsistency undermined
whatever coherence resulted from the Senate's support
for the President.

The Senate Foreign Relations Committee's consideration of the SALT II Treaty contributed to foreign policy coherence. Its findings agreed with the positions

of the Administration, and it recommended approval of the treaty that had been the result of several years of negotiations, without crippling amendments. The attempt by treaty opponents on the Armed Services Committee to make a negative report on the treaty was questionable on procedural grounds, and the existence of official and unofficial reports with contradictory conclusions did create some confusion. By not proceeding to debate the treaty, in the wake of the Soviet invasion of Afghanistan, the Senate opened-up questions about the ability of the U.S. to implement agreements negotiated in good faith by the other parties. When the Administration wanted to see the treaty debated in 1980, the Senate's refusal to do so contributed to foreign policy confusion, even though the Administration also vascilated on the question as the whether or not it was politically opportune to bring the treaty up.

Coherence, unlike consistency, is not merely a hobgoblin of small minds. It is an attribute of an effective and successful foreign policy. While not necessarily the most important factor in all cases, it can be ignored only at the risk of being ineffective and failing to achieve national objectives.

(5) Effectiveness

The most important questions are sometimes the most difficult to answer satisfactorily. The bottom line in evaluating any foreign policy action is whether it is good or bad, right or wrong, in the national interest or not. Immediately, one is in the realm of highly subjective value judgments. This does not mean that there is no answer, but means that there may be as many different answers as there are observers. But there is a standard that is less subjective, effectiveness: Did the foreign policy action of the Congress achieve what Congress intended? Asking the question, "did it work?" is a crucial step in a total evaluation of an action, and while it is not the only step, it is a more manageable task than answering the broader question, "was it good?"

How often do Congress' foreign policy actions have the intended results? It would be easier to answer this question if intent were less problematic. In many cases, intentions are either unclear, mixed, or openly contradictory--all the more so given the fact that Congress is a collective actor. Adopting a rational actor assumption and imputing intent where motives are obscure has obvious faults, but provides at least a point of departure for the estimation of effectiveness.

In the case of policy towards Turkey in 1974, Congress apparently sought to: (1) punish Turkey; (2) respond to a powerful ethnic lobby; (3) assert itself vis-a-vis the executive; (4) apply the law; and (5) provide an example to other nations that receive arms aid. Deciding to lift the embargo four years later would seem to be at least a tacit admission that some of these objectives were expendable (apply the law, respond to a powerful ethnic lobby), that some had been achieved (punish Turkey, assert itself vis-a-vis the executive), and that some were probably unrealistic in the first place (provide an example to others). On the whole, this was a relatively effective exercise of Congress' foreign policy responsibilities. It would have been even better if, in addition to being effective, it would also have been coherent, i.e., if Congress had responded earlier to Administration requests to lift the embargo. Imposing the embargo may have been a good thing; lifting it was a better thing.

SALT provides mixed findings with respect to the question of effectiveness. The Senate's consideration of the SALT II Treaty was incomplete, stopping after the hearings by the Foreign Relations Committee. As far as they went, these hearings (and collateral hearings by the Armed Services and Intelligence Committees) were effective in that they: (1) provided an opportunity to air the major issues; (2) allowed key senators a chance to work their will on the treaty; and (3) laid the groundwork for the floor debate to come. Refusal to debate the treaty reflected several objectives: (1) reacting against a disorderly world; (2) punishing the Soviet Union; and (3) signaling a change in U.S. policy; (4) avoiding a tough political issue in an election year. The Senate did avoid confronting this issue in 1980, and did signal a change, for better or worse, in U.S. policy. But the other objectives do not seem to have been realized by refusing to debate the treaty. As a reaction against a disorderly world, refusing to debate the SALT II Treaty was meaningless, a futile gesture with respect to concrete issues such as the Iranian hostage crisis and the invasion of Afghanistan. And it is difficult to see how the Soviet Union was punished by the U.S. failure to approve and ratify the SALT II Treaty; quite the opposite, the Soviet Union achieved a propaganda victory by making the U.S seem at best irresolute, or, worse, hostile to the objective of arms control. The failure of the Senate to act in 1980 did have an ironic consequence, largely unintended but still important. Those who supported the treaty and feared that it would not receive the necessary two-thirds majority were reluctant to have a floor debate in 1980. Since the treaty was pending business at the end of the 96th Congress, it was returned to the Foreign Relations Committee. The Reagan Administration was then presented with an option that it would not have had otherwise: to abide by the terms of the SALT II Treaty, even though it had never been approved by the Senate.

On the whole, the Senate's failure to act on SALT II was politically expedient, but of questionable effectiveness--at least, not intentionally effective.

The Senate's action on Panama indicates several ostensible objectives: (1) exerting existing authority vis-a-vis the President; (2) impressing public opinion that the Senate was acting responsibly; (3) improving the terms of the agreements with Panama; and (4) demonstrating the statesmanship of particular senators. In most respects, the Senate succeeded in realizing these objectives. An independent Senate role in treaty approval was established, and the basis laid for an argument that the Senate had acted only after careful consideration in the face of much public hostility. Whether the terms of the treaties were improved is arguable, but at least the treaties were not seriously weakened. And key senators, particularly Byrd and Baker, emerged with greatly enhanced reputations. The Senate's action in this case was further strengthened by the fact that it was generally in line with Administration policy, thus contributing to coherence in foreign policy.

In the case of the Indian nuclear fuel, the House and the Senate came to different conclusions. The House action seems predicated on the desire to: (1) retain the spirit and the letter of nonproliferation policy; and (2) to dispose of a low salience foreign policy question in an election year. On the basis of these considerations, the House voted against the Administration's decision to supply nuclear fuel to India. The Senate's action seemed to be based on these same premises and one additional consideration, the desire to improve the U.S. position in South Asia. It was this additional consideration that seemed to tip the scales in the Senate in favor of the President's position, especially since senators could do so and still be consistent with the letter of the existing legislation. But the Senate's action did not have the effect of improving relations with India. At best, it could be argued that relations were prevented from deteriorating further. This marginal goal has to be weighed against the confusion resulting from the fact that the two Houses of Congress could not agree, and the fact that in the wake of the decision to supply nuclear fuel to India the overall direction of U.S. nonproliferation policy was more in question than it would have been had the House position prevailed.

In establishing the right to review and possibly disapprove arms sales, Congress was pursuing at least three objectives: (1) asserting its institutional prerogatives vis-a-vis the executive; (2) seeking to limit the volume of arms being exported by the U.S.; and (3) seeking to assure that the particular arms sales would be consistent with Congress' definition of national interest. The Saudi AWACS example suggests that Congress had been effective in at least two of these objectives. Congress' right to be consulted was confirmed, and the Senate succeeded in winning some concessions from the Administration with respect to the substance of the arms transfer in question. But the size of the Saudi agreement--more than $8 billion--points to the fact that Congress' involvement in reviewing arms sales has had little impact in reducing the volume of arms exported. With the exception of the limited restraint exercised during the Carter Administration, arms sales to foreign governments continue to grow, and are increasingly perceived as a necessary instrument of American foreign policy.

Overall Congressional Performance

Within the limits to which it is possible to generalize on the basis of these policy studies, Congress appears to have performed its foreign policy responsibilities reasonably well, better perhaps than it is generally given credit for.

Out of 25 possible "yes" ratings, Congress scored 13 yeses and 6 qualified yeses. (See Table 8.1) More important, the negative ratings tend to cluster in two problem areas--coherence and effectiveness. Most "buts" arise with respect to legitimacy problems. These are the areas, then, where possible reforms in congressional handling of foreign policy are most appropriate.

Institutional Improvements

Of the problem areas, effectiveness does not seem very susceptible to institutional reforms. Although procedures and analytic capability can obviously have an impact on effectiveness, ultimately it is more the result of wisdom and good judgment than information or organization. In none of the policy studies did a lack of information or an inability to bring information to bear in a timely and effective manner seem to be a fundamental problem. If Congress failed to be effective, it was because it exercised questionable judgment. Stated another way, in some cases political considerations or short-term concerns loomed larger than a detached view of the broader, long-term national interest. Beyond the exhortation to "elect good men," there is a limit to what can be done to improve the exercise of wisdom.

The major area where institutional remedies may be relevant would seem to be with respect to policy coherence: there are ways of making Congress' foreign

TABLE 8.1
Evaluating Congress' Foreign Policy Performance

	1	2	3	4	5
U.S.-Turkey Relations, Arms Embargo	Yes	Yes	Yes	No	Yes, but...
Nonproliferation, Indian Nuclear Fuel	Yes but...	No	Yes	No	No
Panama Treaties	Yes, but...	Yes	Yes	Yes	Yes
SALT II Treaty	Yes, but...	Yes	Yes and No	No	No
Arms Sales, Saudi-AWACS	Yes, but...	Yes	Yes	Yes	Yes

1. Legitimacy
2. Interest Articulation and Public Information
3. Expeditious Consideration
4. Coherence
5. Effectiveness

policy actions more consistent with those of the executive and coordinating the foreign policy activities of
the two Houses of Congress. Reestablishing a national
consensus on foreign policy, stregthening party organizations, and centralizing leadership within Congress
would all contribute to foreign policy coherence. In
particular, the possibility has been repeatedly raised
(e.g., the 1975 Murphy Commission Report) that some
sort of a national security committee be established to
deal with major foreign policy issues. It is argued
that consultation between the executive and the Congress is hampered by the fact that congressional committee jurisdiction is confused and overlapping, making
it either difficult to know whom to consult with or
making the list of members and staff to be consulted so
long as to be unmanageable. Many national security issues clearly overlap the present jurisdictions of Foreign Relations, Armed Services, and Intelligence Committees, making consultation cumbersome in normal times
and nearly impossible in times of crisis. A National
Security Committee would provide a small, select group

of members of Congress with whom the executive could
consult. Logically, such a consultative committee
might be composed of the party leaders in each House,
and the chairmen and ranking members of the Foreign
Relations, Armed Services, and Intelligence Committees, with perhaps the addition of key figures on Appropriations Committees. It might be a joint committee or, more likely, a similarly constituted committee
in each House.

Changes in committee structure in Congress in recent years have gone in two directions: towards the
formation of more functionally specific committees such
as the Energy Committees, and of committees that have
broader jurisdiction and membership such as the Joint
Economic Committee. There are cases in which the formation of a new committee has resulted in the reduction
of jurisdiction of other, established committees as
happened when the Intelligence Committees assumed oversight functions previously exercised, if on a limited
basis, by the Armed Services Committees. However, in
most cases committees have simply been added to the
existing list, resulting in even greater jurisdictional
overlap. This is the primary objection to the organization of a National Security Committee--it would very
likely add additional members and more staff to the
numbers of foreign policy interlocutois on the Hill,
without concentrating the consultation process. On the
other hand, the possibility that such a committee might
gut the established jurisdictions of committees such as
Foreign Relations and Armed Services has been sufficient to prevent Congress from responding favorably to
the National Security Committee proposals that have
been made to date.

There has been some informal realization of the intent of this proposal. Ad hoc consultation by the executive branch often follows the pattern of the National Security Committee idea. Executive agencies such as
the CIA and State Department make a habit of informing
the leadership of both Houses and key committee members
of foreign policy events and problems in the offing.
During the Iranian hostage crisis, Secretary of State
Vance or Deputy Secretary Christopher regularly briefed
a select group of senators. If this pattern of consultation is successful on an ad hoc basis, it is difficult to see why it should not be formalized with the
organization of a National Security Committee. But
practically, as long as a prudent President satisfies
Congress' demands for consultation informally, there is
likely to be little pressure from the Hill for institu-
tionalizing this pattern of interaction. It is only
when Congress feels that it is being left out of important foreign policy decisions that demands for the
formation of a National Security Committee or other institutional innovations are likely to be strong.

Possible reforms or changes that address the manner in which Congress carries out otherwise legitimate functions have already been discussed. One device used by Congress, the legislative veto, has apparently been struck down as a means for exercising congressional oversight of the executive branch. With respect to treaty approval, both Senate approval by a simple majority or joint House and Senate approval by simple majorities would seem to be reasonable alternatives to the constitutional two-thirds provision. But short of overwhelming dissatisfaction with the way the Senate performs its treaty responsibilities, changes in the Constitution seem unlikely.

Setbacks and Successes

There is little prospect for substantial changes in the way Congress participates in the foreign policy process. The 1980s are likely to be an extension of the 1970s with a mix of successes (e.g., the SALT I agreements, the opening to China, the Panama treaties, the Camp David accords) as well as foreign policy setbacks (the oil embargo, the fall of South Vietnam, the Iranian hostage crisis, the lack of progress toward a comprehensive peace in the Middle East). As an active participant in making foreign policy in this period, Congress shares responsibility for both the successes and setbacks. Congress' exercise of its foreign policy prerogatives, as measured in the policy studies in this volume, has been positive on the whole. Congress does not deserve to be perceived as a problem in the policy-making process.

The congressional foreign policy reassertion in the last decade coincided with a dramatic shift in position of the U.S. in world politics. Friends in Western Europe and Japan and adversaries such as the Soviet Union have grown in power, reducing America's relative position in the international system. Perhaps more important, the role of great powers generally has been reduced as regional, local, and subnational forces have asserted themselves. These changes in the world probably have had a greater impact on U.S. foreign policy than any changes in policymaking within the U.S. If American foreign policy seems less certain today than a decade ago, it is because the world is less certain, not because Congress is an active participant in the foreign policy process.

Bibliography

Baker, Howard. <u>No Margin for Error</u>. New York: Times
   Books, 1979.
Carter, Jimmy. <u>Keeping Faith--Memoirs of a President</u>.
   New York: Bantam, 1983.
Crabb, Cecil V. Jr. and Pat M. Holt. <u>Invitation to
   Struggle: Congress, the President, and Foreign
   Policy</u>. Washington: Congressional Quarterly
   Press, 1980.
Dodd, Lawrence C. and Bruce I. Oppenheimer, eds. <u>Con-
   gress Reconsidered</u> (2d ed.). Washington: Congres-
   sional Quarterly Press, 1981.
Fenno, Richard F. Jr. <u>Congressmen in Committees</u>.
   Boston: Little, Brown, 1973.
Franck, Thomas M. and Edward Weisband. <u>Foreign Policy
   by Congress</u>. New York: Oxford University Press,
   1979.
Frye, Alton. <u>A Responsible Congress: The Politics of
   National Security</u>. New York: McGraw-Hill, 1975.
Fulbright, J. William. <u>The Crippled Giant</u>. New York:
   Random House, 1972.
Fulbright, J. William and John C. Stennis. <u>The Role of
   Congress in Foreign Policy</u>. Washington: American
   Enterprise Institute, 1971.
Haass, Richard. <u>Congressional Power: Implications for
   American Security Policy</u>. Adelphi Papers, no. 153,
   1979.
Holt, Pat M. <u>The War Powers Resolution: The Role of
   Congress in U.S. Armed Intervention</u>. Washington:
   American Enterprise Institute, 1978.
Javits, Jacob K. <u>Who Makes War--The President Versus
   Congress</u>. New York: Morrow, 1973.
King, Anthony, ed. <u>Both Ends of the Avenue: The Presi-
   dency, the Executive Branch, and Congress in the
   1980s</u>. Washington: American Enterprise Institute,
   1983.
Kissinger, Henry. <u>The White House Years</u>. Boston:
   Little, Brown, 1979.

LaFeber, Walter. The Panama Canal: The Crisis in His-
    torical Perspective. New York: Oxford University
    Press, 1978.

Nathan, James A. and James K. Oliver. Foreign Policy
    Making and the American Political System. Boston:
    Little, Brown, 1983.

Neidle, Alan F., ed. Nuclear Negotiations: Reasses-
    sing Arms Control Goals in U.S.-Soviet Relations.
    Austin: Lyndon B. Johnson School of Public
    Affairs, 1982.

Piper, Don C. and Ronald J. Terchek. Interaction: For-
    eign Policy and Public Policy. Washington: Ameri-
    can Enterprise Institute, 1983.

Pierre, Andrew J. The Global Politics of Arms Sales.
    Princeton: Princeton University Press, 1982.

Pierre, Andrew J., ed. Arms Transfers and American For-
    eign Policy. New York: New York University Press,
    1979.

Platt, Alan. The U.S. Senate and Strategic Arms Policy
    --1969-1977. Boulder: Westview Press, 1978.

Platt, Alan and Lawrence D. Weiler, eds. Congress and
    Arms Control. Boulder: Westview Press, 1978.

Schlesinger, Arthur Jr. The Imperial Presidency.
    Boston: Houghton Mifflin, 1973.

Stern, Lawrence. The Wrong Horse. New York: Times
    Books, 1977.

Spanier, John and Joseph Nogee, eds. Congress, the
    Presidency and American Foreign Policy. New York:
    Pergamon, 1981.

Talbott, Strobe. Endgame: The Inside Story of SALT II.
    New York: Harper & Row, 1979.

Vandenberg, Arthur H. Jr., ed. The Private Papers of
    Senator Vanderberg. Boston: Houghton Mifflin,
    1952.

Index

About the Editors and Contributors

Editors

HOYT PURVIS is director of the Fulbright Institute of International Relations at the University of Arkansas, where he teaches political science and journalism. He served for many years as an aide to Senator J. W. Fulbright and then as foreign/defense policy advisor to Majority Leader Robert Byrd and as deputy director of the Senate Democratic Policy Committee. He formerly taught at the Lyndon B. Johnson School of Public Affairs, University of Texas.

STEVEN J. BAKER is associate professor of international policy studies at the Monterey Institute of International Studies. He served as SALT II Treaty consultant and foreign policy advisor to Majority Leader Byrd. He was formerly on the faculty of the University of Texas at Austin.

Contributors

JOHN OPPERMAN has a master's degree from the Lyndon B. Johnson School of Public Affairs. He contributed to a volume on Foreign Economic Policy Decision-Making and has served on the staff of the Texas Legislature.

J. PHILIP ROGERS is a fellow at the Center for International Security and Arms Control at Stanford University. He is a Ph.D. candidate in government at the University of Texas, Austin.

TURA CAMPANELLA has master's degrees in Middle East studies and in public affairs from the University of Texas. She contributed to a published study on U.S. Policy and the Third World. She writes on foreign policy and energy issues and translates Arabic.

229